T0261623

Real Life Cryptology

# Real Life Cryptology

*Ciphers and Secrets in Early Modern Hungary*

*Benedek Láng*

*Translated from Hungarian by Teodóra Király and Benedek Láng*

Atlantis Press | Amsterdam University Press

Originally published as: 'Titkosírás a kora újkori Magyarországon' 2015, ISBN 9789635069514,
Balassi Kiadó, Budapest

Cover design: Coördesign, Leiden
Lay-out: Newgen / Konvertus

ISBN        978 94 6298 554 4
e-ISBN      978 90 4853 669 6
DOI         10.5117/9789462985544
NUR         685

Printed and bound by CPI Group (UK) Ltd, Croydon, CR0 4YY

# Table of contents

# Abbreviations

| | |
|---|---|
| AR | *Archivum Rákóczianum, II Rákóczi Ferenc levéltára* (Rákóczi Archives) (Budapest: MTA Tört Biz. Kiad. 1873–1935) vols. 1–12. |
| ÖStA HHStA | Österreichisches Staatsarchiv, Haus-, Hof- und Staatsarchiv, Vienna |
| MNL OL | Magyar Nemzeti Levéltár, Országos Levéltar, Budapest (Hungarian National Archives, Budapest) |
| MTT | *Magyar Történelmi Tár* (Hungarian Historical Records), (Pest, Magyar Tudományos Akadémia, 1855–1934) |
| OSZK | Országos Széchényi Könyvtár (National Széchényi Library) |
| Teleki | *Teleki Mihály Levelezése* (Correspondence of Mihály Teleki) (Budapest: Magyar Történelmi Társulat, 1905–1926), vols. 1–8. |

# Note on terminology

In theory, cryptology is a discipline composed of two fields, cryptography, that is secret writing, and cryptanalysis, that is codebreaking (cryptanalysis is a modern term forged by William Friedman). In the period under study, no such methodical distinction was used, ciphering, encryption, "translating", "working with chiffres" and many other terms are applied somewhat inconclusively in the sources. Therefore, throughout the book, differentiation between cryptology and cryptography will be neither systematic nor analytic. Whenever I refer to the practice of ciphering in general, I will use cryptography, unless I want to particularly emphasize that besides encryption, codebreaking is also included in the activity, because then I will use cryptology.

All other terms – open text, plain text, monoalphabetic, homophonic, and polyalphabetic ciphers, frequency analysis, probable word method, entropy, etc. – will be explained in the book at their first occurrences.

# Note on names

In the early modern times, person names were used inconclusively: sometimes in the language of the country of origin of a given person (which is not necessarily identical with his or her nation), sometimes in Latin, and – particularly in the countries under the Habsburg crown – sometimes in German. I made an attempt at using those name versions in each case that were the most frequently used in the sources and in the secondary literature for a given historical actor. These were most often those variations that refer to the country of birth. I did not wish to follow those scholars, who anglicize the Hungarian, German, Italian and other names, which have never been used in English (and write Francis Rákóczi, instead of Ferenc Rákóczi). I only anglicized emperors' names, such as Charles V or Ferdinand I, when these are the most widespread versions in the secondary literature.

# 1.   Introduction

What do the following people have in common: the Hungarian poet whose private life is in crisis while he is in litigation with his family; the Serbian secret agent whose life is in danger while he is sending crucial information to the imperial court; the Transylvanian master of the mint who is eager to protect his technical knowledge; the Hungarian magnate who despises both the Turkish and the Habsburg powers; the Emperor in Vienna who corresponds with his ambassador in Constantinople; and the Archbishop who is writing to his Italian delegate? These people stood on various levels of social hierarchy. Though they were all literate, their education and cultural backgrounds differed, as did their political power and influence on history. Yet, they all applied the same means when trying to protect their messages from prying eyes: the technology of ciphering.

Even though they and their secret writings have long been known, this monograph is the first systematic work on the history of ciphers of early modern Hungary. Its conclusions have been formed through the systematic collection and analysis of sources that come in remarkably high numbers. The most important argument of this book, as stated in the lines above, is that the social and political background, the intentions, the cryptographic skill and choice of tools of those using cryptographic methods in the sixteenth and seventeenth centuries show a much more significant variation than the traditional scholarship – concentrating primarily on the practice of diplomacy – had shown. The second argument – closely related to the first one – is that studying the variety of attitudes of this wider social environment of cryptography and the many ways people made use of enciphering methods is an approach that will help reintegrate the history of ciphers in the growing scholarship on secrecy. In other words, studying cryptography not only as a scientific technology, but rather as a complex system of social practices, will enrich the traditional "internalistic" approach to this branch of the history of science and will situate it in the context of social history.

The source material used as a sample to demonstrate these arguments comes from early modern Hungary that – because of its history particularly rich in conflicts in this period – provides ample resources for such an examination. I do not wish to claim that no other region could have provided this richness of resources to such research, as I will show in detail later. The assumption that Hungarian history is more abundant in secret writings than other countries is in itself to be examined and presently I would refrain from taking sides in this matter. It is argued that a similar demonstration might be carried out relying on the source material of other regions as well, and the conclusions aim to bear general relevance to the history of secrecy.

The research discussed here has yielded two results. First of all, it is a text-based analysis of a very common type of source which is inherently connected to a number of research areas within the discipline of history. Furthermore, it enables us to draw general implications connected to social history and research methodology, thus becoming relevant even for those readers who are interested in socio-historical developments rather than in coded letters.

In the following chapters I will first review the literature on the topic to prove that this study fills a niche, and then, having summarized the international developments in the historiography of secret writing, I will discuss the Hungarian contributions. Subsequently, through the analysis of sources, some of which was printed, some of which only exist in the archives in manuscript form, I will reach more general conclusions, which I will use to adequately support my two main statements above. Thus, this book starts out from the technical and source-centered aspects to reach finally more general socio-historical conclusions.

# 2. Uncovered fields in the research literature

## 2.1. Neglected secret writings in secrecy studies

Secrecy as a historical phenomenon has received increasing scholarly attention in recent decades. The communication of secrets and the secret ways of communication, keeping diplomatic, scientific or technological information secret, hiding private or sexual information, and strategies of learning about the secrets of others have increasingly been regarded as crucial not only in large-scale societies, communities, and religions of the past, but also in smaller units such as professions, spiritual sects, and families.

This relevance is reflected in a number of recent publications. William Eamon has surveyed the wide variety of genres and topics in the literature of secrecy in late medieval and early modern Europe, and has demonstrated that books of secrets played an essential role in history of science.[1] Edited by Agostino Paravicini-Bagliani, a thematic volume of the Micrologus Series collected several topics of and approaches to medieval secrecy ranging from theological mysteries to magical arcana and political secrets,[2] while another volume, edited by William Newman and Anthony Grafton, concentrated more on the notion of the occult in early modern alchemy and astrology.[3] A German collection of essays gave an even wider picture, and included such historical themes as diplomatic secrecy, sexual secrecy, intimacy, and the place of secrets in art.[4] Karma Lochrie's *Covert Operations* concentrates on women's secrets, gossips, confessions, and sexuality – an area where secrecy overlaps with intimacy.[5] Tanya Luhrmann studied the psychological, social, or sometimes even healing effects of initiation into secret mysteries in rites of contemporary groups of magic, trying to

---

1    William Eamon, *Science and the Secrets of Nature: Books of Secrets in Medieval and Early Modern Culture* (Princeton: Princeton University Press, 1994).

2    *Il Segreto / The Secret*, ed. A. Paravacini Bagliani, Micrologus, vol. XIV (Florence: Sismel, 2006).

3    William Newman and Anthony Grafton, eds. *Secrets of Nature: Astrology and Alchemy in Early Modern Europe* (Cambridge, MA: The MIT Press, 2001).

4    Gisela Engel, Brita Rang, Klaus Reichert and Heide Wunder, eds. *Das Geheimnis am Beginn der europäischen Moderne* (Frankfurt am Main, Klostermann, 2002).

5    Karma Lochrie, *Covert Operations: The Medieval Uses of Secrecy* (Philadelphia: University of Pennsylvania Press, 1999).

discover how the act of sharing a secret becomes a tool of group formation and group cohesion.[6]

Pamela Long juxtaposed the openness of mining treatises with the secrecy of alchemical writings while exploring the role of authorship in the history of technology in an age when the notion of intellectual property had to be reinterpreted.[7] One of the many merits of her analysis is that she makes an effort to define the notions of *secrecy* and *openness* appropriately. Going back to the fundamental work of the philosopher Sissela Bok from 1982,[8] Long defines secrecy as "intentional concealment", and distinguishes it, first of all, from privacy and secondly from the unknown, such as the secrets of nature.[9]

Walking in Long's footsteps, Koen Vermeir makes the relationship of secrecy and openness more explicit. By conducting a concept analysis as well as providing historical examples, he argues that the two concepts are not necessarily negating one another, and therefore they cannot be defined as each other's opposites. He claims that both secrecy and openness are categories with a range: things are not either completely secret or absolutely public – they are partly hidden to certain groups, while being partially public for another audience.[10] (This argument is not entirely novel. As early as 1970 John Cohen wrote that the secrecy of a given information is not an absolute feature; rather, it should be seen as a scale measuring how carefully one hides information, what risks one takes to keep it secret, and what obstacles anyone who wants to uncover this secret might face. As Cohen mentions, secrecy can only be defined in relation to a community with which one wishes to share the secret information.)[11]

Vermeir goes on to emphasize that "secret as content" and "secrecy as action" do not necessarily coincide, however close these two categories may seem to be at first sight. Many handbooks – both historical and contemporary – that contain "secrets" that only a selected audience is supposed to know are in fact widely publicized (secret without secrecy), while the secrets of some esoteric circles seem banal or empty once they are uncovered

---

6    Tanya Luhrman, "The magic of secrecy," *Ethos* 17 (1989): 131–165.

7    Pamela O. Long, *Openness, Secrecy, Authorship: Technical Arts and the Culture of Knowledge from Antiquity to the Renaissance* (Baltimore: Johns Hopkins University Press, 2001).

8    Sissela Bok, *Secrets: On the Ethics of Concealment and Revelation* (New York: Vintage, 1989.)

9    Long, *Openness* 1–15.

10   Koen Vermeir, "Openness versus secrecy? Historical and historiographical remarks." *The British Journal for the History of Science*, 45 (2012): 165–188.

11   John Cohen, *Homo Psychologicus* (London: George Allen and Unwin Ltd, 1970), 133–138.

(secrecy without a secret). The *rhetoric of secrecy* is a recurring feature of early modern science – several kinds of knowledge had the exciting trademark of secrecy that in effect could easily be obtained by any literate person. Similarly, advocacy of the value of "publicity" in the seventeenth century did not mean actual publicity – as it does not mean it today, either. Many writers argued in the past and argue today that open access to information is a value, when the reality is that, because of the special customs of publication, or because of intentional secrecy, these writers' knowledge is not widely accessible at all.[12]

The overview of the history of secrecy should be closed by mentioning two monumental undertakings. The first is *Sigila*, a French-Portuguese journal completely devoted to a 'transdisciplinary' study of secret. It publishes short studies, essays, works of literature and visual art, it reviews publications on the topic of secret and lists conferences and presentations that are relevant in the field. The thematic editions since 1998 cover the topics of forgetting, confession, secret symbols, code names, dissimulation, feminine secrets, music, intimacy, orientalism, shame, silence, nighttime, secret languages, guardians of secret, and in the 2005 issue (no. 15) the relationship of secret and science.[13] The other major work is the three-volume monumental multi-authored overview edited by Aleida and Jan Assmann that is less historically oriented, and devotes more attention to literature and cultural history; nonetheless, it marks a growing interest in the field of secrecy by leading contemporary scholars.[14] Both undertakings are fine examples of the growing need on the part of contemporary leading researchers to unfold the concepts of secret.

The list can easily be continued to include many more publications on secret,[15] dealing with its different aspects. William Eamon, the first important voice on the topic, writes that in 1982 his first conference lecture on secret books was received with vague looks, from 2000 on, however, one conference has been organized after the other on the early modern history of secret – one of these was precisely that workshop in Cambridge in 2008,

12 Vermeir, *op. cit.* and Pamela O. Long, "The Openness of Knowledge: An Ideal and its Context in 16th-Century Writings on Mining and Metallurgy," *Technology and Culture* 32 (1991): 318–355.
13 *Sigila*, publication semestrielle transdisciplinaire consacrée à l'analyse de la figure du secret, 1998-.
14 Aleida Assmann and Jan Assmann, eds. *Geheimnis und Öffentlichkeit* (Schleier und Schwelle I, Munich: Fink, 1997); *Geheimnis und Offenbarung* (Schleier und Schwelle II, Munich: Fink, 1998); *Geheimnis und Neugierde* (Schleier und Schwelle III, Munich: Fink, 1999).
15 Among others: Philippe Dujardin, ed. *Le Secret* (Lyon, Presses Universitaires de Lyon, 1987)

where he made this observation when presenting his views on the future research directions of secret books.[16]

The secondary literature, just like the topic itself, is rather rich. Authors make a serious attempt at contextualizing the phenomenon of secret by reconstructing the social background, aspects and consequences of secrecy. A common characteristic of them, however, is that they rarely mention a major means of secrecy, that is, secret writing (cryptography and code breaking), and when they do, they concentrate on its application in the political domain and on its technological evolution. The neglect of cryptography in secrecy studies is fairly surprising; one cannot but agree with Dejanirah Couto, who argued in her article on early modern espionage in the Ottoman Empire, that "without cryptography, secrecy lacks material form or readability".[17] The context of secret writings is secrecy, and the context of studying them should be the literature of secrecy.

## 2.2.    Secrecy in the history of science

The contrasting concepts of secrecy/openness are much discussed in historiography of science. Robert Merton's four well-known scientific norms – universalism, communalism, disinterestedness, and organized skepticism – have had a long-lasting influence on how researchers approached the issue.[18] One of the norms, communalism is particularly relevant here. According to this norm, scientific achievements should be made freely available to anyone, since knowledge is the common intellectual property of society, not of the individual. Merton, of course, was fully aware that his norms do not necessarily describe the reality of scientific research. He looked at them as the ethos of scientific research, a set of values that would guarantee the free and effective progress of science, and one that academic institutions of democratic societies strive to achieve in an ideal world. In historiography, however, the norms were taken up in a somewhat simplified way. Researchers simply accepted the view that openness is a

---

16   William Eamon, "How to Read a Book of Secrets" in Elaine Leong és Alisha Rankin, eds. *Secrets and Knowledge in Medicine and Science 1500–1800* (Surray: Ashgate, 2011), 23–46, particularly: 39.

17   Dejanirah Couto, "Spying in the Ottoman Empire: Sixteenth-Century Encrypted Correspondence," in Francisco Bethencourt and Florike Egmond, eds. *Cultural Exchange in Early Modern Europe* (Volume III) – Correspondence and Cultural Exchange in Europe, 1400–1700 (Cambridge: Cambridge University Press, 2007) 274–312, particularly: 278.

18   Robert Merton, "Science and technology in a democratic order," *Journal of Legal and Political Sociology* 1 (1942): 115–126.

positive value that supports academic research, and that secrecy, which is more characteristic of the history of technology, was fortunately abandoned by modern science. Science, on this understanding, has become open, whereas technology remained secretive.[19]

This view was, of course, challenged both in regard to the past and the present of the scientific practice. John Ziman pointed out that Merton's norms are constantly being violated in the twentieth century, and these violations are somewhat natural in the so-called post-academic phase of science.[20] Since corporations are taking the place of national academic institutions in financing scientific research, they exert a growing influence on the object of research along with the degree of its publicity. In the meantime, historians examining early modern science and technology realized that retaining, hiding, or restrictedly sharing information had a much greater and more constructive importance in science and craft industry than previous authors had believed.[21]

A recent thematic issue of *The British Journal of the History of Science* illustrates vividly how historiographical research has moved from the conventional and unreflective view that contrasted openness and secrecy, mapping this pair of opposites onto another one, that of science and technology.[22] Editors Koen Vermeir and Dániel Margócsy argue that the focus of the research on secrecy has been narrowed down too much to the very topic of secrets themselves, when in fact practices of secrecy would be a more fruitful object of investigation. As Georg Simmel put it, in what is perhaps the first systematic analysis of the social role of secrecy, it functions as the principle of social hierarchy: "Secrecy gives the person enshrouded by it an exceptional position; it works as a stimulus of purely social derivation, which is in principle quite independent of its casual content."[23]

19  David Hull, "Openness and secrecy in science: their origins and limitationsm," *Science, Technology* and *Human Values* 10 (1985): 4–13; Ernan McMullin, "Openness and secrecy in science: some notes on early history," *Science, Technology and Human Values* 10 (1985): 14–23.

20  John M. Ziman, "Postacademic Science: Constructing Knowledge with Networks and Norms," *Science Studies* 9 (1996): 67–80.

21  See Koen Vermeir and Dániel Margócsy, "States of secrecy: an introduction." *The British Journal for the History of Science*, 45 (2012): 153–164; Karel Davids, "Craft Secrecy in Europe in the Early Modern Period: A Comparative View," *Early Science and Medicine*, 10 (No. 3, Openness and Secrecy in Early Modern Science) (2005): 341–348; Stephan R. Epstein, "Craft Guilds, Apprenticeship, and Technological Change in Preindustrial Europe," *The Journal of Economic History* 58 (1998): 684–713.

22  *The British Journal for the History of Science* 45 (2012), Special Issue: States of Secrecy. Editors: Koen Vermeir and Dániel Margócsy.

23  Georg Simmel, "The sociology of secrecy and of secret societies," *American Journal of Sociology* 11 (1906): 441–498, particularly: 464 and 478.

Vermeir and Margócsy regard secrecy in science as more than a tool for protecting knowledge from intellectual competitors: in their view it is a dynamic social practice, a self-maintaining force that creates and organizes a group, establishes and manages hierarchy within it, and fundamentally influences the mechanisms of exclusion-inclusion. Often, the content of the secret is not really relevant in the study of the dynamics of secrecy; the ability to withhold or share information in itself becomes a power enabling social control, regardless of the object of secret.[24]

Simmel, Vermeir and Margócsy and the authors they cite unanimously share such observations that help make sense of the seemingly unexplainable secrecy practices in early modern Hungary. Presently, however, I would like to point out that the history of secret writings is the neglected stepchild of not only the research of secrecy in general, but specifically of the history of scientific secrecy. The use of cryptography and scientific secrecy of some seventeenth-century figures such as Galileo Galilei, John Wilkins, Robert Hooke, Christian Huygens, John Wallis, Giambattista Della Porta,[25] or Robert Boyle[26] have been studied to some extent. The close relationship of mathematics and decoding has also been analyzed.[27] With the exception of a few remarkable yet sporadic studies, however, little effort has been made to include the use of secret writings into the careful and socially sensitive analyses of historiography.

This is illustrated by the third volume of The Cambridge History of Science.[28] Focusing on early modern science, this volume offers an excellent perspective on the present state of contemporary research, as it is reflected in its outstanding group of authors (Katharine Park, Lorraine Daston, Steven Shapin, William Eamon, Peter Dear, Anthony Grafton, Paula Findlen, William Newman, Brian Copenhaver, etc.) as well as in the topics it covers (among many others: the meaning of experiment, evidence and persuasion, and the old and new scenes of science, such as: markets, squares and towns, libraries, schoolrooms, botanical gardens, anatomical theaters, laboratories

---

24  Vermeir and Margócsy, "States of secrecy."

25  Kristie Macrakis, "Confessing secrets: secret communication and the origins of modern science," Intelligence and National Security 25 (2010): 183–197; Mario Biagioli, "From ciphers to confidentiality: Secrecy, Openness and Priority in Science," The British Journal for the History of Science, 45 (2012), 213–233.

26  See the publications of Lawrence M. Principe, e.g.: "Robert Boyle's Alchemical Secrecy: Codes, Ciphers and Concealments," Ambix 39 (1992): 63–74.

27  Peter Pesic, "Secrets, Symbols, and Systems: Parallels between Cryptanalysis and Algebra, 1580–1700," Isis 88 (1997): 674–692.

28  Katharine Park and Lorraine Daston eds. The Cambridge History of Science, Volume 3, Early Modern Science (Cambridge, Cambridge University Press, 2006.)

and coffee houses.) Secret and secrecy are recurrent themes of the volume, yet cryptography is only mentioned once, and even there it is somewhat mixed into the history of constructed languages.[29] All this is rather surprising in light of the fact that the first golden era of cryptography coincides with the early modern period. Besides the publications of Macrakis, Biagioli and Principe, the above-mentioned publication on the 2008 Cambridge conference provides a more refreshing example.[30] Secret writings are mentioned in relation with the alchemic diaries of Boyle, and with a collection of medical formulas compiled for Eleanor, the daughter of Sir Peter Temple.[31] The questions addressed on both occasions are particularly relevant for our present interest: what the reason for using encryption really was (why did Temple encode formulas that were publicly available at the time in a printed form), who was meant to be excluded from the communication, how cryptographic secrecy helped define and limit a community, and, finally, how ciphers appeared in areas remote from the practice of diplomacy such as a research journal and a compilation of private recipes. If only for the length of a few pages, this publication does integrate the practice of cryptography into the framework of secrecy research.

In spite of these exceptions, one may draw the conclusion: the social history of cryptography and the integration of secret writings into the practices of secrecy do not seem particularly relevant for the most progressive movement of contemporary history of science.

## 2.3. The need for social history in cryptography studies

Thus far, there has been little success in finding cryptography in the literature on secrecy. It is worthwhile now to look at the same issue from another angle, and see how secrecy appears in the studies on ciphers. Cryptography has been the subject of considerable secondary literature in recent decades. The beginning of the twentieth century marks the birth of two richly documented volumes of Aloys Meister,[32] who studied the European beginnings

---

29  Mary Baine Campbell, "Literature," in Park and Daston, *Early Modern Science*, 756–772, cryptography appears: 762.

30  Elaine Leong and Alisha Rankin, eds. *Secrets and Knowledge in Medicine and Science 1500–1800* (Surray: Ashgate, 2011).

31  *Ibid.* 9–10, 100–101.

32  Aloys Meister, *Die Anfänge der modernen diplomatischen Geheimschrift* (Paderborn: Ferdinand Schöningh, 1902); *idem, Die Geheimschrift im Dienste der päpstlichen Kurie von ihren Anfängen bis zum Ende des 16. Jahrhunderts* (Paderborn: Ferdinand Schöningh, 1906).

of the history of ciphers, more specifically the diplomatic cryptography of Italian cities and the papal court in the late medieval and early modern periods. He reconstructed several hundred code keys in these volumes and published a number of crucial cryptographic treatises.

Though several useful articles, sources and monographs were published in the previous and following decades on Italian,[33] Spanish,[34] French,[35] German[36] and Polish[37] ciphers, one can say without exaggeration that the history of cryptography as a discipline was born as late as in 1967, when the *Codebreakers*, a lengthy monograph by David Kahn was published.[38]

Kahn, relying on the information available at the time, carried out a systematic investigation on the history of ciphers from the beginnings to WWII. The primary focus of his research was the twentieth century. Though the story of Enigma was not incorporated into the book as it was still classified at the time, Kahn was a pioneer in publishing many details of other areas. Despite the emphasis on modern times, his review on the early modern era is a highly rich and useful introduction even today.

Kahn's oeuvre was fundamental in establishing the field of cryptography: he was a co-founder of *Cryptologia, the* journal on the history of cryptology that has published studies and reviews related to the history of cryptography since 1977.[39] Kahn is also a prominent figure of the great biannual

---

33   Luigi Pasini, "Delle scritture in cifra usate dalla Repubblica Veneta," in *Il Regio Archivio Generale di Venezia*, (Venezia: Pietro Naratovich, 1873). 291–328; Bartolommeo Cecchetti, "Le scritture occulte nella diplomazia veneziana," *Atti del Regio Istituto Veneto* 14 (1868–69): 1186–1211.

34   J. P. Devos, *Les chiffres de Philippe II (1555–1598) et du Despacho Universal durant le XVIIe siècle* (Brussels: Académie Royale de Belgique, 1950); Henry Biaudet, "Un chiffre diplomatique du XVIe siècle: Étude sur le cod. Nunz. Polonia 27. A. des archives secretes du Sant-Siège," *Annales Academiae Scientiarum Fennice* (Helsinki: 1910); Pierre Speziali, "Aspects de la cryptographie au XVI siècle," *Bibliothèque d'humanisme et Renaissance* 17 (1955): 188–206.

35   J. P. Devos and H. Seligman, eds. *L'Art de Deschiffrer: Traité de Déchiffrement du XVIIe Siècle de la Secrétairerie d'Etat et de Guerre Espagnole* (Belgium: Université de Louvain, 1967.)

36   Ludwig von Rockinger: "Über eine bayerische Sammlung von Schlüsseln zu Geheimschriften des sechzehnten Jahrhunderts," *Archivalische Zeitschrift* 1892: 21–96; Franz Stix, "Die Geheimschriftenschlüssel der Kabinetskanzlei des Kaiser," *Nachrichten von der Gesellschaft der Wissenschaften zu Göttingen, Philologisch-Historische Klasse*, Neue Folge, Fachgruppe II, 1936: 207–226, and 1937: 61–70.

37   Liisi Karttunen, "Chiffres diplomatiques des nonces de Pologne vers la fin du XVIe siècle: Extraits des archives des princes Chigi à Rome," *Annales Academiae Scientiarum Fennice* (Helsinki: 1911).

38   David Kahn, *The Codebreakers. The Story of Secret Writing* (London: Weidenfeld and Nicolson, 1967); amplified edition: *The Codebreakers: The Comprehensive History of Secret Communication from Ancient Times to the Internet* (New York: Scribner, 1996).

39   *Cryptologia* comes out with four issues a year. Taylor and Francis took over publishing it in 2006: http://www.tandfonline.com/toc/ucry20/current

professional meetings of the history of cryptology in Maryland, which is organized by the National Security Agency (NSA) of the United States. The National Cryptologic Museum, located near the conference site, bought up Kahn's thematic book collection, thus becoming the most concentrated library on the history of cryptography.[40] The field has been energized by its journal, conferences and numerous publications, and the source material is so rich that it feeds a steady stream of reviews and monographs.[41] Among these works Simon Singh's *The Code Book* has been the most successful among lay readers.[42]

A common feature of these publications, however, is that they focus primarily on the evolution of enciphering and decoding methods, which are rarely contextualized in their wider social environment. Early modern cryptography is researched almost exclusively from two points of view. First, it is well documented how certain authors from the fifteenth to seventeenth centuries (Leon Battista Alberti, Johannes Trithemius, Giambattista Della Porta, Gustavus Selenus, Blaise Vigenère, and John Falconer, etc.) put forward sophisticated methods in their famous summaries on steganography and cryptography. These were complicated intellectual techniques, too complicated in fact for diplomatic, military, or private use by their contemporaries; thus, only limited application of them can be documented until the eighteenth century. Considerably less sophisticated methods were applied in real life: enciphered dispatches, secret letters used in spy communications and conspiracies, and deciphering manuals in early modern Italy, Spain, France, and Germany followed a system that, due to its simplicity, was beneath the expertise of the above-mentioned intellectuals–and this diplomatic application is the second major topic of

40  http://www.cryptologicfoundation.org/;  http://www.nsa.gov/about/cryptologic_heritage/museum/index.shtml.

41  Edmond Lerville, *Les Cahiers secrets de la cryptographie* (Paris: Rocher, 1972); L. Sacco, *Manuel de Cryptographie* (Paris: Payot, 1951); Gerhard Strasser, *Lingua Universalis: Kryptologie und Theorie der Universalsprachen im 16. und 17. Jahrhundert* (Wolfenbütteler Forschungen, Vol. 38.) (Wiesbaden: Harrassowitz, 1988); Fred B. Wrixon, *Codes, Ciphers and other Cryptic and Clandestine Communication* (New York: Black Dog, 1998); Friedrich L. Bauer, *Entzifferte Geheimnisse: Methoden und Maximen der Kryptologie* (Berlin: Springer, 2000) English translation: *Decrypted Secrets. Methods and Maxims of Cryptology* (Berlin: Springer, 2002); Klaus Schmeh, *Codeknacker gegen Codemacher: Die faszinierende Geschichte der Verschlüsselung* (Dortmund: W3L, 2014); *idem, Nicht zu knacken: Von ungelösten Enigma-Codes zu den Briefen des Zodiac-Killers* (Hanser, 2012); Craig Bauer, *Secret History: The Story of Cryptology* (CRC: Chapman Hall, 2013); *idem, Unsolved!: The History and Mystery of the World's Greatest Ciphers from Ancient Egypt to Online Secret Societies* (Princeton: Princeton University Press, 2017).

42  Simon Singh, *The Code Book: The Science of Secrecy from Ancient Egypt to Quantum Cryptography* (New York: Doubleday, 1999).

the secondary literature. Outside the realm of theoretical inventions and their practical use in the diplomatic sphere, cryptography is rarely investigated, even though noblemen, scientists, medical doctors, university professors and students, alchemists, engineers, and "everyday" members of society often used enciphering methods for their own – not necessarily diplomatic – purposes. The wider context of secrecy is rarely mentioned in monographs and articles on cryptography, even though motivations behind everyday use of cryptography can be hardly understood without integrating the application of ciphers in the larger context of secrecy.

The historiography of cryptography as a field is unduly internalist. The internalist historical approach primarily looks for the intellectual content in the history of a science, and documents the birth and growth of such concepts, theories and methods that are the predecessors of the theories and methods presently in use. The so-called externalist approach, by contrast, includes the social, economic and institutional aspects of a given area of science. It investigates the social environment in which a certain technology was used and which often affected scientific content itself.[43]

With the exception of a few articles on specific topics,[44] general studies on the history of cryptography regard encryption as a scientific technology and mostly fail to consider its real life use and its social context. This tendency is vividly exemplified in an influential article by David Kahn from 2008 in which he enumerates the tasks and questions of the field that remain to be solved. He draws attention to a number of basic and so far under-researched topics, but these are mostly connected to the origin and history of certain cryptographic methods, such as the polyalphabetic secret writing or the nomenclature, not the social history of secret writings.[45]

I have argued first that though the phenomenon of secrecy has received considerable socially sensitive attention, this hardly affected secret writings. Second, I pointed out that cryptography is barely integrated into the context of secrecy, and is often portrayed as a technology and as a diplomatic practice, detached from its broader social environment.

43   Steven Shapin, "Discipline and Bounding: The History and Sociology of Science as Seen through the Externalism-Internalism Debate," *History of Science* 30 (1992), 333–369.

44   A number of case studies can be quoted here, most frequently published in *Cryptologia*, which do take real life situations into account. Even these, however, focus on the political and diplomatic application of cryptography, and consider issues of secrecy rarely.

45   David Kahn, "The Future of the Past—Questions in Cryptologic History," *Cryptologia* 32 (2008):56–61.

## 2.4. Cryptography in Hungary

This lack of attention is even more striking in Hungary, a country which, due to its historic conflicts and dividedness, provided rich soil for the use of ciphers, a fact that the historian Ágnes R. Várkonyi has more than once warned about.[46] This issue, however, is rather neglected in Hungarian research, despite the fact that several valuable initiatives have been made by Hungarian scholars.

An early example is Ágoston Ötvös' 1848 publication, a highly representative selection from the encrypted correspondence of the era of György Rákóczi I, Prince of Transylvania (prince: 1630–1648). Ötvös, originally a physician, found the letters in the rich collection of the Batthyány library in Gyulafehérvár (Alba Iulia, today Romania), and by all appearances it was he himself who had deciphered the enciphered letters, and who had reconstructed at least six different codes.[47]

Not counting a few sporadic source publications, there was a long pause in the historiography of Hungarian cryptography following Ötvös, until 1970 when lieutenant colonel Zoltán Révay became interested in the field, supposedly as a result of his military intelligence position. First he published a general monograph,[48] then a reference book describing the ciphers that survived from the freedom fight of Ferenc Rákóczi II (1703–1711).[49]

Révay's monograph is rather confusing. On the one hand, it must be praised for being the first Hungarian report on the post WWII developments of decoding, based partly on David Kahn's *Codebreakers*, partly on the personal experience of the author. In addition, the author compiled a useful list of the relevant publications related to the history of cryptography in Hungary, and he described a number of hand-written sources from diverse archives and manuscript collections for the first time. On the other hand, the work displays certain typical shortages of the amateur historian:

46 Ágnes R. Várkonyi, "A tájékoztatás hatalma" (The power of information), in *Információáramlás a magyar és török végvári rendszerben* (Information flow in the Hungarian and Turkish military zones), ed. Petercsák Tivadar and Berecz Mátyás (Eger: Dobó István Vármúzeum, 1999), 9–32, particularly: 17.

47 Ágoston Ötvös, *Rejtelmes levelek első Rákóczy György korából* (Secret letters from the time of Rákóczi György I), (Kolozsvár, 1848).

48 Révay Zoltán, *Titkosírások. Fejezetek a rejtjelezés történetéből* (Secret Writings: Chapters from the History of Cryptography) (Budapest, Zrínyi Katonai Kiadó, 1978.)

49 Révay Zoltán, *II. Rákóczi Ferenc és korának rejtjelezése (XVIII. század)* (Cryptography of Ferenc Rákóczi II and his Age) (Budapest: Magyar Néphadsereg Híradó Főnökség Kiadása, 1974).

haphazard references, misunderstood sources, including a horoscope depicting astrological symbols, mistakenly labeled as the earliest Hungarian example of secret writing.[50] More importantly, Révay touches on plagiarism when introducing the findings of Ötvös. He does cite his source, but at one point forgets to mention that the messages were decoded by the nineteenth-century physician-historian,[51] and in several places he explicitly claims to be the decoder.[52] And, as if that was not enough, he paints a distorted picture of the process of deciphering. He gives a detailed description of his own decoding process, but what he describes is in effect the typical case of backwards reasoning relying on the knowledge of the solution, a procedure that is really hard to follow when one does not happen to have the key.[53] Despite all of these contradictions, the book is a good starting point for anyone wishing to study early modern cryptography in Hungary. Révay's second book, *Cryptography of Ferenc Rákóczi II and his Age*, is a remarkably useful source analysis. It presents and analyzes one by one those nearly seventy cipher tables that survived from the freedom fight of Rákóczi. This is a groundbreaking work despite the fact that Révay had worked from the nineteenth-century copies of the Hungarian Academy of Sciences,[54] not the original sources held in the National Archives of Hungary.[55]

Interestingly enough, the other important achievement of the seventies is also connected to a lieutenant colonel of the Hungarian national army, Ottó Gyürk. Parallel with Gábor Gilicze, then a university student, he found how to break the cipher system of the secret diary of the writer Géza Gárdonyi (1863–1922).[56] Subsequently, he started to work on a statistical analysis of the mysterious Rohonc codex held in the archives of the Library of the Hungarian Academy of Sciences. This second manuscript, however, resisted his decoding efforts.[57]

During the following decades of Hungarian historiography, ciphers of Prince György Rákóczi, of the Wesselényi movement and of Prince Ferenc Rákóczi were mentioned several times (most often in the studies of Ágnes

50  Révay, *Titkosírások*, 60.
51  Révay, *Titkosírások*, 90.
52  Révay, *Titkosírások*, 81.
53  Révay, *Titkosírások*, 95.
54  Hungarian Academy of Sciences, Manuscript Collection, Ms 4951/5.
55  MNL OL G 15, Caps. C. Fasc 43–44
56  Gyürk Ottó, "Hogyan fejtettem meg Gárdonyi titkosírását?" *Élet és Tudomány* 24/47 (1969): 2211–2216; Gárdonyi Géza, *Titkosnapló* (Secret diary) (Budapest: Szépirodalmi Kiadó, 1974.)
57  Gyürk Ottó, "Megfejthető-e a Rohonci-kódex?" (Is the Rohonc codex decipherable?) *Élet és Tudomány* 25 (1970), 1923–1924.

R. Várkonyi),[58] but they hardly ever stood in the spotlight. One of these studies will be brought up more than once here: the correspondence of Archbishop Péter Pázmány and C. H. Motmann, his source of information from Rome. This extremely complex code was reconstructed by the historian Péter Tusor, and the analyst Imre Máté, retired head of the National Cipher Council.[59] Tusor and Máté achieved this result through using historical reasoning and mathematical analysis in a parallel way.

Among contemporary research, one may cite the code-breaking results of István Vadai and Hanna Vámos, they managed to decipher dozens of enciphered letters from the 17th century.[60] Somewhat beyond our period, Hanna Vámos has also come out with the reconstruction of the polyalphabetic code of the Nagybajom manuscript.[61] These results nicely illustrate the rich potential involved in historical codebreaking.

Finally, I would like to mention my own monograph on the Rohonc codex,[62] a manuscript that has long been regarded with suspicion. As a result of the decryption of Levente Zoltán Király and Gábor Tokai, this 450-page prayer-book will also be available.[63] Though kept in the Library of the Hungarian Academy of Sciences, it is not evident that this (most

58  Ágnes R. Várkonyi, *A rejtőzködő murányi Vénusz* (The hiding Venus of Murany) (Budapest: Helikon Könyvkiadó, 1987), 213–15; eadem, "Az elveszett idő: Zrínyi Miklós nádori emlékirata?" (The time lost: a memorandum of Palatine Miklós Zrínyi?) *Hadtörténeti Közlemények* 113 (2000): 269–328, esp. 291; eadem, "A tájékoztatás hatalma."

59  Péter Tusor, "Pázmány bíboros olasz rejtjelkulcsa: C. H. Motmann 'Residente d'Ungheria': A római magyar agenzia történetéhez" (Cardinal Pázmány's Italian Codebook: C. H. Motmann 'Residente d'Ungheria,' On the History of the Hungarian Agenzia in Rome), *Hadtörténelmi közlemények* 116 (2003): 535–81;

60  Hanna Vámos, István Vadai, "Pázmány Péter és I. Rákóczy György titkosírása" (The cipher of Péter Pázmány and György Rákóczi I), in Alinka Ajkay and Rita Bajáki eds. *Pázmány nyomában* (Following Pázmány) (Vác: Mondat, 2013), 461–479; *eidem, Kuruc titkosírások megfejtése* (Solutions of Kuruc ciphers), in István Mercs, ed. *Kuruc(kodó) irodalom* (Kuruc(izing) literature) (Nyíregyháza: Móricz Zsigmond Kulturális Egyesület, 2013), 209–221; István Vadai, "Titkosírás" (Cryptography) in *Magyar Művelődéstörténeti Lexikon* (Encyclopaedia of Hungarian cultural history), vol. 12, ed. Péter Kőszeghy Péter and Zsuzsanna Tamás (Budapest, Balassi, 2011), 60–65; *idem*, "Két XVII. századi titkosírás megfejtése" (Solution to two seventeenth-century ciphers) in *Pálffy Kata leveleskönyve: Iratok Illésházy István bujdosásának történetéhez (1602–1606)* (Letterbook of Kata Pálfyy: Texts relevant for István Illésházy's exile), ed. Ötvös Péter (Szeged: Scriptum Kft, 1991), 183–89.

61  Hanna Vámos, "Leleplezett titok: Pálóczi Horváth Ádám titkos, szabadkőműves dokumentuma," (Unrevealed secret: the Freemason document of Ádám Pálóczi Horváth) in István Csörsz Rumen and Béla Hegedüs, eds., Magyar Arión (Hungarian Arion) (Budapest: rec.iti, 2011), http://rec.iti.mta.hu/rec.iti

62  Benedek Láng, *A rohonci kód* (the Rohonc code) (Budapest: Jaffa, 2011); *idem, The Rohonc Code: Tracing a Historical Riddle,* forthcoming.

63  The publication of Gábor Tokai and Levente Zoltán Király is forthcoming.

certainly) sixteenth-century codex is related to Hungarian history. It is not likely either that we deal with a real cipher here, the context of constructed languages seems more probable. In my monograph, I give a historiographical overview of fascinating and occasionally almost ludicrous theories associated with the Codex and discuss the possible interpretations of the manuscript: as a Biblical commentary, as an apocryphal gospel, as a secret book written for and by a sect. I also provide an overview of the secret writing systems known in the early modern times, and an account of numerous efforts to create an artificial language or to find a long-lost perfect language, as both endeavors were especially popular at the time the Codex was most probably made. The book tests a number of codebreaking methods in order to decipher the codex and finally presents a solution (the solution of Király and Tokai) to the enigma of its content.

To sum up: there are useful case studies available on the cryptographic practice of the region, but neither a systematic summary, nor a socially oriented overview has been published. It is high time the social history of the secret writings of the Carpathian basin was researched.

# 3. Secret writings and attitudes – research questions

This research has two objectives in order to fill the gaps in the study of cryptography and secrecy. First, it aims to reconstruct the social milieus of the applicants and the reception of cryptography, not only in diplomacy (where ciphers were used in the largest quantity and in their most professional form), but also in science, religion, artisanal tradition, university context, espionage, medicine, and in the private lives of noblemen, engineers, and everyday people, where previous research had neglected its role. Second, it aims to integrate cryptography into the larger intellectual context of secrecy, in private, medical, scientific, religious, alchemical, magical, and political practices of secrecy, that is, in the context where it *sui generis* belongs.

The number of research questions to be answered is extensive. What was the relationship between various practices of intentional secrecy and cryptography? On what occasions were secret writings used and what were the alternative tools available at the time?

What was the content of the hidden knowledge: politics, sexual secrets, or scientific knowledge? What type of information did the contemporaries want to be secret? The question is not only whether we can solve the ciphers, but also: Can we figure out which texts were seen as important enough to be enciphered? This is even more relevant when the given information does not seem today valuable enough to be hidden. It is worthwhile to compare in a given source the enciphered contents with and those that were not to better understand people's attitudes to secrecy.

The ways of knowledge transfer would be equally important to discover. How did techniques of cryptography spread in society, e.g. by way of printed texts, by manuscripts, or by personal transfer? Was the source of their knowledge the diplomatic practice or the manuals of such classic authors of cryptography as Johannes Trithemius, Athanasius Kircher, and Giambattista Della Porta? Which deciphering methods in the region were results of endogenous development, and which came from the Ottoman Empire? Was there any knowledge transfer between the considerably more developed Arabic tradition the slowly improving European cipher practices? If such transfer did take place, did this happen in the territory of Hungary, where the Islamic and European cultures confronted each other, and where double spies were familiar with both the Eastern and Western methods? If, on the other hand, such transfer did not take place, what was the reason for its lack?

How widespread were the encryption and decrypting methods outside the political sphere? Is there any correlation between the quality and sophistication of a cipher system being used and the social status, education, and the distance of the user from the practice of diplomacy?

How much trust was laid in these methods? What was the exact purpose for enciphering a text: to make it cryptic and hidden from the contemporaries, or something else? Why did certain diaries use ciphers that were easily solvable? How can we identify whether a specific cipher key was used for diplomatic missions or for the communication of private secrets?

How can the perception of risk that justified enciphering be reconstructed on the basis of the sources? What are the – often civilian – practitioners' attitudes towards the technology they used? How far could they make use of the techniques, how far did they realize the potential of the given methods? What complications took place because of misunderstood encryption? Which mistakes were typically made by users when applying ciphers, or more precisely, how might they have decreased the efficiency of their techniques? What measures were made to protect the secret of a specific key? How frequently did users change their encryption? To what extent were they aware that the key might be broken by their enemies? How developed and practical was the diplomatic practice of cryptography? Was encryption and code breaking carried out by the clerks or did the ruler himself felt obliged to spend precious time enciphering and deciphering secret reports?

The questions abound. To summarize the, one can use a paraphrase of Jacques Le Goff's famous words:[1] what is common to the university student, the emperor's clerk, and the master of the mint as far as their attitudes to and practices of cryptography were concerned?

---

1    The *histoire des mentalités* operates at the level of the everyday automatisms of behavior. Its object is that which escapes historical individuals because it reveals the impersonal content of their thought: that which is common to Caesar and his most junior legionary, Saint Louis and the peasant on his lands, Christopher Columbus and any one of his sailors. The *histoire des mentalités* is to the history of ideas as the history of material culture is to economic history. Jacques le Goff and Pierre Nora, *Constructing the Past: Essays in Historical Methodology* (Cambridge: Cambridge UP, 1985), 169.

# 4. Theory and practice of cryptography in early modern Europe[1]

## 4.1. Vulnerable ciphers: the monoalphabetic way

We would not have to waste a lot of words on the pre-1400 history of cryptography if it were not for the Arabs. Most of the cryptographic methods in Latin and later in national languages remained on the level of simple substitutions until the late medieval centuries. In the beginning only vowels were substituted for signs that were made up of dots and then graphic symbols. Later every single letter of the plain text was replaced by a corresponding numeral, letter or symbol. That means that, as the ciphertext was being constructed, the user took the letters from the plain text one by one and wrote their corresponding symbol down in the secret (or rather encrypted) text.[2] This method assigned one single string of symbols, numerals or letters to the original alphabet, in other words, it used one single code alphabet to encipher the plain text, and therefore this encryption is called the monoalphabetic cipher.

Cum Amorato de Torollis. Jam diu.

| | | | | | | | | | | | | | | | | | | | | | | |
|---|---|---|---|---|---|---|---|---|---|---|---|---|---|---|---|---|---|---|---|---|---|---|
| a | b | c | d | e | f | g | h | i | k | l | m | n | o | p | q | r | s | t | u | x | y | z |
| ç | y | x | u | t | s | r | q | p | o | n | 1 | 2 | 3 | 4 | 5 | 6 | 7 | 8 | 9 | ⊤ | 7 | ⊬ |

Monoalphabetic cipher from Mantua (1395)[3].

Monoalphabetic ciphers are rather vulnerable. It may seem at first that in the case of a 22-letter alphabet, the codebreaker must choose from 22! (twenty-two factorial), that is 22x21x20...x3x2x1 = 1 124 000 000 000 000 000 000 possibilities, which is a highly time-consuming task, almost impossible without the help of a computer. Fortunately, the life of the codebreaker is not this difficult. There is a range of mathematical methods

1 This chapter is the elaboration and amplification of the 6th chapter of my *Rohonc Code*.

2 Medieval methods are classified in helpful categories in Bernhard Bischoff, "Übersicht über die nichtdiplomatischen Geheimschriften des Mittelalters" *Mitteilungen des Instituts für Österreichische Geschichtsforschung* 62 (1954): 1–27, see also: Kahn, *The Codebreakers*; Meister, *Die Anfänge der modernen diplomatischen Geheimschrift, idem, Die Geheimschrift im dienste der päpstlichen Kurie.*

3 Meister, *Die Anfänge der modernen diplomatischen Geheimschrift*, 41.

available with which one can radically narrow down the number of possibilities to break this type of cipher. The best-known method of this kind
is frequency analysis. This is quite a down-to-earth method in which the
codebreaker counts each character of the ciphertext and tries to match the
most frequent ones to the most frequent letters of the supposed language
of the plain text. The reliability of this method is based on the fact that languages are strongly characterized by the frequency of their letters, a feature
that is rather constant in every text written in the given language. All of this
is only true, of course, if the encryption did not substitute all the vowels
with 'e' for example, did not intentionally make spelling mistakes, and did
not use a technical terminology. Military jargon, for example, uses a smaller
number of articles.

In present English the letters E T A O I N S H R D L U are the most frequent, in this order, with Z being the least common. In French these are
E N A S R I U T O L D C, in German, E N R I S T U D A H G L, in Italian,
E I A O R L N T S C D P, in Spanish, E A O S R I N L D C T U, while the
Hungarian table of frequency starts with the letters E A T L N. The relative
frequency table of any language can be easily created by counting all the
letters of half a page of text, or even more simply, by downloading a ready-
made graph from the Internet.

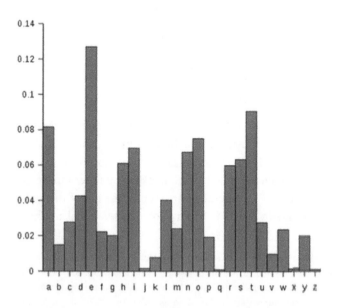

The characteristic frequency of letters in the English language
Source: Wikipedia http://en.wikipedia.org/wiki/Frequency_analysis

Since in the monoalphabetic cipher identical codegroups are substituted for identical letters repeating the pattern of the plain text in the ciphertext, and different codegroups stand for different characters, it takes only a few attempts to match the tallest columns in the frequency chart of the original language to the similarly tall columns in the frequency chart of the language of the coded text. The longer the secret writing available to us is, the more precisely it can be fitted to the frequency chart of the original language – most often a half-page sample is enough for this operation. This assigning process, of course, almost never works automatically, it takes several attempts to successfully match the string of the most frequent characters to the string of the most frequent letters.

Besides the frequency of letters, advanced codebreakers also analyze the frequency of bigrams (a sequence of two letters), trigrams (a sequence of three letters) and digraphs (a pair of letters used to write one speech sound). The most frequent bigram in the English language is TH, the most frequent trigram, not surprisingly, is THE. The most frequent digraphs are SS, EE and TT. In light of this kind of linguistic statistical data, the monoalphabetic cipher cannot be considered secure.

Though the methods described above make the job of the codebreaker a lot easier, in reality many people use simpler (so-called brute force) ways to decipher monoalphabetic secret writings: they look for a prominent pattern in the flow of characters and assign it to the most frequent syllables of the supposed language of the plain text. An excellent example of this is the Cipher Challenge of Simon Singh that he published in the original edition of his book on the history of secret writings, *The Code Book*. Singh offered valuable prize money for the deciphering of ten coded messages. Having worked together for one year, a group of amateurs and professionals coming from all over the world finally solved the Challenge in October 2000. They published their codebreaking methodology, so we know from first hand that instead of applying difficult computer-assisted algorithmic methods, they used pen and paper and brute force to decode the first few (simplest) tasks of the challenge.[4]

Now that we learned how easy it is to solve monoalphabetic ciphers in theory either by frequency analysis or by brute force, it should be emphasized that with historic ciphers this optimism is rather unfounded. The method of simply looking at a text and recognizing its linguistic structures immediately obviously depends on whether word boundaries are indicated in the code text, whether the original language is known, whether this

4    http://www.simonsingh.com/Cipher_Challenge.html

language is well known and whether the scribe had used consistent spelling. In case there are no word boundaries and the codebreaker is uncertain about the language, they are not likely to be successful with the 'take a glance at' technique. It is in such instances that letter-frequency methods should be applied. A seventeenth-century Hungarian text, nonetheless, may prove to be quite a challenge even for proper statistical methods. One may be disappointed if they expect the same character not to stand three times in succession within the same word on the grounds that there are no Hungarian words with the same letter repeated three times. As a matter of fact, scribed often made mistakes, they left out characters or accidentally noted a code number twice. One may be disappointed if one expects a coherent spelling – nothing was further from the scribe than the wish to conform to our modern-day expectations about spelling coherency. It is not obvious, for example, whether he had spelled the Hungarian word 'hogy' (meaning: that) as 'hogy' or as 'hogi'. It is not evident if he had used different signs for the accented vowels (and there are many such vowels in Hungarian!), if he had used a simplified alphabet containing no accents, or whether he had a mixed approach. One cannot be sure if he had a distinct *v* and *u* letters or if he had used the same sign for both. Whether he had a distinct *i* and *j* letters or if he had used the same sign for both.

Knowing the relative frequency of letters in today's Hungarian does not help, and neither does creating our own frequency charts based on the old texts published – according to the publishing conventions of the day – in a more or less modernized way. One may, of course, use a letter-perfect transcript of a manuscript for this purpose. It has to be decided in this case, however, whether the accented vowels should be taken into consideration in creating the frequency charts, or whether the letters *u* and *v*, and *i* and *j* should be considered as two or as one character. In case the codebreaker is not sure whether the text is Hungarian, German, Latin or French, the problems are multiplied. For now, let it be enough to remark that even though a seventeenth-century letter had been encrypted by a monoalphabetic method – without knowing the word boundaries, the base language and without trusting that a coherent spelling was used – the historian may not be successful with the frequency analysis or with any other statistical methods, they will also be required to apply historical and linguistic considerations. This is why the difficulties created by some letters encrypted in the monoalphabetic way – which survived, as we will see later, in surprisingly high numbers from the early modern period of Hungarian history – should not be belittled.

After this detour into modern day deciphering problems, let us now redirect our attention to the people of the past. They faced fewer obstacles because they usually knew the original language of a coded message, just as they were thoroughly familiar with the language of their time (and not confused by a modernized and unified language form that is only to come centuries later). This is why we should not be surprised that although the contemporaries of Julius Caesar, Charlemagne, medieval papacy and the North-Italian city-states apparently did use monoalphabetic ciphers but not frequency analysis, most of the time they did not entrust their diplomatic secrets to this unreliable tool. The vulnerability of the messages was further enhanced by the fact that a great percentage of pre-fifteenth-century letters was only partially enciphered. Sometimes only vowels were coded, and sometimes letters of the plain text were simply substituted by the following letter of the same alphabet (writing *b* instead of *a*, *c* instead of *b*). Dozens of ciphered letters as well as numerous cipher keys survived from before 1400; most of the time, however, non-cryptographic methods were preferred to hide important messages. Letters were, for example, simply hidden in the clothes of the messenger.

## 4.2.    An Arabic contribution: the cryptanalysis

In the Western world, the birth of the science of cryptography in the strictest sense did not take place until the fifteenth century, when the simple monoalphabetic substitution method was started to be replaced by new strategies. This only happened around 1400 despite the fact that medieval Arab scientists had already achieved significant results. Beginning from the twelfth century, Western culture already owed a great deal to Arab science in several other fields. They became familiar with the achievements of the Arab world, the fundamental texts of which were being assiduously translated. The Arabs were equally fruitful in the fields of astronomy, mathematics, optics, logic, philosophy, alchemy, astrology and practical magic. Their texts were read and translated into Latin by dozens of translators. In the course of the reception, these translations had to be examined from the perspective of Christian theology: it had to be decided what to adopt from the science of Aristotle, Galen, Ptolemy and the Arabs and what to reject. This reception, which was initially characterized by enthusiasm more than depth, but then it was gradually replaced by careful analyses, recognized and reacted to the scientific superiority of the Arabs.[5]

---

5    Marie Thérèse d'Alverny, *La transmission des textes philosophiques et scientifiques au Moyen Age,* ed. Charles Burnett (Aldershot: Variorum, 1994); Charles Burnett, *Magic and Divination in*

This recognition and reaction did not characterize the reception of cryptography, although Arab writers described precisely how to decipher monoalphabetic ciphers with methods based on language statistics and were already designing newer and better encrypting methods. We have only recently recognized the real impetus of the achievements of the Arabs, more precisely since historians have started publishing the *Arabic Origins of Cryptology*, a series containing the most crucial documents: sources that were found in the manuscript collections of Istanbul.[6] In light of these we can argue that cryptology, by origin, is a truly Arabic discipline. In other areas of science, such as mathematics, philosophy and logic, the Arabs might have acted as mere transmitters (though decisive ones), but the science of cryptography was not taken over from the Greeks or the Romans to be developed further – it was created by the Arabs from almost nothing. To be sure, there had been simple encrypting methods in the ancient Greek and Roman world too, but it was the Arab writers who attempted for the first time to systematize the methods of decrypting ciphers. This is how the actual science of cryptology was born, covering both cryptography (secret writings) and cryptanalysis (code-breaking).

Editors of the texts of Arabic cryptology explain its birth with four mutually influential reasons, two of these related to the development of linguistics. To begin with, the Arabic culture had made serious efforts to translate into Arabic such texts that had been written in other, often somewhat obscure, languages. Secondly, the Arabic language was itself an object of meticulous study that sometimes even applied statistical methods. The third reason lies in the well-known advancement of Arabic mathematics, hence the very common *sifr* stem (meaning *number* in Arabic) in many a cryptological term (e.g. chiffre). Note how Arabic numerals were necessary for doing efficient language statistics, being more suitable for mathematical manipulations than the traditional Roman numerals. Finally, the fourth reason behind the advancement of cryptology could be the growth of administration in the rapidly expanding Arab states. The editors

---

the Middle Ages: Texts and Techniques in the Islamic and Christian Worlds (Aldershot: Variorum, 1996); David Pingree, "The Diffusion of Arabic Magical Texts in Western Europe," in La diffusione delle scienze Islamiche nel Medio Evo Europeo, ed. B. Scarcia Amoretti, 57–102 (Rome: Accademia Nazionale dei Lincei, 1987).

6     The series publuished by KFCRIS & KACST and edited by Mohamad Mrayati, Yahya Meer Alam, and M.Hassan at-Tayyan, has thus far six volumes: al-Kindi's Treatise on Cryptanalysis (2003); ibn Adlan's Treatise (2003); ibn ad-Durayhim's Treatise (2004); ibn Dunaynir's Book (2005); Three Treatises on Cryptanalysis of Poetry (2006); Two Treatises on Cryptanalysis (2007).

cite important writers from all four major areas that support the claim that these fields were explicitly interrelated, often with the same authors active in them.[7]

The first of these, a scholar from Baghdad, also prominent in the fields of philosophy, geometry, optics, etc. was Ya'qūb ibn Isḥāq Al-Kindi (801?-873?). As early as twelve hundred years ago, Al-Kindi was already familiar with the letter-frequency analysis for solving ciphers. This means that in the ninth century he could easily have broken the kind of monoalphabetic codes that the Western world used as late as in the fourteenth century in diplomacy. During the next half millennium, Arab cryptology flourished in the life and works of scholars, poets and linguists from Damascus and Cairo, as seen from the handbooks of ibn 'Adlan, (1187–1268), ibn Dunajnir (1187–1216), ibn ad-Durajhim (1312–1359), al-Qualquashandi (1355–1418) and others.[8] The majority of the ciphers described by these authors, however, remains basically monoalphabetic. For example, they suggest assigning letters of a different language (Hebrew, Greek, Mongolian, Armenian, Persian, etc.) to the letters of the Arabic alphabet so the text is written in Arabic, but with foreign characters. Alternatively, they point out, one could even make up one's own imaginary system of characters. Al-Kindi introduces a method in which sometimes one, and sometimes two letters of the plain text are substituted with one ciphertext character. al-Qualquashandi mentions a procedure where two Arabic letters of the ciphertext correspond to one letter of the plain text in a way that the numerical values of the two letters equal the numerical value of the substituted character (note that each letter of the Arabic alphabet has a numerical value).[9] Moreover, at least three hundred years before the idea of a homophonic cipher first occurred to the Westerners, an anonymous writer's handbook from the tenth-eleventh centuries entertained the possibility of assigning several code characters to the more frequent letters of the plain text.[10] These methods considerably go beyond simple monoalphabetic substitutions, and might efficiently resist frequency analysis.

---

7   Mohammed Mrayati, Yahya Meer Alam, M. Hassan at-Tayyan, eds. *al-Kindi's Treatise on Cryptanalysis* (The Arabic Origins of Cryptology, 1), (Riyadh: KFCRIS, 2003), 44–74.

8   Besides the publications above, see also: Ibrahim A. Al-Kadi, "Origins of cryptology: The Arab contributions," *Cryptologia*, 16 (1992): 97–126.

9   Abdelmalek Azizi and Mostafa Azizi, "Instances of Arabic Cryptography in Morocco," *Cryptologia* 35 (2011): 47–57.

10  Mohammed Mrayati, Yahya Meer Alam, M. Hassan at-Tayyan, eds. *Two Treatises on Cryptanalysis*, 25.

Discussion of the code-breaking methods, that is, cryptanalysis, is even more important in the Arabic handbooks than these sophisticated encrypting methods. Cryptanalysis starts with the careful study of the plain text's language: the frequency of letters, letter pairs, letter combinations, and an analysis of the typical word patterns. The authors suggest examining which letters stand together regularly, and which ones never stand next to each other; which letters stand typically at the beginning of words and which never; which ones are usually doubled in an average Arabic text. As for the cipher text, they recommend counting the characters in order to identify the language, identifying which characters could signal word boundaries, as well as trying the method of probable word break. This last technique, which was not applied in the West until the sixteenth century, means taking a word that we suspect to be contained by the ciphertext, and simply try it on the cryptogram looking for a string of signs with a similar structure.

These methods constitute and impressing early advance in the science of cryptanalysis, however, since the time of Al-Kindi the frequency analysis was considered to be the main tool: Al-Kindi, ibn 'Adlan and the others produced ample statistics on the relative frequency of the letters and letter combinations of the Arabic alphabet.

## 4.3.    New methods in the literature: the polyalphabetic cipher

Despite the fact that through these achievements the Arabic legacy became far more advanced in this field by the fourteenth century, there is no sign that they became either a source of inspiration, or a powerful opponent for Western cryptography for the coming centuries. As if the treatises discussed above had hidden in the archives of Istanbul, to sit quietly, waiting till the end of the twentieth century to be discovered. Apparently, Western cryptography took off unaware of the achievements of the Arabs, partly due to a number of theoretical studies, partly to the practicing cryptologists of various Italian diplomatic services. As for the theory, it was the leading scholars of the age who authored the monographs on cryptography too.[11] If we look into the books of Leon Battista Alberti,[12] Johannes Trithemius,[13]

---

11   Kahn, *The Codebreakers*, 106–188.

12   Leon Battista Alberti, "De Componendis Cyfris," in Meister, *Die Geheimschrift*, 125–141, *idem*; *A Treatise on Ciphers* (Torino: Galimberti, 1997.)

13   Johannes Trithemius, *Polygraphiae libri sex* (Oppenheim: Haselberg de Aia, 1518), *Steganographia: ars per occultam scripturam* (Frankfurt: Becker, 1606)

Giambattista Della Porta,[14] Gustavus Selenus,[15] Blaise Vigenère,[16] or the English John Falconer[17] we are at first astounded to find the great array of methods available to early modern users.

Some of these were elementary operations based on monoalphabetic substitution, or on transposition (mixing up the letters of the plain text), ciphers that could easily be broken by frequency analysis, by a vowel-identifying algorithm, or by any other paper-to-pen method. These writers, the first of whom is the reputable fifteenth-century architect, Leon Battista Alberti (1404–1472), nevertheless, describe more complex polyalphabetic ciphers too. In these the consecutive letters of the plain text are replaced by characters that are selected from several different code alphabets. In other words, letters of the plain text are not replaced by letters from one single code alphabet, but several ones. As we encode each letter we regularly switch the code alphabets, according to a certain, easy-to-follow system. Initially, Alberti's method was to switch alphabets only after every few words, but more frequent changing of the alphabets is also possible. Alberti's famous disk helps us understand the procedure.

There are twenty uppercase letters and four numerals in the outer ring, for the plain text. The letters A J, K, Y and H are not represented, partly for the sake of simplicity, partly because of the way the system is operated. The rotatable inner ring displays the lower-case letters of the cipher alphabet in a mixed order. When we start working with the plain text, we fix the inner ring and write down the lower-case letter that is opposite B. Then we start encryption, and do not rotate the ring until we do not wish to change code alphabets. If we do, however, we insert one of the four numerals 1, 2, 3 or 4 in the plain text, and the letter corresponding to these in the ciphertext. Then we rotate the rings so this lower-case letter is opposite B, and continue the process until we decide to change the code alphabet again. The strength of the method lies in the fact that the code alphabet is mixed, and the way it is changed is unpredictable and arbitrary.

14   Giambattista Della Porta, *De furtivis literarum notis vulgo de ziferis liber quinque* (Naples: Johannes Baptista, 1602), *De occultis literarum notis, seu artis animi sensa occulte aliis significandi* (Starssbourg: Zetzner, 1606).

15   Gerhard Strasser, "The Noblest Cryptologist: Duke August the Younger of Brunswick-Luneburg (Gustavus Selenus) and His Cryptological Activities" *Cryptologia* 7 (1983): 193–217; *idem*, "Die kryptographische Sammlung Herzog Augusts: Vom Quellenmaterial für seine Cryptomenytices zu einem Schwerpunkt in seiner Bibliothek" *Wolfenbütteler Beiträge* 5 (1982): 83–121.

16   Blaise de Vigenère, *Traicte des Chiffres* (Paris: Abel l'Angelier, 1586).

17   J. Falconer, *Rules for explaining and deciphering all manner of secret writing* (London: Printed for Dan. Brown and Sam. Manship, 1692).

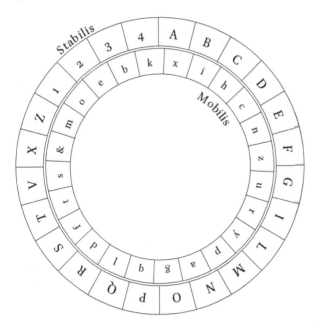

Alberti, *De Componendis Cyfris*, 1446

This polyalphabetic method was further developed by Trithemius, J. B. Bellaso, Della Porta and later Vigenère. It was Trithemius who introduced the polyalphabetic table (a list of alphabets), in which he looked up the first letter of the plain text in the first row of the table, and encrypted the following letters of the plain text according to the corresponding letters in the following alphabets.

Vigenère added a twist to the use of this table. We take a code word (in honor of the inventor let it be *alberti*) and we encrypt the consecutive letters of the plain text according to the alphabets starting with the letters of the word *alberti*. We look up the equivalent for the first letter in the row starting with the letter *a*, the second letter in the row starting with the letter *l*, and so on, till the seventh letter in the row starting with the letter *i*, and then we start again: the eighth letter is looked up in the row starting with the letter *a*. This is the way we go through the letters of the word *alberti* again and again, until we are finished with the process. The main strength of this method compared to monoalphabetic, or even homophonic systems is that it significantly raises the level of entropy in the text.

But what is entropy, and why does it need to be increased? Simply put, entropy is the measure of disorder. Mathematicians use this and similar ways to define the entropy of X:

$$H(X) = \sum_{i=1}^{n} p_i \log_2 \left( \frac{1}{p_i} \right)$$

We could start out from this equation too, but let us use another, more expressive example to explain the idea of entropy. Every text written in a natural language shows strong patterns. In Latin and Neo-Latin languages, for example, the letter $q$ is always followed by the letter $u$, and $h$ often comes after $t$ in English, but rarely the other way around. In Hungarian, the sequence $az$ (the definite article: 'the') and $hogy$ (meaning 'that') are very frequent, but $za$, $ogyh$ and $gyoh$ are less common, and most likely the $hgyo$ sequence never occurs naturally. In English, $the$ occurs in high numbers, but not $eth$, in Latin $que$ is very common, but $euq$, $uqe$ do not exist, and $equ$ can hardly ever be found. In every language, the number of existing letter combinations is relatively restricted compared to the number of all such possible combinations. The stronger the structure, the higher the order in a given language, and entropy (or disorder) is smaller. Higher order, nevertheless, means higher predictability of the words of a given language, that is why smart phone software so successfully predicts the continuation of the words we are writing. The more predictable a system, the less secret it is, the easier it becomes to decipher. Once part of the text is decoded, the rest becomes easier to guess.

Monoalphabetic ciphers do replace every letter of the plain text, but the ciphertext will display the same patterns as the original text. Should the combination 22-17-46 occur in a relatively high number in an originally English ciphertext, we are right to suppose that this sequence stands for the letters of the article *the*. The polyalphabetic cipher, in contrast, mixes up the characteristic patterns of the base language, concealing the typical structures of the plain text and raising the level of entropy (or disorder). Each *the* word in an English text will look different, for these three letters will be enciphered according to three different alphabets each time.

Note, however, that in classic polyalphabetic methods the code alphabets are used in the same strict order. With a sample long enough, we are likely to find a pattern in the plain text (two *the* words, for example, that are coded in the same way, using the same succession of three code alphabets). The weak point of the system is, therefore, periodicity, the fact that the code alphabets are used in the same order. Using this feature, it becomes possible to break a ciphertext – an idea that was served as the base of the ingenious method of Charles Babbage (1791–1871) and Friedrich Kasiski (1805–1881), who finally broke the polyalphabetic cipher.[18] However complex, developed and twisted the upgraded polyalphabetic system of Vigenère may seem, certain writers, like Sacco, plausibly argue that it is actually a step back compared to the less predictable system of Alberti.[19] Code alphabets were ordered, their selection was periodic, and the code word was often a meaningful, existing word, making this algorithm predictable and breakable. This was not to be recognized until much later. During the period we are now examining, however, it was regarded very powerful, and the idea that it could be broken did not even emerge until the nineteenth century.

A special case of polyalphabetic ciphers is Ádám Pálóczi Horváth's secret writing mentioned above, which was deciphered by Hanna Vámos. The first letter of each word was left unchanged, the second was substituted by the letter following it in the alphabet, the third letter by the second letter that stands after it in the alphabet, and so on. Instead of *et*, we write *eu*, instead of *purissimo*, *pxtmyzpty*. Although this is undeniably a polyalphabetic cipher, where each letter of a given word is enciphered by a different code alphabet, it is apparent that the plain text does not become disorganized enough, leaving strong structures in the code text. A simple shifting of the alphabet by one (encoding each letter by an alphabet that is the neighbor of the previously used alphabet), and the fact that this shifting cycle starts again with the beginning of every word makes this code vulnerable. This certainly does not lessen the merit of the codebreaker who recognized this pattern in the seemingly jumbled-up text.[20]

Let us now return to the major cipher handbooks from the sixteenth century. Beside encryption methods in the strictest sense, the works of Trithemius, Della Porta, Vigenère, Selenus, and Falconer also discuss a number of techniques for actually hiding messages, not so much connected to the area of cryptography, as to that of steganography (the art of concealing messages). One example is when only certain letters of a seemingly intelligible, but unimportant text should be read, the rest should be left out. Gustavus Selenus discusses such methods in great length, including those in which only the first letter of each word should be considered as relevant elements of a message, or only every second

---

18    See Kahn, *Codebreakers*, 207–213.
19    Sacco, *Manuel de Cryptographie*, 36–41, 296–304.
20    Vámos, "Leleplezett titok".

word-starting letter.[21] Similarly popular are the syllable methods in these monographs. These assign a text character to a plain text syllable, or double characters to letter pairs, and so on.

## 4.4.    Practice in diplomacy: the homophonic cipher

This rich diversity in the theory did not result in a similar variety in the practice. In sharp contrast with the sophistication exposed in the handbooks, the majority of the considerable cipher methods that were actually used (besides the old monoalphabetic procedure) in the fifteenth to seventeenth centuries fall under the same subcategory of a single method, and one that is hardly mentioned in the handbooks above: the homophonic cipher.[22]

The homophonic cipher was formed gradually during the late fourteenth-century practice of Italian diplomacy. Official cryptography appeared in the decades following 1395 in the chancellery of the Pope as well as in Venice, Florence and a number of other Italian towns. The sporadically used methods based on vowel substitution slowly merged into code alphabets where each letter was replaced by a letter, number, or a graphic sign, and then, step-by-step, second or third signs (homophones) were added to these monoalphabetic alphabets to replace the most common vowels. Meanwhile, another coding tradition was channeled into the practice, which applied a so-called nomenclature, a list of code signs for the most common words, political figures and geographic names. Around 1400, these code signs were inserted into the cipher keys so that the regular names and expressions do not stand out from the ciphertext. Finally, nullities, signs without meaning, were more regularly employed. As a consequence of these improvements, it has become problematic for the codebreaker to figure out if a character stands for a letter, a political figure, or nothing.[23] Homophonic ciphers were born practically from the realization that through

21  Selenus, *Cryptomenytices*, Book 3.

22  About the gap between the theory and practice of early modern cryptography, see: Kahn, *Codebreakers*, 156. for different approaches to the same issue: see Strasser, *Lingua Universalis*, 249; and de Leeuw, "Cryptology in the Dutch Republic: a case-study" in idem and Jan Bergstra, eds. The History of Information Security: A Comprehensive Handbook. Amsterdam: Elsevier, 2007: 324–364, particularly: 329–330.

23  Meister, *Die Geheimschrift*, 21–23, 171–176, *idem, Die Anfänge*, 14–15.

frequency analysis, the monoalphabetic methods had become rather frag-
ile. The first complete code keys of this type containing a full code alphabet, homophones for the vowels, a list of nomenclatures and nullities all in
one, first appeared in 1411 in Venice, then in 1412 in the papal court, and in
1414 in Florence.

The more important Italian political centers soon employed their own
codebreaker who occasionally also wrote a treatise on cryptology. Some
of them are well-known: Gabriel de Lavinde served in the court of anti-
pope Clement VII, Antoine Elio worked first in the court of Paul III, then
of Paul IV; and the Argentis: Giovanni Battista Argenti, and his nephew,
Matteo were the codebreakers of Sixtus V and Gregory XIV, popes in the
late sixteenth century. A good indicator of the prestige surrounding code-
breaking is the fact that members of this profession were highly regarded,
they worked separated from scribes doing the simple, mechanic part of enciphering, and assistants were often assigned to help their activity. Both in
the papal court and in the Republic of Venice this field was institutional-
ized around 1540 to the extent that they opened an official codebreaking
office. In Venice, the codebreakers' room was directly in the Doge's Palace,
above the Secret Chamber. They were not to be disturbed in their work, and
legend has it that they could not leave their room until they had broken the
incoming ciphers.

The homophonic cipher thus became the dominant method of the
late medieval and early modern times. It was simple, easy-to-follow and
practical, and one only needed one or two pages of the cipher table. These
tables – in their mature form – consisted of the following five categories.

1) Three or four different characters, that is, homophones assigned to each
letter of the alphabet. More common letters are usually assigned more
characters than the less common ones. The role of homophones is to
make frequency analysis unhelpful, and also to hide characteristic word
structures in order to hinder probable word break.

2) Special characters for the most common double letters. This category was not yet included in the earliest homophonic keys, but became
more common during the fifteenth century, and grew an inevitable
part of the sophisticated systems in the sixteenth century. Every language has its special set of double letters, therefore concealing them
with one character is an important means to slow down the process of
code-breaking.

3) Special characters for syllables. This method, which also became widespread by the sixteenth century, makes decoding practically impossible. However, the price of this increased security is longer encoding and decoding times, which seemed too big a sacrifice in wartime situations, and thus syllable-substituting characters were often abandoned.

4) Nullities, i. e. characters that do not carry meaning. They confuse a codebreaker, unless a less careful scribe only applied them at the beginning and at the end of a row, which was sometimes the case.

5) Finally, the table of nomenclature, the list of those code words that stand for the most common conjunctions and prepositions, geographical names and political actors. Since these are given a special sign or number (and they are not spelled letter by letter), the system is more likely to resist the "probable word break method", which looks for a word that is most probably found in a plain text, and tries to find its characteristic pattern in the ciphertext.

If one takes two or three homophones for each letter, that makes up an alphabet of approximately one hundred characters. There are usually no more than ten nullities, and the same number of letter pairs. Characters standing for syllables usually number between 100 and 150, while a dictionary of code words could contain 300 items or more (although a very high number of code words makes ciphering very impractical). All this could fit on one big or two smaller pages. This method was followed in the early modern diplomatic correspondence of Italy,[24] Spain,[25] France,[26] Germany[27] and Hungary.[28]

24  Meister, *Die Geheimschrift*; idem, *Die Anfänge der modernen diplomatischen Geheimschrift*; Karttunen, "Chiffres diplomatiques"; Pasini, "Delle scritture in cifra"; Gaetano Platania, "La Polonia nelle carte del cardinale Carlo Barberieni Protettore del regno," *Accademie e Biblioteche d'Italia* 56 (n. s. 39) (1988) n. 2. 38–60; Cecchetti, "Le scritture occulte."

25  Devos, *Les chiffres de Philippe II*; Biaudet, "Un chiffre diplomatique"; Speziali, "Aspects de la cryptographie."

26  Devos, Seligman, *L'Art de Deschiffrer.*

27  Rockinger: "Über eine bayerische Sammlung," Stix, "Die Geheimschriftenschlüssel".

28  Tusor, "Pázmány bíboros olasz rejtjelkulcsa"; Révay, *Titkosírások.*

a  b  c  d  e  f  g  h  i  l  m  n  o  p  q  r  s  t  u  x  z  9  &  ɣ

ℶ  o-  ↳  ꝗ  ⊥  7  ꝗ  π  4  =  ⊨  ഠഠ  Ɔ  ∓  ⋇  ⊘  c  ᴄ  A  ᴢ  6  R  &  ◌

o  ꝑ  ꝑ  ꝑ  n  c̃c̃  e  :·  e  ꝗ  ··  o⊦  ε  ꝗ  4  ꞇ  ﬀ  ÷  a  ꝫ  ⸗  ⊢  8  ⫼

4        ·    ×        z            φ                10

Gemme:
| bb | cc | dd | ff | gg | mm | nn | pp | rr | ss | tt |
|----|----|----|----|----|----|----|----|----|----|----|
| d | d̶ | d̲ᵃ | dᵒ | d̲ₚ | dˡ | dᵒ | d̲ᵧ | dⁿ | dʳ | d̲ˣ |

Nihil importantes:  ✚  ♭  ℼ  Δ  nᵒ  ♄  mᵃ

Quicquid positum fuerit inter hec signa  Ɛ ꓱ
nihil importabit.

| Che | per | come | quando | anchora | pertanto |
|-----|-----|------|--------|---------|----------|
| g | g⁻ | gᵃ | gᵇ | gᵍ | gᶜ |

| | | | | | |
|---|---|---|---|---|---|
| Papa | Lᵒ | El Sʳᵉ de Favenza | Lʳ | Voy | bᵗ |
| Cardinali | Lᵗ | Pace | ⨑ᵗ | Noy | bᵉ |
| Re Ferrando | L² | Guerra | ⨑² | Expedito | b³ |
| Duca di Milano | L³ | Cavalli | ⨑³ | Con conditione | b⁴ |
| Duca de Ferrara | L⁴ | Fanti | ⨑⁴ | In boni termini | b⁵ |
| Duca de Calabria | L⁵ | Gente darme | ⨑⁵ | In male termini | b⁶ |
| Fiorentini | L⁶ | Victualie | ⨑⁶ | De questa cosa | b⁷ |
| Lorenzo de Medici | L⁷ | Carestia | ⨑⁷ | Facilmente | b⁸ |
| Marchese de Mantua | L⁸ | Abondantemente | ⨑⁸ | Dificilmente | b⁹ |
| Sʳᵉ Constantio | L⁹ | V. Sʳⁱᵃ | ⨑⁹ | In stato | bⁱᵒ |
| Bolognesi | Lᵃ | S. Exᵗⁱᵃ | ⨑ᵃ | Acordato | bᵃ |
| Senesi | Lᵇ | Ambasatori | ⨑ᵇ | Essere | bᶜ |
| Suyceri | Lᶜ | Italia | ⨑ᶜ | Non essere | bᵈ |
| Venetiani | Lᵈ | Campo | ⨑ᵈ | In effecto | bᶠ |
| S. Roberto S. Severino | Lᵉ | Inimici | ⨑ᵉ | Assecurare | bᵍ |
| La Sᵐᵃ liga | Lᶠ | Tractato | ⨑ᶠ | Li potentati de | |
| Card. Roano | Lᵍ | Concluso | ⨑ᵍ | Italia | bʰ |
| Card. de Milano | Lʰ | Dicto | ⨑ʰ | Li potentati de | |
| Card. de Novara | Lᵏ | Facto | ⨑ᵏ | la liga | bⁱ |
| Card. de S. Pietro | | Rasonato | ⨑ˡ | La Vʳᵃ Ex. | bᵐ |
| in vinculis | Lᵐ | Venuto | ⨑ᵐ | La S. Sᵗᵃ | bⁿ |
| Vicecancellario | Lⁿ | Mandato | ⨑ⁿ | La S. Mᵗʰ | bᵒ |
| Collegio de Cardinali | Lᵖ | Ritornato | ⨑ᵒ | | |
| Consistorio | Lᑫ | Andato | ⨑ | | |

Homophonic cipher in 1483 in Milan. It contains first the homophones, then the characters standing for double letters, than the nullities, some conjunctions, and finally the code words in a nomenclator table.[29]

---

It should be noted that homophonic tables embody two different cipher methods. Signs assigned to letters and syllables, in other words, units that do not carry meaning but which make up a word fall in the category of cryptography. Statistical analysis and mathematical methods are needed to break them. Nomenclatures, however, are strictly speaking not units of a cipher, they are code signs. These units carry their own meaning regardless of the structure of the given word. Nomenclature tables are in fact dictionaries which assign complete words and ideas to foreign words, or, in our case, code signs. Not so much mathematical analysis is needed to break this code, they should be rather approached as an old language that nobody speaks any more. Breaking a code requires a great deal more encoded texts than breaking a cipher. A further difference is that solution of a cipher composed of letters and syllables can ideally be complete, whereas broken codes often remain partly unsolved – even if the codebreaking was successful, the meaning of some code units might be left unidentified. All in all: the strength of the homophonic cipher comes from a fortunate combination of the advantages of the two kinds of encrypting: ciphers and codes.

Beside the popular homophonic keys, another type of cipher table was in use, although on a much smaller scale, and almost exclusively in the practice of the Papal diplomacy.[30] Instead of assigning several signs to each letter, the so-called polyphonic cipher assigns the same sign to two or sometimes three letters of the alphabet of the plain text. As seen in the first table below, the numeral 4 can equally stand for the letters *a* and *m*, or, in the second example, the numeral 9 can stand both for the letters *a* and *s*. While there are thirty to one hundred homophones in the alphabet of an average homophonic system, the polyphonic method only operates with nine to ten signs, that is, the cipher alphabet is shorter than the alphabet of the plain text. How can such a system function successfully and what are its advantages? The major advantage is that it effectively nullifies frequency analysis, but not because it has assigned more signs to the most frequent letters, but because it has assigned fewer. Deciphering the ciphertext is not that difficult, though undoubtedly lengthy. The addressee writes in several rows the open alphabet letters taken from the code table under the lines of the enciphered text, then, using his linguistic ingenuity and contextual knowledge, composes a meaningful text, selecting in each case from the two or three options. Though ingenious, this method never really became widespread. Mostly it were the secretaries of the Papal office who used it, and only around the mid-sixteenth century.

---

30  Meister, *Die Geheimschrift*, 286–298, 316–323. Sacco, *Manuel de cryptographie*, 34–35; 291–293.

Cifra con il Sig. Cosmo Furtado Falcornio in Portogallo.

| am | bs | cg | du | fe | ni | lt | po | rz | Nulla |
|----|----|----|----|----|----|----|----|----|-------|
| 4  | 5  | 7  | 8  | 9  | 0  | 1  | 2  | 3  | ·6·   |

| qua | que | qui | che | non | cifra |
|-----|-----|-----|-----|-----|-------|
| 66  | 33  | 000 | 99  | 77  | 44    |

Polyphonic cipher from the papal court from around 1584, from the collection of Matteo Argenti[31]

Con il Toletani.

| as | bd | ce | fi | gl | mn | np | ro | tx | Nulle |
|----|----|----|----|----|----|----|----|----|-------|
| 9  | 7  | 5  | 4  | 2  | 1  | 3  | 6  | 8  | 99 . 33 |

| Il Signor Iacopo B.. | 44 | Il Duca di     | 88 | Il Re di   | 44  |
|----------------------|----|----------------|----|------------|-----|
| Il Papa              | 37 | Il Cardinal di | 88 | Il Padre   | 999 |

Polyphonic cipher from the papal court from 1580, from the collection of Matteo Argenti[32]

The homophonic method prevailed until the end of the seventeenth century in both military and diplomatic correspondence. Progress within the system was due to the appearance of syllable codes, on the one hand, and the fact that the nomenclature or code dictionary was becoming longer and longer. By the time of Louis XIV, nomenclatures of five hundred words were not at all uncommon. This, however, can only be regarded as progressive in one sense. When a cipher (in which letters and combinations of letters are assigned to characters) develops into a code system (in which complete words are substituted by code characters), it becomes much more secure, practically unbreakable. One disadvantage, however, is that both sender and addressee must own a rather thick dictionary that contains the correspondence of the numbers and the words. Security is not cheap and the price one pays is decreased user-friendliness. The message becomes more secure as the passing on of the key becomes more complicated. On the other hand, even this increased security is relative – if there is enough sample, the codebreaker may draw logical conclusions from the supposed content, the context and the relationship of the code words. And if the codebreaker happens to obtain a copy of the dictionary of the code words (either by stealing it, or in case of a historian, simply looking it up in the archives), he will have an easy job.

If he does not, his task is almost impossible. The story of *The Man with the Iron Mask* illustrates this well. Originally a story by Voltaire, it is elaborated

---

31  Meister, *Die Geheimschrift*, 293.
32  Meister, *Die Geheimschrift*, 291.

on by Alexandre Dumas in his novel: Louis XIV in 1691 ordered a young man to be shipped in utmost security to the island of Sainte-Marguerite on the Mediterranean. The prisoner, wearing an iron mask, was looked after by the governor of the prison himself. Nobody could meet him during his life, and not even in his death in 1703. A number of theories have been formulated about the identity of this mysterious prisoner, and the source of one of these is a letter which contains the most important piece of information – the name of the prisoner – in the form of a number group serving as nomenclature. The supposedly quite extensive nomenclature dictionary was never found despite the best efforts of historian cryptologists, so the scientific debate is left open on the real name of the man with the iron mask that was concealed by this particular combination of numbers.[33]

33 David Kahn, "The Man with the Iron Mask: Encore et Enfin: Cryptologically," *Cryptologia* 29/1 (2005): 43–49; Emile Burgaud et commandant Bazeries, *Le Masque de fer, révélation de la correspondance chiffrée de Louis XIV* (Paris: Firmin-Didot, 1893).

# 5. Ciphers in Hungary: the source material

## 5.1. Frameworks of data collection

A historian of early modern Hungary, Ágnes R. Várkonyi examined the causes of the "particularly widespread" practices of cryptography in the region.[1] It is hard to judge how far her impressions were right compared to the source material of neighboring countries, because there is no systematic study on the Polish, Czech and Austrian enciphered source materials in the early modern period, and prior to the present monograph, there was no general overview about the Hungarian sources, either. However, as will be evident in the following sub-chapter, the percentage of surviving code tables and ciphered messages is considerably high, my – far from being confirmed – impressions are similar to those of Várkonyi.

Although it is neither necessary nor possible to summarize the history of Hungary in the sixteenth-seventeenth centuries here,[2] it is worth pointing out that this high percentage of enciphered sources is by no means surprising in light of Hungary's political history. This region became a clash zone in these centuries where Christian and Ottoman armies fought, Western culture was confronted by Islamic culture, Catholicism was challenged by the Reformation, and, to a certain degree, Western Christianity met Eastern Christianity.

Hungary, covering the whole of the Carpathian Basin, was seen by contemporaries as a powerful and rich country in the fifteenth and early sixteenth centuries until 1526, when it was first defeated and then, after the fall of its capital, Buda, in 1541, partly occupied by the Ottoman Empire. Subsequently, as one historian has recently put it, Hungary became "a complicated set of lands caught up in an intricate network of alliances, belonging to and claimed by several ruling houses and dynasties".[3] As a result of a series of internal fights, the kingdom became divided into three. Its central part remained occupied by the Ottoman sultan until the end of the seventeenth century. Its western and northern regions continued their existence

---

1   Várkonyi, "A tájékoztatás hatalma," 9 és 27.
2   For an overview of the sixteenth-century history of Hungary, see Géza Pálffy, *The Kingdom of Hungary and the Habsburg Monarchy in the Sixteenth Century* (Boulder, CO: Center for Hungarian Studies and Publications, Inc., 2009).
3   Dóra Bobory, The Sword and the Crucible: Count Boldizsár Batthyány and Natural Philosophy in Sixteenth-Century Hungary (Newcastle upon Tyne: Cambridge Scholars Press, 2009), 10.

as the Kingdom of Hungary under the Habsburg kings but, due to its geographical situation, became a permanent battlefield between the Turkish and Christian armies. And third, the Principality of Transylvania started enjoying a limited independence as a vassal state of the Ottoman Empire and ruled by the so-called Prince of Transylvania.

Borders were constantly changing and a large part of the population lived in the border regions.[4] In this unstable, hence eventful region it was especially important to hide and discover diplomatic, military, scientific and religious secrets. Hungary's richness in enciphered sources makes it an outstanding sample for the study of the social history of secrecy. Other geographic and political areas remain to be revealed by further research, and I hope my studies may offer a helpful example.

But what does "the early modern Hungarian source material" refer to precisely? Where are the frontiers of Hungary, and where are the limits of the early modern period? It is neither possible, nor necessary to draw exact lines, it is, nonetheless, possible to give the rough space and time coordinates for the collection of the sources.

Chronological boundaries are easier to deal with. While the history of secrecy obviously does not conform to political eras and their boundaries, the spread and use of the homophonic cipher do mark the two centuries of the early modern period rather well. They replace monoalphabetic ciphers (which though do not completely disappear until 1700) around the third decade of the sixteenth century to be widely used in Hungary's diplomacy until they too give way to even more complex methods (extensive code books) in the eighteenth century. The use of cryptography in Hungary reaches its summit in the time of the Rákóczi freedom fight (1703–1711) both regarding its quality and its quantity – mainly because prince Rákóczi led intensive and independent foreign policy. Partly due to a quieter political situation, there is a radically decreased number of ciphers surviving from the second decade of the eighteenth century. In this way, therefore, the source material marks its own boundaries from 1526 to 1711.

Geographical coordinates prove to be less self-evident, and give way to endless debates. All studies of this kind face these obstacles, because it is impossible to build up a perfectly sound selection system. As a guideline, effort was made to be practical in this research: I regarded all editions and secondary sources as potential sources for my studies that were on the history of Hungary, i. e. that are traditionally regarded as such by scholars in research and education (and not the least by library catalogs). The most important collections

4    Várkonyi, "A tájékoztatás hatalma," 16.

of Hungarian history provided the source material: the National Archives of Hungary, the Manuscript Collection of the National Széchényi Library, the Ráday Archives, the Military Archives of Hungary, the Manuscript and Rare Books Collection of the University Library of ELTE, and the Hungarica, Turcica and Polonica collections of the Haus-, Hof- und Staatsarchiv in Vienna. When doubt arose about a source, I tended to be more inclusive than exclusive. I included the code keys of the correspondence of Ferdinand I and Charles V, kept in the National Széchényi Library, and the letters of the Constantinople envoy of the Habsburg Emperor kept in the Manuscript and Rare Books Collection of the University Library of ELTE. Even though these correspondences did not necessarily discuss matters related to Hungary, I aimed at giving as wide a picture of the sources found in Hungary's archives as possible. I did not, however, include all the code keys of the Saatskanzlei in Vienna. They may be all from Emperor's capital and connected to the Habsburg's diplomacy, but my focus was on cipher collections directly connected to Hungarian history.

Whether a particular cipher key or ciphered message is included in the list of sources or not is an important issue, more important is that the background of a source should be taken into account on all occasions before being used in an argument. For example, the code keys of Andreas Dudith, envoy from Habsburg Emperor Maximilian to the Polish king, have been included in the database, one has to remember, however, that these do not enable us to draw conclusions about the development of 'Hungarian' cryptography, since they only talk about the diplomacy of the Habsburgs, in which a Hungarian nobleman happened to take part.

Obsession about setting sharp geographical boundaries should be avoided also because general tendencies of the history of cryptography – as we will see – are rarely modified by the appearance or exclusion of a new source.

## 5.2.    General description of the sources

The sources relevant to the history of cryptography in early modern Hungary are scattered in the archives, mostly unidentified and unpublished. Catalogs often fail to mention that a few paragraphs of a text are written in a cipher.

A few code key collections containing dozens of *claves* from the history of Habsburg diplomacy, Hungarian family correspondences, and anti-Habsburg uprisings, however, are exceptions to the rule. These were probably placed in a particular fascicle or fond, or under a call number because their one-time collector must have thought that sources of one kind (most typically one-page documents) belong together and should be kept in one specific place. The folder collecting the nineteenth-century copies of Antal Gévay in the Manuscript Collection of the National Széchényi Library contains almost fifty Hungarian-related sixteenth-century code keys of the Habsburg diplomacy.[5] The Staatskanzlei sources of the Haus-, Hof- und Staatsarchiv of Vienna contain several hundred keys (that Gévay may also have used) in rough alphabetical order.[6] This exceptionally rich collection, only partially related to Hungarian history, sketches beautifully the four hundred years of Habsburg diplomacy.[7] Ten claves of Mihály Teleki are found in the National Archives of Hungary among the materials of the Teleki family archives of Marosvásárhely (Targu Mures, Romania).[8] Twenty-two code keys and five ciphered letters, captured in the mop-up of the Wesselényi movement, are also gathered in Vienna.[9] The cipher tables of Rákóczi's freedom-fight can be found under three call numbers, two of which refer to the documents of Rákóczi that he took with him into exile. These are kept in the National Archives of Hungary, and luckily survived the big fire of 1956 that happened to decimate exactly the Rákóczi's documents.[10] The third call number refers to the documents of Pál Ráday in the Ráday Archives.[11] There are approximately one hundred thirty keys under these three headings, but many of them are in duplicates, so the actual number of different keys is considerably lower. Smaller collections containing fewer than ten keys can be found in the Mednyánszky family archives from the correspondence of György Rákóczi II and Jónás Mednyánszky[12] and among the letters of Pál Esterházy, also in the National Archives of Hungary.[13]

Apart from these concentrated collections of cipher keys, it is generally true for many other keys and the letters themselves that one needs a lot of effort, good luck, and the help of other researchers to be able to identify them. That is why, the nearly three hundred code keys and almost one thousand six hundred letters consulted for this monograph are not a mere addition to the study, but the result of the most laborious part of my research. Future studies will hopefully complete, correct and benefit from the list of sources compiled.

---

5   National Széchényi Library (OSZK) Quart. Lat 2254.
6   I thank István Fazekas and Géza Pálffy for calling my attention to these sources.
7   ÖStA HHStA Staatskanzlei Interiora 13–16. Chiffrenschlüssel.
8   National Archives of Hungary (MOL) P 1238 Teleki Mihály collection, miscellanous documents, cipher keys.
9   ÖStA HHStA Ung Act. Spec. Fasc. 327. Konv. D. Chiffres 1664–1668.
10   MNL OL G 15 Caps. C. Fasc 43 and 44.
11   Ráday Archives C64-4d2-25.
12   MNL OL P 497 Mednyánszky family, 3. fasc.
13   MNL OL P 125 No. 119772.

A peculiarity of the region is the multitude of languages used in the sources. The powerful and long-lasting presence of Latin in the early modern period in all of the Central European region is widely known. While the national languages were gaining strength, Latin remained central for a long time.[14] It was the language of home and foreign affairs (in the Hungarian Diet, for example, or in important peace treaties) and science (Gauss wrote his publications in Latin as late as the nineteenth century). Even commoners spoke Latin sometimes (rumor has it that when Henry Valois arrived in Poland in 1573 to take its throne, he was welcomed by Latin-speaking innkeepers). Latin was sometimes even used even by people arguing for the use of national languages. It is no surprise that ciphered diplomatic and military correspondence was written in Latin too. German was common in the countries of the Habsburg empire – diplomats and captains of German origin naturally liked to write in their mother tongue, in the same way as Hungarian was preferred by Hungarian nobles among themselves. Curiously enough, even the pasha of Buda used Hungarian for decades in his Hungary-related correspondence with the governing bodies of the Habsburgs, excluding the Hungarians themselves from this communication. Spies, typically of Serbian and Bosnian origin, sent their reports in Italian from Constantinople or Ragusa via Venice to Vienna, while the Italian language was gaining importance as the language of the homeland of diplomacy and cryptography. Turkish was present due to the Ottoman occupation. French was also surprisingly popular, even dominant at times, and not only when the leader of the anti-Habsburg appraisal, Ferenc Rákóczi II, was negotiating with his ally, Louis XIV, but also in his letters to his Polish allies.

An important question is how the quantity of the sources presented below relate to the full body of extant manuscripts. This ratio can be best examined according to the three different source types: the cipher tables, the published and the handwritten enciphered documents.

In case of the cipher tables, I was aiming at giving a full picture. This type of source is typically hand-written, it can be found in manuscript collections and archives. Few of them have been published, while one part of the actually published tables are in fact reconstructed, that is, they did not survive as manuscripts, but are based on the enciphered letters that have been broken by the given historian. While I cannot be completely sure that I have found every extant key in the archives (my account is constantly growing, though at a slower pace), in my estimate probably about eighty percent of the extant materials have been taken into account.

---

14 Peter Burke, "'Heu domine, adsunt Turcae': a Sketch for a Social History of Post-Medieval Latin," in *idem, The art of conversation* (Cambridge, Polity Press, 1993): 34–65.

Similarly, the aim was to collect all enciphered letters to be found in source publications and secondary literature. Eighty percent completion has presumably been achieved. It was useful to have a big part of the literature in digital form, especially the source publications of the nineteenth century. These editions are outdated and not always reliable, yet, they are useful for several reasons. A large number of the original letters are now missing, one only knows about them from the publications. Also these digitized sources can be used well for quantitative studies on the mechanisms of secrecy, explicit statements related to the practice of cryptography can be easily identified in them.

As for the original, handwritten documents, I have collected more than a thousand of them, sufficient enough to support the arguments about the historical tendencies related to cryptography. To estimate the total number of enciphered letters kept in the archives is not possible, only approximations are feasible through specific examples. In an archival fascicle related to a military conflict, each and every letter might have been enciphered, but this ratio is more the exception than the rule. In the archive of a family that was involved in high politics, every hundredth letter was enciphered. In other types of archival sources, however, this percentage could be smaller. Having examined numerous archival funds containing primarily diplomatic and private letters, I gathered the impression that on an average as much as one percent of the extant sources are partially or completely enciphered. This may not sound a large quantity at first. However, if we imagine how daunting a task would be to collect one percent of the complete early modern literature, it becomes evident that this is a vast sum. If this estimate is right, collecting the relevant source material is the undertaking of several future generations, of which my studies can only aspire to serve as the basis. Nevertheless, I hope that the sources to be discovered later will only specify, and not modify all that is going to be outlined in the following.

## 5.3.    Cipher keys

### 5.3.1.    The structure of the tables

A precondition of enciphered messaging, at least in the sixteenth-seventeenth centuries, was that both corresponding partners own a copy of the code table, in other words, the cipher key or *clavis*. It ensures that the encryption and the decryption are symmetric, that is, the addressee reads exactly what the sender wrote.

Cipher tables are usually one-page documents. They are usually large sheets, sometimes smaller scraps of paper, even more rarely, parchment sheets neatly written with colored ink. Even the complex systems with many elements were tried to make to fit on one single foldable page, and only a low percentage of the keys required – due to the high number nomenclatures – several pages. Effort was made to arrange the elements so that they are easy to use, and can be reviewed with one glance. As these sheets become quickly worn by use, the claves were usually copied on harder and thicker, cardboard-like paper.

There is a variation in sizes, nonetheless. The smallest ciphers only assign signs, letters or numerals to the letters of the alphabet, and they do so sparingly. These are written in Latin, so in addition to assigning not more than one character to each letter, vowels with accents and the letter *k* are completely missing, and *u* and *v* are identical. As a result, often twenty-two or fewer signs are sufficient for the cipher. Needless to mention, these systems are highly vulnerable.

This is why, additions appeared in the sixteenth century. Bigrams are often assigned special signs or numerals, more frequent letters are assigned several ciphers, nomenclatures and nullities turn out to be more common, and it becomes regular that syllables are systematically assigned a symbol. In addition, by the turn of the seventeenth and eighteenth century, the end of our studied period, Latin is often replaced by the national languages, and the special German, French and Hungarian characters are assigned symbols of their own. As a consequence, keys grow to contain over a hundred, sometimes three or four hundred, or even a thousand items.

The appearance of the code keys may vary, but most often they show the letters of the alphabet in the top row, with the corresponding homophones underneath. Syllables, words and nomenclature are listed in 6 to 14 columns, in alphabetical order. It is not unusual to have the meaningless syllables listed and numbered separately from meaningful words and geographical and political names. Nor is it rare to have the names of the months and nullities given separately, in one of the last columns. Sometimes common titles get their code numbers, and these also are often listed separately. This table of Ferenc Rákóczi, a mature and well-defined Latin system illustrates these categories well.[15]

---

15   MNL OL G 15 Caps. C. Fasc 43.

As one goes on to a deeper study of the source material, one has to revise the previous simplified differentiation between the monoalphabetic and the homophonic cipher systems. The transition from the former to the latter was not the result of one big logical step, nor was it a linear evolution. Between the two kinds of ciphers there was a logical progression, but the stages, that may be distinguished, did not necessarily follow each other, but were more or less coexisting:

1. Classic monoalphabetic cipher, in which only letters of the alphabet are assigned a symbol such as in Szapolyai's cipher message to Hieronym Łaski from 1528:[16]

or the key of Jónás Mednyánszky and György Rákóczi II, from 1658:[17]

The monoalphabetic system occasionally involved fairly "immature" solutions, such as the simple alphabet shift (in its weakest form it is only a shift of one letter, where A becomes b, B becomes c, and C: d,) or when the first and second halves of the alphabet are mutually assigned to each other. These often appeared in the mid-sixteenth-century diplomacy,[18] as well as in the end of the century in ciphers of the poet Bálint Balassi,[19] but, surprisingly, it was also not outdated enough in the middle of the seventeenth century for Prince György Rákóczi II to use them with his envoys.[20]

17  MNL OL P 497 Mednyánszky family, fasc. 3. Cipher keys, fol. 9.
18  Cipher table of Johann Weze, Archbishop of Lund and Ferdinánd I in 1536-ból: OSZK Quart. Lat 2254. 29, and the table of Kaspar Seredy and Leonhard von Fels OSZK Quart. Lat 2254. 21.
19  Balassi's cipher will be discussed below.
20  Ágoston Ötvös, *Rejtelmes levelek,* keys III-VI. See also: Révay, *Titkosírások,* 76–86.

2. Monoalphabetic cipher completed with a short list of nomenclatures, such as the table of David Ungnad, Habsburg envoy in Constantinople,[21] and another table of Jónás Mednyánszky and György Rákóczi II:[22]

21    OSZK Quart. Lat 2254. 23r-v.
22    MNL OL P 497 Mednyánszky family, fasc. 3. Cipher keys, fol. 11–12.

3. Weak homophonic cipher, where only the most frequent vowels are assigned several symbols, with the major part of the alphabet remaining monoalphabetic – such as the clavis of György Martinuzzi,[23] and that of Ferdinand I from 1530:[24]

23   ÖStA HHStA Staatskanzlei Interiora Kt. 13. Chiffrenschlüssel: Kt. 13. Nr. 41. fol 133.
24   OSZK Quart. Lat 2254. 1.

4. Weak homophonic cipher with nomenclatures, such as a key of Andreas Dudith used in messages to the chancellery in Vienna from 1573,[25] and another table of Mihály Teleki:[26]

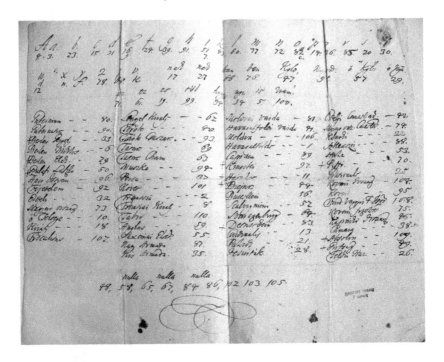

25   Lech Szczucki and Szepessy Tibor, eds. *Epistulae / Andreas Dudithius*, Vol. 3, 16–17.
26   MNL OL P 497 Mednyánszky family, fasc. 3. Cipher keys.

5. Mature homophonic cipher (with several symbols assigned to each letter of the alphabet) and nomenclatures, such as the clavis of Mihály Teleki and István Vitnyédi:[27]

27   MNL OL P 1238 Mihály Teleki collection, Miscallenous documents, Cipher keys.

6. Finally, the most detailed homophonic system including nomenclatures, frequent words, nullities, bigrams, and a complete system of syllables as seen in the near 500-item Hungarian cipher system of Ferenc Rákóczi II and Sándor Nedeczky:[28]

This complex picture is further complicated by two factors. One results from the users being human. A homophonic cipher key may offer several options for each letter in vain if the scribe never made the effort to use other than always the first ones, in which case the method is actually reduced to the level of a monoalphabetic cipher.

The other factor is that the historical development towards a higher level of complexity (from monoalphabetic into homophonic) in reality did not quite respect the six stages that were so nicely outlined above. Some systems used a simple monoalphabetic alphabet, but introduced such a complex system of syllable and nomenclature symbols that in effect the cipher became virtually impossible to break. It also happened that the clavis contained syllables, but no nomenclature, or vice versa, a lot of nomenclatures without any syllables.

28  Ráday Arcvhives C64-4d2-25. 14.

In addition to a growing complexity, we can see another tendency to be formed during this era. In the medieval ages and in the sixteenth century, designers of ciphers seemed to have shared the conviction that the more abstract the signs, the harder it is to break a cipher. Consequently, the dominant cipher of this period is made up of graphic symbols. With time, of course, they realized how difficult it is to design a large number of different symbols – we can experience these difficulties it if we try to come up with four hundred different graphic signs in one sitting – and also that graphic symbols are impossible to arrange in any logical order – something that made the process of decoding infinitely complicated. For this reason, certain modifications were introduced in the structure of the symbols so they can be grouped better (for example the symbols assigned to the letter *A* all looked somewhat similar), and there was also a growing preference towards numerals instead of graphic symbols. In the international diplomatic correspondence of the Rákóczi freedom fight most keys are numeric, graphic signs occur only in the weaker systems used only for inside communication.[29] Mixed systems of numerals and graphic signs were rather rare albeit not totally missing.

The advantage of numeric ciphers is their user-friendliness, although this can easily turn into a disadvantage too. In more than one cases, the designer assigned the numbers to the units of the language, the syllables and the nomenclatures in some order. If he was extremely negligent, he also numbered the letters of the alphabet in their original order or backwards, making the task of the codebreaker easy. This can be observed in several claves of Mihály Teleki,[30] in the correspondence of Ferenc Rákóczi II to his envoy, László Kökényesdi,[31] and even in several of his claves that he used in writing to the French ambassadors Rivier and Bonnac, channels that we would expect to have employed a more advanced level of technology:[32]

---

29   War History Archives E. 1705/18, cipher table of Sándor Károlyi and Miklós Bercsényi, and AR I. vol. 4. Appendix, the cipher table of Rákóczi and Bercsényi.

30   MNL OL P 1238 Mihály Teleki's collection, miscellanous documents, cipher keys.

31   MNL OL G 15 Caps. C. Fasc 43. and Ráday Archives C64-4d2-25. 6.

32   MNL OL G 15 Caps. C. Fasc 44.

A typical case for a too methodical correspondence is when every letter is assigned ten different numbers, but A is assigned the numbers from 100 to 109, B from 200 to 209, and so on, in a perfectly predictable way.[33] Once the codebreaker recognizes the system, it is quickly reduced to the level of a monoalphabetic cipher. The above-mentioned Teleki-Vitnyédi clavis faces a similar problem. The key goes like this: A: 2, 22, 32; B: 8, 18, 28; C: 6, 16, 26.[34] In another, seventeenth century clavis A: 1, 11, 21; B: 2, 12, 22, and E: 5, 15, 25,[35] and in a third one from the Rákóczi freedom fight A: 25, 50, 75, 100; B: 24, 99, 74, 48, and E: 21, 46, 71, 96.[36] The systematic approach is an advantage and a disadvantage at the same time: the cipher is easy to handle and it is just as easy to break.

In most cases, however, the designer was more careful, and the letters of the alphabet are assigned random numbers. The problem is that nomenclatures and syllables are even in such cases numbered as they come in alphabetical order. This enables the addressee to look up geographical or political names assigned to the nomenclature numbers fast, but simplifies the task of the codebreaker too, since he is right to suppose that if 112 is the code

33    Ráday Archives C64-4d2-25. 25.

34    MNL OL P 1238 Mihály Teleki's collection, miscellanous documents, cipher keys.

35    ÖStA HHStA Ungarische Akten Specialia Verschwöreakten VII. Varia, Fasc. 327. Konv. D. Chiffres 1664–1668, fol 15.

36    Ráday Archives C64-4d2-25. 9.

sign of absque, 113 stands for aliter, 114 for ante, 115 for autem, 116 for admiral and 118 for Austria, then 117 is more likely to be Anglia than for example Turcica.[37] Further examples that assign words to numbers in alphabetical order are two claves of Palatine Pál Esterházy,[38] the famous flower-patterned clavis that Rákóczi used with the French court, and a few of his other tables in which even the letters are assigned to every second number, in a recognizable way.[39] In case of these cipher structures, even a fifty-percent solution makes the rest of the nomenclature table easy to fill in.

A more clever system is in which the nomenclatures are numbered, not vertically, however, in alphabetical order, but horizontally as they appear on the page. The addressee can decrypt the ciphertext with the same ease, but the hostile codebreaker has a harder task because the numbers do not follow the alphabet but rather the way words were randomly placed next to each other in the columns of the nomenclatures.[40]

37 MNL OL G 15 Caps. C. Fasc 43.
38 MNL OL P 125 No. 119772.
39 MNL OL G 15 Caps. C. Fasc 44.
40 MNL OL G 15 Caps. C. Fasc 43 and 44.

Similar problems arise when the different categories of the cipher (letters, syllables, nomenclatures, nullities) are corresponded different types of code signs. For example, letters are always assigned two-digit numbers, and nomenclatures three-digit ones,[41] or when the system is made up of graphic symbols but the symbols for the nomenclatures look different from the symbols for the letters.[42] This procedure, which was used in sixteenth-century diplomacy as well as in the Wesselényi movement or the Rákóczi freedom fight, enables the addressee to quickly find the right category in the big and complex table, but it helps the codebreaker just as much, who will be able to differentiate between letters and nomenclatures just by looking at them, and will soon leave the latter out of the frequency analysis.

According to the proper modern terminology, these cipher tables are 'structured'. An advanced stage is represented by the so-called 'unstructured' tables, in which the code words follow each other completely randomly, giving no clue whatsoever to the codebreaker. Entirely 'unstructured' nomenclature tables, nonetheless, are rather rare, especially among the extensive ones.

These problems are partly due to the fact that both encryption and decryption were done by the very same table. There are a few exceptions, when the encryption works with a different *type* of table than the decryption, and both processes can be optimized to fit their own purposes. The nomenclature words of the encoding table are organized into alphabetical order, while the decoding table is arranged in the order of the code numbers. One A4-size chart of Ferenc Wesselényi (*ad scribendum*) gives the code numbers of syllables and nomenclatures in alphabetical order, while the other (*ad legendum*) lists the cipher signs in a numerological order. One system, two different perspectives.[43] Similarly, a chart of Rákóczi, called *reducta*, helps the addressee in the decryption process by showing the system from his perspective, whereas another table of the same cipher follows the logic of the encryption.[44] These double tables, however, are the minority. Most ciphers use one type of table for both processes.

41   OSZK Quart. Lat 2254. 51–52; ÖStA HHStA Ungarische Akten Specialia Verschwörerakten VII. Varia, Fasc. 327. Konv. D. Chiffres 1664–1668, fol 12–13; MNL OL G 15 Caps. C. Fasc 43.

42   OSZK Quart. Lat 2254. 27.

43   ÖStA HHStA Ungarische Akten Specialia, Fasc. 327. Konv. D. Chiffres 1664–1668, fol 1–2.

44   MNL OL G 15 Caps. C. Fasc 43.

The language of the tables should also be taken into account. Sometimes, when only the letters of the alphabet and maybe a few syllables accompanied by numbers can be seen, it is hard to decide what the original language of the key was. Naturally, since these tables were mostly used by sixteenth-century diplomats, we have reason to think of Latin. In other cases, though, the words of the nomenclature table precisely identify the language.

Latin kept its vital role in cipher tables. At least one third of all extant tables were used for a text written in Latin. In the Hungarian archives, there are not more than two to three percent of Italian claves and only a bit more German. Most of the German ones, by the way, were ciphers caught or broken in the Rákóczi freedom fight. By the end of the early modern period, particularly in the Rákóczi freedom fight, French becomes more dominant – ten percent of all extant tables are in French, and not only in messages directly related to Louis XIV, but in other directions too, for example with the Polish. Thirty percent of all tables are in Hungarian. Their ratio gradually increases by the end of the period. Finally, several claves survived that were apparently used in more than one language, and several others had Latin, Hungarian, and French versions too.

### 5.3.2. Letters of the alphabet

The letters of the alphabet of the open text are most often matched with graphic signs or numbers in code tables. Assigning other letters in the code alphabet to the original letters is not infrequent either. Different parts of a grid can also make a code alphabet, like in the famous Pigpen cipher of the Freemasons. Other examples of this kind are two tables from 1658 of Jónás Mednyánszky and György Rákóczi II.[45]

45   MNL OL P 497 Mednyánszky family, fasc. 3. Cipher keys, fol. 9 and 10.

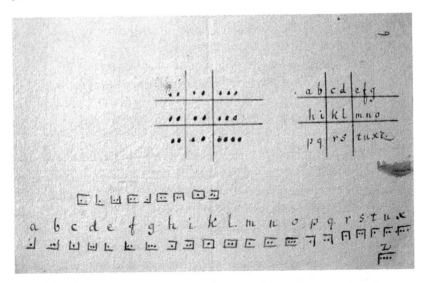

Particularly exceptional, however, is the *clavis musicalis* of Ferenc Rákóczi II, a three-page nomenclature table that assigns Latin words to political and geographical names, and musical notes to letters. Due to these musical notes, the system is spectacular, but even this does not change the fact that its alphabet remains basically a vulnerable monoalphabetic cipher.[46]

46  MNL OL G 15 Caps. C. Fasc 43.

Code alphabets may reflect how the language of the open text functions. When the designers first realized the danger in double letters and tried to hide them by making up a special sign for the most typical ones (in Latin: *rr, ll, ss*), they were apparently aware of the recognizable features of the language. Special German characters also appeared relatively early: an example is from around 1570, in the clavis of David Ungnad, the Habsburg court's

ambassador to Constantinople.[47] The typically Hungarian letters appear in
the tables from the second half of the seventeenth century: first *Ö* and *Ü*,
then *Ty, Sz, Ny, Cs, Cz* and *Ly*.[48] Curiously enough, the most frequent accented letters, *Á* and *É* were only assigned special numbers in the beginning of
the eighteenth century, by the time *Ö* and *Ü* were already much used.[49]

### 5.3.3.    The nomenclatures

In a recent article cryptology historian David Kahn denotes the systematic study of the development of nomenclatures as one of the tasks to
be achieved in the field.[50] Nomenclatures, this list of proper names and
frequent words carries truly valuable information for historians regarding both the political situation of the time and the use of cryptographic
technology.

As mentioned above, the code signs of the nomenclatures were visually separated from the rest of the cipher table. In the correspondence of
Ferdinand I and Johann Malvezzi, envoy to the Ottoman Porte, for example, single signs are assigned to letters, numbers for double letters, and
two- or three-letter words for nomenclatures.[51] This distinction remains
to be quite common later, and is related to the tendency of renaming nomenclatures by other code words. In the correspondence of András Dudith
and the Habsburg court, *Niger* stands for Laski, *Accursius* for the Pope,
and *Lethargici* for the Lithuanians.[52] In a mid-sixteenth-century table
*Veneti* stands for mirantur, *Ragusei*: insignis, *Orator*: utinam, *Passa*: otium,
*Turchi*: paxes.[53] Free association and some humor were not absent from the
name giving procedure.

Most claves of the sixteenth century included only a few, not more than
ten to twelve nomenclatures for the most important political and geographical names. The 1531 table of Sigismund Herberstein and Hyeronim
Łaski contains merely two nomenclatures: one for *Emperor Suleiman* and

---

47   OSZK Quart. Lat 2254. 23r-v.

48   MNL OL P 1238 Mihály Teleki collection, Miscallenous documents, Cipher keys; ÖStA HHStA
Ungarische Akten Specialia, Fasc. 327. Konv. D. Chiffres 1664–1668, fol 16; MNL OL G 15 Caps. C.
Fasc 43.

49   MNL OL G 15 Caps. C. Fasc 43.

50   David Kahn, "The Future of the Past," 58.

51   War History Archives, 1548/3.

52   Lech Szczucki, Szepessy Tibor, eds. *Epistulae / Andreas Dudithius*, Vol. 4, 18–22.

53   OSZK Quart. Lat 2254. 20.

one for Łaski' lord: *János Szapolyai*.[54] The 1545 table of Johann von Tarnow, Polish ambassador to Ferdinand I uses only one: *Sigismund junior Ploniae Rex*,[55] and the 1658 table of Jónás Mednyánszky, acting on behalf of Prince György Rákóczi II, only contains seven: *Nádasdi, bishop, porta ottomanica, Rákóczy, chancellar, king, palatine*.[56] In the longer tables of the Rákóczi freedom fight *Caesar, Rex* and *Princeps* are often the first words. By the end of the early modern period the lists grew to include several hundred, occasionally a thousand items.

The enrichment of the list of nomenclatures is a good illustration for the growing awareness of the vulnerability of codes. The names of the months are rarely included in the nomenclature lists in the sixteenth century[57] but they are almost compulsory elements by the time of the Rákóczi freedom fight, because the dates, that always had to be indicated at the beginning or end of a letter, are the most critical part of every enciphered letter where codebreakers can easily find a breaking point. The same is true for numbers in general, punctuation marks, and the obligatory greetings at the beginning of a letter, all of which became part of the nomenclature lists by the end of the seventeenth century. In the table of Rákóczi and Ferenc Horváth, the phrase "Your humble and unworthy servant" is simply 887, Ferenc Horváth (obviously as a signature) is 888, the question mark is 1013, and the days of the month from 1 to 31 remain unchanged – a daring and clever invention. Numbers used for other purposes have their own codes, so for example eight is 683.[58]

A close reading of the nomenclature tables serve for painting a vivid picture of the political environment of a period simply by showing who or what was important enough for the corresponding partners to include in the list. They put those names on the cipher table that occurred often enough in the text for a codebreaker to identify them and use the probable word method. The major foreign relationships of Rákóczi can be well mapped out just by looking at the diplomatic cipher tables used during the freedom fight. Another example is a nomenclature table from the correspondence of Mihály Apafi, prince of Transylvania, and palatine Pál Esterházy which shows clearly who and what was important to them: *peace, mining towns, Telekij, frontier armies, Tököly, Wesselényi*. A mere glance on the keys of the

54  OSZK Quart. Lat 2254. 12.
55  OSZK Quart. Lat 2254. 24.
56  MNL OL P 497 Mednyánszky Family, fasc. 3. Cipher keys, fol. 11–12.
57  OSZK Quart. Lat 2254. 7, and 47.
58  MNL OL G 15 Caps. C. Fasc 43.

Wesselényi movement confiscated by the Habsburg court is informative about the network of the conspiracy, these were indeed the participants: Our graceful Lord Palatine, Lord Nádasdy, Lord Péter Zrínyi, István Csáki, the bishop of Győr, etc.[59] Naturally, these tables reveal details that had been long known to those who study the period, but it is still fascinating to see how a single-page table can tell us, who were the really relevant figures in a specific historical situation.

There are cases, however, where we can reach more important conclusions based on the nomenclature table. The most detailed table from the Gévay collection (a table that surpasses most eighteenth-century claves in its richness) was apparently not used in a correspondence related to the diplomacy of the Hungarian Kingdom. However developed and clever this cipher may be, the code words themselves prove that they were not connected to Hungarian history in any way.[60] An even more compelling conclusion can be drawn from the choice of nomenclatures of one table of Rákóczi that will be discussed in further detail in a later chapter. This cipher key is completely void of the names of the relevant political figures and military scenes, but it is full of French terms denoting different emotions. Based on the table, and, as we will later see, further external evidence, we have reason to suppose that Rákóczi used the key with his Polish ally and lover, Elżbieta Helena Sieniawska.[61] In contrast, the table that was supposedly used by him and his lawful wife includes a most traditional, politically relevant nomenclature list – a telling sign that his marriage will not be long-lasting.[62]

### 5.3.4.  Nullities

Nullities, code signs with no meaning that were only used to confuse codebreakers, are denoted by several different terms in the tables such as *non-valeurs, nullitas, errantes, nihil significantes, superflua.*

59  ÖStA HHStA Ungarische Akten Specialia Fasc. 327. Konv. D. Chiffres 1664–1668, fol 12–13.
60  OSZK Quart. Lat 2254. 49.
61  MNL OL G 15 Caps. C. Fasc 44.
62  Ráday Archives C64-4d2-25. 5. On the back of the table: "Mme la Comtesse de Transylvanie"

It is not uncommon to have ten to twenty consecutive numbers as nullitas for the sake of simplicity, but in more careful tables such as that of Rákóczi and Daniel Ernest Jablonsky systematic descriptions define nullities: for example all numbers with an apostrophe.[63] Another table by the same people instructs the reader to consider every letter a nullity that is not listed in other parts of the key.[64] In the table of Malvezzi presented above nullities are meaningful Latin words (*atque, etiam, cum, idcirco*).[65] In certain cases certain numbers are not only nullities by themselves – they annul the words preceding them in the ciphertext.[66] Most commonly, though, a few, sometimes a dozen numbers are simply listed in a separate rubric of the table, under the heading *numeri nihil significantes*.

### 5.3.5. Grammatical elements

Cipher tables traditionally list letters, syllables and nouns. It was a considerable improvement when grammatical categories were taken into account, and specific symbols were introduced for plural, accusative, genitive, dative and ablative. In two systems of Mihály Teleki – both of which are otherwise fully constructed of numbers – the indicators of the grammatical cases are graphic symbols.[67] It is hard to overestimate the significance of this extension. With the introduction of grammatical signs, cipher systems took a step towards artificial languages, then highly popular. I am going to investigate this issue in the chapter on the transfer of knowledge.

63  Ráday Archives C64-4d2-25. 2.
64  Ráday Archives C64-4d2-25. 3.
65  War History Archives, 1548/3.
66  MNL OL P 1238 Mihály Teleki collection, Miscallenous documents, Cipher keys.
67  MNL OL P 1238 Mihály Teleki collection, Miscallenous documents, Cipher keys.

| | | |
|---|---|---|
| .S. | | |
| .SS. | 210 | |
| .Sa | 211 | *Signa Casuum* |
| .Se | 212 | |
| .Sed | 213 | nominat. Sine Signo |
| .Si | 214 | Genitivus . . . — |
| | 215 | |
| .Secretum | 216 | Dativus . . . ⋅v |
| .So | 217 | accusativus    θ |
| .Su | 219 | ablativus . . .    + |
| .T. | 221 | |
| t t | 222 | Quando debebit intelligi |
| ta | 223 | in plurali, tunc ponetur |
| Transilvani | 224 | Supra ∩ |
| Tartari | 225 | |
| te | 226 | |
| ti | 227 | *Numeri nihil* |
| to | 228 | *Significantes* |
| tu | 229 | 1. 27. 40. 44. 97. |
| Turcæ | 230 | 117. 142. 155. 159. |
| U     231 | 232 | 171. 197. 218. 220. |
| va | 233 | |

## 5.4.    Encrypted messages

There is a striking contrast between the excitement of the readers roused by some novels that contain ciphers, and the usual indifference historians display towards the content of the real enciphered messages. A long row of authors of classic literature, bestsellers and detective stories give a central role in their stories to codes and ciphers – Edgar Allan Poe (*The Gold-Bug*), Isaac Asimov (*1 to 999*), Arthur Conan Doyle (*The Adventure of the Dancing Men*), Agatha Cristie (*The Four Suspects*) Edgar Wallace (*Code No. 2.*), Umberto Eco (*Foucault's Pendulum*), Jules Verne (*Cryptogram*), Dan Brown (*The Da Vinci Code*), Dorothy Sayers (*Have his Carcase*) or Ken Follett (*Key to Rebecca*).[68] Each issue of the journal *Cryptologia* contains useful reviews on the recently published secondary literature, and among these, in the "fiction" section it also gives informative reports on crypto-novels and detective stories.

---

68  John F. *Dooley, "Codes and Ciphers in Fiction*: An Overview," *Cryptologia* 29 (2005), 290–328.

A recent research lists 150 relatively well-known novels in which ciphers play an important role.[69]

In sharp contrast with this popularity, the extant historical ciphers give a somewhat boring impression. A ciphered message is nothing but a mere sequence of symbols or numbers. Even if the content of the message becomes readable – either because the late addressee had written the solution above the line, or because a modern researcher has reconstructed the key – there are surprisingly few cases which provide information still unknown to the historians specialized on the given age.

Nevertheless, the central thesis of this monograph is that the research on the early modern enciphered messages is relevant from a different aspect. Beyond the content of the secret messages they are rich information resources of their age. The attentive reader can get insight into the attitudes of the people involved, into their notion of secrecy and into the details of their use of technology.

In order to gain the appropriate information from the sources, one either has to examine the original document, or a trustworthy edition of it. Since a portion of the sources ever edited can no longer be found in the archives, and since manuscripts have the disadvantage of not being digitally searchable, source publications, however bad their quality may be, should be included in the research. These source publications are highly different in nature.

The least useful ones for this present research are those that do not indicate which part of the letter was originally enciphered – either because the published text is a regesta (summary), or because this information about the ciphertext did not seem relevant for the nineteenth century editors. Luckily enough this policy was only applied in a small percentage of the text editions.[70]

More informative are the editions that indicate (in italics, or in some other way) exactly what part of the text had originally been typeset in *chiffre*, that is, enciphered. The crypto-historian can thus compare what part of the message was considered worthy of hiding, what words were thought to be dangerous, and what was left as plain text. Scribes often followed awkward strategies and enciphered contents that today we think could easily have been reconstructed on the basis of the rest of the plain text. Another quaint

69  http://www.staff.uni-mainz.de/pommeren/Kryptologie/Klassisch/o_Unterhaltung/Lit/.

70  Such as the correspondence of Ferdinand I and Giambattista Castaldo in: Samu Barabás, "Erdély történetére vonatkozó regesták" (Regestae related to the history of Transylvania) 5–6, *Magyar Történelmi Tár*, III/15 478–492 and ibid. 651–683.

observation is how typical the quality and quantity of the enciphered parts within a message are for a given author. Some people cover up only proper names and certain military and financial data, some other encode virtually the complete message.

The majority of publications, for example most volumes of the series *Archivum Rákóczianum,* set ciphered texts in italics.[71] Their advantage lies in the fact that both the enciphered parts and the explicit references to the use of cryptography are easily searchable, especially if they are digitized. It is due to this feature that I tried my best to enumerate as many of the published enciphered letters in my constantly growing database as I could. Their disadvantage, however, lies in the fact that they usually contain no information whatsoever on the cipher method employed, with a few exceptions that publish the keys in an appendix, as in an Ágoston Ötvös publication of the enciphered letters of György Rákóczi I,[72] or the modern-day publication of András Dudith's letters.[73] The average source publication unfortunately does not contain any reference to the method (monoalphabetic, homophonic or other) or to the meaning of the particular numbers and signs, making it impossible to identify the cipherkey. The reason for that in some cases is that instead of the original ciphertext, the publisher used the book of letters that only contained the underlined parts that were to be ciphered. In other words, the publisher himself never actually saw the enciphered message.[74] More often, nonetheless, the publication was based on the enciphered original, however, the publisher used the reconstructed text that the addressee or his secretary wrote above the lines of the code symbols. Interested mainly in the content of the message, the publisher may have just disregarded the ciphertext.

Finally, the publications most useful for us are those that use skillful and fastidious typesetting to show the code numbers right underneath the corresponding words of the plain text, as in a Károly Széchy publication of Miklós Zrínyi's letters to the prince of Transylvania,[75] or the published diary of Mihály Bay.[76]

71    AR, vol. I. 2 (Budapest: Magyar Királyi Tudományegyetem, 1872).

72    Ágoston Ötvös, *Rejtelmes levelek.*

73    Lech Szczucki, Szepessy Tibor, eds. *Epistulae / Andreas Dudithius,* Vol. 2, 22–23; Vol. 3, 16–17; Vol. 4, 18–19; ibid. 19–20; ibid. 20–22

74    AR, I. vol. 1. 472–474. 13.; 477–478., 16.; 504–506., 35; 512–513., 42.

75    Károly Széchy, ed., *Gróf Zrínyi Miklós 1620–1654* (Count Miklós Zrínyi), vols. I-V (Budapest: Magyar Történelmi Társulat, 1896–1902), vol. III, 335–338, vol. IV, 252–268.

76    "Diary of Mihály Bay" in: Kálmán Thaly, ed., *Késmárki Thököly Imre és némely főbb híveinek naplói és emlékezetes írásai 1686—1705* (Diaries and memorable writings of Imre Thököly of Kežmarok and some of his main followers 1686—1705), (Monumenta Hungariae Historica,

Much to the dismay of the historian, the addressee occasionally leaves a few words coded here and there in the ciphertext, and not owning a copy of the key, the editor could not decode these either.[77] A vivid example of this is the following excerpt from a letter of Ferenc Rhédey to Mihály Teleki from 1678: "Our Lord Bethlen and his company, especially Farkas is not writing to Your Lordship as much as he used to, and is not very fastidious in forwarding the letters of the Porte to Your Lordship. Indeed, these days 140. 131. 124. 123. are *most evil*."[78] The words *most evil* were originally in cipher, but were published decoded. However, the preceding numbers, which are apparently nomenclatures and must have stood for the names of particular people, remained in cipher. Modern-day historians are left wondering who Rhédey regarded as most evil. It is not uncommon either to have all the enciphered text of a message unbroken, even though these sources only make up a small percentage of the published letters.[79]

It is symptomatic that in those cases when the late addressee did not decrypt the ciphertext, it has typically remained unbroken for decades or centuries, even if theoretically it was never unbreakable. The author of children's books, Beatrix Potter (1866–1943) wrote her encoded diary between 1881 and 1897, which, though not at all beyond the capacities of a well-prepared codebreaker, was not broken until 1958. Similarly, a typical problem with modern-day publications of Hungarian enciphered texts is that instead of deciphering them, they merely publish those that had been decoded by someone from the time of the ciphertext (most typically the addressee). In case a code was left undeciphered for a few weeks after it was written, it has been most often left undeciphered since then.[80] This is in spite of the fact that the cryptologically informed historian can use mathematical and statistical methods, or – if they are lucky to enjoy the comfort of having the cipher key – they can simply match the ciphertext with the key and thus reconstruct sources previously not available to historians.

When preparing the publication, the editors – but often the addressee himself, whose reading the editor uses – almost always *reconstruct* the

Magyar Történelmi emlékek 1868, II. 23/2.) 461—578. In the manuscript (MNL OL G. 15. Caps A.1. Fasc 24. fol. 75- 124r.) a hand (a secretary?) wrote the solution above the numbers, on the basis of which the editor amended the text.

77   Teleki 8. 135–140., 123. In the the decoded text, two numbers, 500 and 42, are left undeciphered.

78   Teleki 8. 306–307. 283.

79   Among others: Teleki 8. 19–20., 20; ibid. 20–21., 21; ibid. 27., 25; ibid. 290–292., 266.

80   Exceptions are the sources in Révay, *Titkosírások*, in Ötvös, *Rejtelmes levelek*, and the aboce quoted articles by Péter Tusor, István Vadai and Hanna Vámos, where historical sources are published in modern decoding.

message, which involves indicating word boundaries not marked in the enciphered text, and differentiating between vowels with and without accent even if the same symbol encoded the letters 'a' and 'á'. In other words, the editor modernizes the text in the editing customs of his own time. This is a necessary procedure in every text edition which aims not at retaining a letter-perfect transcription for linguistic purposes, but rather readability and usability for historical purposes. Still, it is quite evident that aiming at reader-friendliness leads to significant information loss concerning the use of ciphers.

Ciphertext decoded by the addressee: Letter of Rákóczi's French delegate Jean Tournon to Pál Ráday. An advanced homophonic cipher from 1707.[81]

One can get real insight into early modern practice of cryptography through examining the original manuscripts. When the historian starts to make a meaningful message out of a ciphertext by statistical methods or with the help of the key, they will directly realize how hard it is to break a string of symbols when it lacks word boundaries, a correct orthography, and contains a lot of mistakes.

81   Ráday Archives C64-4d2-10.

Undeciphered ciphertext with symbols, for which there is a key available: the correspondence of Ferdinand I and ambassador Malvezzi on 23 January, 1548. Advanced homophonic system.[82]

82  War History Archives, 1548/3.

A recently deciphered ciphertext with numbers: A letter from the Wesselényi movement. A monoalphabetic cipher.[83]

83   MNL OL E 199. fasc 8., pallium 1.

An experience with such ciphertexts helps appreciate the kind of obstacles addressees were faced even with the legitimate cipherkey at hand,
why they had spent the whole night decoding a letter, why they could
sometimes be uncertain whether they had used the right clavis, and how
they could misunderstand the ciphered text so often. Similarly, one needs
to have the manuscript at hand when one tries to reconstruct if these
methods could stand against the most frequent codebreaking approach,
the probable word method. In reconstructed editions the messages containing the same words are identical, though not necessarily in the original
manuscripts. One can also observe if the given code numbers are identical
too, making it easy for the codebreaker to use the probable word method,
or if he had broken identical words into different syllables each time, or
had always assigned a different homophone for the letters to give the codebreakers a tough job. In addition, published sources do not display nullities,
but the manuscripts indicate precisely that less diligent encoders tended
to place the meaningless numbers at the beginning and end of each row,
something that codebreakers must have quickly found out about. Furthermore, in the manuscripts one can see how long a scribe used the same key,
how many different keys an important politician applied with his or her
correspondents, or to which extent the user (a secretary, but sometimes
the prince himself) exploited the capabilities of the enciphering method.
Finally, one has to go back to the archival sources too in order to see at what
pace the awkward systems of graphic symbols were replaced by the more
advanced, number-based methods. A text edition says nothing about how
much more sophisticated encoding Rákóczi had used in his letters to the
French ambassador than to his general Bercsényi – it simply publishes the
messages.

# 6. Ciphers in action

## 6.1. Sharing the key

A recurrent theme in early modern Hungarian military, political, and diplomatic correspondence is the use, or improvement, of cryptography and all the entailing problems. These topics are usually covered at the very beginning or end of a letter in a few explicit remarks, and it is mentioned here which cipher worked and which did not, what letters they had sent or received. Such an example can be found in the second sentence of a 1662 letter sent to the Transylvanian politician Mihály Teleki, where his correspondent reported that he had earlier received both the letter and the cipher key. "As to a good-willed lord, I am at your service. An officer handed me your letter together with the clavis a few days ago."[1]

Ciphered correspondence did not work in the early modern period if the corresponding partners had not previously exchanged a cipher key or clavis. The key was usually not more than a folded paper. Since at least two claves were needed for a ciphered correspondence to work, one for the sender and one for the addressee, and because often it was the secretaries who did the administrative tasks around the correspondence, it is not surprising that some keys have survived in several copies.

Political actors often noted that without a proper cipher key, they were not able or not willing to write about things that really mattered. The Transylvanian magnate, Dénes Bánffy, who was writing to Mihály Teleki, noted that "Since I have no clavis, I do not dare to write, because if my letter were caught, they would know that we were betraying our lord and our nation, and that we are asking for money for this reason."[2] Bánffy writes again, in another letter, "Do not fail to send the clavis because there is no correspondantia without it."[3] Prince Ferenc Rákóczi II wrote to his correspondent in 1711 from Gdansk, "I do not dare to write without a clavis..."[4] Chancellor of Transylvania, János Bethlen emphasizes in a 1667 letter that "we can trust a letter with private information if it is written with a clavis".[5]

It is no surprise, then, that people regularly asked each other to write their letters with a clavis, or, if they had no clavis, they requested one,

---

1    Teleki 2. 253–254, 186.
2    Teleki 4, 297–98.
3    Teleki 4, 461–463.
4    AR, I. vol. 3. 698–701.
5    Teleki, 4. 47–49.

usually the less important person from the more important one. Mihály Teleki is writing to János Nemes in 1678. "Dear brother, please write to me better and more truthfully with a clavis."[6] Miklós Bethlen is writing in 1678, "therefore I suggest that you only write about significant topics with the clavis"[7] Mihály Teleki in 1678, "Because Lord Rédei was also there, I have used a clavis to make this more secret. We pray to God that it would remain secret."[8] Ferenc Rákóczi II is writing to Antal Esterházy in 1710, "Please write to me by post via couriers, in casu necessitatis using the clavis of Újvár."[9] Ferenc Palkovics is sending a letter to General Bercsényi from Simontornya in 1709, "As the enemy is going to encircle us more, I advise my Lord to have some claves made and use them in writing to us here."[10]

István Dalmady, childhood friend of Teleki is asking for a clavis from him: "If it is not too much of a trouble, please make a clavis with secret letters so we could write to each other with bigger confidentia."[11] The lawyer István Vitnyédi makes the same request to his patron, the magnate Miklós Zrínyi: "It would be good if Your Lordship could send a clavis that I could trust because I think things will occur that I will need to write to Your Lordship about."[12]

A similar letter from the same correspondence: "As I see it I will soon need to have a secret writing to Your Lordship, so I am asking Your Lordship to send me a clavis as Your Lordship promised to do when we parted from each other so I could write without fear in case a servant reports something that I need to tell Your Lordship about, or if I hear some other news."[13] People asked for a clavis from a higher dignity because they wanted to share private and sensitive information with them, in other words, they wanted to offer their services to a more preeminent politician, this time for example, to Zrínyi. Though Vitnyédi wished to send ciphered letters to the lord, he was not in a position to ask Zrínyi to use a clavis that he, as his inferior, had made.

Requests for a clavis were often granted and claves were exchanged, as Rákóczi writes in the last sentence of his letter to Antal Eszterházy, sent from the fort of Senthe in 1706, "In order that we can be more confident

---

6   Teleki 8. 4–5, 4.

7   Teleki 8. 216–217, 178.

8   Teleki 8. 78. 68.

9   AR I. vol. 3. köt. 253–257. 26.

10  AR I. vol. 9. 714–715. 538.

11  Teleki 1. 311–312.

12  *Magyar Történelmi Tár* (Hungarian Historical Records, MTT) (Pest, MTA, 1855 – 1934) II/3. 237–239.

13  MTT II/4. 37–41.

in the correspondentia, I am sending to Your Lordship a clavis with which Your Lordship could cipher if not the whole letter, in casu interruptae et periculosae correspondentiae, the most relevant pieces of information."[14] Márton Kászoni says goodbye at the end of his letter in 1663, "Please find attached the new clavis. (...) You can be securus that I am going to report any news, as I am asking you to do the same. May God bring you back to us with good news."[15] György Lippay starts his letter to Prince György Rákóczi I in 1637 in this way, "I have written to you recently and have sent it by a man of the voivode. I have also sent a clavis. He must have been delayed because I should have received a reply from you by now."[16]

There were several ways to exchange a clavis. They were often sent together with the ciphered letter, sometimes by a separate courier, or occasionally a personal meeting was arranged, this being the most secure option, of course.

Archbishop György Lippay sent the clavis in an attachment to his letter to Prince György Rákóczi in 1637 from Vienna. The clavis itself has survived too: [17] "...in order to carry it out more appropriately, I am sending Your Lordship the clavis too. There are things I would be happy to share with Your Lordship. If Your Lordship had received this clavis, I might be able to write more."[18] Rákóczi reacts assuring that he has received the key, noting that "I took the letter and the clavis included in it from the man of the voivode four days ago..."[19] Then once more a few days later, "We received your letter four weeks ago from the man of the voivode dated from 16 July, together with the clavis."[20]

It was vital to indicate that a clavis had been successfully delivered to the addressee as Mihály Teleki writes on the back of a monoalphabetic clavis this polite request, "Rogo responsum an reciperit hanc cartam nisi duo verba."[21] A similar request can be read on the back of one of the biggest nomenclature dictionaries of our period, a table with one thousand and three hundred items that survived in Vienna, "Please write me recipisset."[22]

14   AR I. vol. 563–565. 82.
15   Teleki 2. 660–661, 453.
16   MTT III/5. 147, 35.
17   MTT III/5. 146, 34.
18   MTT III/5. 144–146, 34.
19   MTT III/5. 280–281, 37.
20   MTT III/5. 283–284, 39.
21   MNL OL P 1238 Teleki Mihály Collection, Miscallenous documents, Cipher keys
22   ÖStA HHStA Ungarische Akten Specialia Verschwörerakten VII. Varia, Fasc. 327. Konv. D. Chiffres 1664–1668, fol 4–11.

The first lines of another letter to Teleki make us think that the clavis was delivered by a separate messenger. "I have replied to your letter. If it was not taken elsewhere, it must have been delivered to you by now. I have been delivered the clavis."[23]

Despite being complex and confused, the letter of László Rédei from Hust, Ukraine (Huszt) in 1660 nicely illustrates how difficult it was to arrange a ciphered correspondence: "I have often regretted that I did not take information concerning the clavis when I was at His Lordship, but I had not expected these things to happen; although I did not know about it so far, I am only learning it, but to no avail, if my lord does not know my clavis. You might have a copy, and if you do not, you might write these words with a clavis, but if you do not have a key, and you cannot write to His Lordship using a clavis, you might take the courage to send my letter to His Lordship, you may succeed because I have written only that much to His Lordship, but I have not written to His Lordship where you should be, because I cannot. So His Lordship may not understand a word from my letter, but if you could either send this letter to His Lordship, or write to him in clavis these few words..."[24]

After the appropriate claves were sent, delivered or exchanged, the corresponding partners put them into use. That was when a new problem arose. How should one name the different cipher keys? They evidently had to be differentiated since a high-ranking political figure had several significant relationships in which he used ciphered letters, to which end he used a number of different keys.

Ciphers were often named after the sender or the addressee, supposing (rightly or not) that the given person was only using one ciphered channel of correspondence. The writer would sometimes specify below the signature and the date at the bottom of the page which cipher was used for encoding the letter, or part of the letter. "We have written this letter with the clavis that Lord Szalai has."[25] "We have written to you this letter with the clavis of His Lordship."[26] "I have used the clavis of Lord Absolon."[27] "I have written to Your Lordship with the clavis of Lord Fajgel."[28]

In other cases the keys are described less precisely. Teleki notes that "I have written to Lord Simon Kemény the names with the clavis that Your

23   Teleki 2. 259–260, 189.
24   MTT II/5. 101., 25. sz.
25   Teleki 8. 249, 222.
26   Teleki 8. 265–266, 238.
27   Teleki 8. 433–435, 413.
28   Teleki 8. 68–69, 63.

Lordship has sent me, I wonder if you know which one I am talking about."[29] "My brother has written to Your Lordship using the clavis that Your Lordship had made for me for the alphabet, so when Your Lordship is writing to me, please use only that."[30] Jónás Mednyánszky's instructions on his message for the Transylvanian noble (later prince) János Kemény were hardly explanatory: "Your Lordship can understand it using the clavis that our lord owns."[31] Since the ciphered parts of this letter had not yet been decoded, one suspects that the one-time addressee could make no sense of the faint reference either.

Sharing the key was a need often discussed in the letters, but its usage was hardly problem-proof. In a 1710 letter to his general, Miklós Bercsényi, Prince Rákóczi brings up the topic of claves twice. First he scorns his commander-in-chief that he did not use the cipher frequently enough in his previous letter, making it accessible to unsolicited readers ("you could have used more encoded text in the letter where you write about negotiations, for it is peasants who deliver these messages from Szolnok (...) and they are not safe from robbers") and then he goes on to lament that he could not "decipher a letter because the key was left somewhere else".[32]

Rákóczi mentions such problems several times – he obviously had a great deal of experience exchanging keys. In 1711 he sends the following letter: "Since Your Lordship has written to me once again with a clavis that previously I have told Your Lordship about that Károlyi also has a copy, I am not sure whether the clavis that Lord Vay had resigned to you in a table is not lost. Until I hear confirmation that Your Lordship has received it, I cannot write any more particularities."[33]

Archbishop György Lippay and Prince György Rákóczi could not successfully share the key either, according to their 1637 correspondence – the prince finds a mistake in the clavis he was sent by the archbishop upon which Lippay, who cannot find any fault with it, asks him somewhat indignantly to mend it quickly so they can use it. "Your Majesty did not wish to use the clavis I had sent and had found some fault in it that I still cannot see," he writes, "but if there was one, Your Majesty could correct it and send me a copy, perhaps my humble service had not been useless to Your Majesty, I do not wish to be of nuisance to Your Majesty. I remain to be full of good intentions."[34] Three days

29  Teleki 2. 262–264, 193.
30  Teleki 1. 389–390, 342.
31  MTT II/6, 86–89.
32  AR I. vol. 3. 133–137, 84.
33  AR I. vol. 3. 673–674, 68.
34  MTT III/5, 286–90, 41.

later he repeats the request: "I have written about that clavis by the courier, please, Your Majesty, correct it and *cum correctione* send me a copy."[35]

It is impossible to prevent all complications, but it is exemplary how careful Chancellor Miklós Bethlen is when he gives orders on sharing the key as well as about what to do if the addressee happens to pass away. "I have sent Harsányi a clavis too, in case he will need it," he instructs. Continuing, he notes that "I have told my messenger whom he should deliver the letter to in case Harsányi had died in the meantime. Your Lordship may see the short *instructio* that I have given to him. *Pro sua prudentia* instructs Your Lordship too. All about these *coram plura*".[36]


## 6.2.    Replacing the cipherkeys

After a key was successfully shared and smoothly used for a while, it was time to think about how to replace it with a newer one. Naturally, a cipher key cannot be in service forever. The longer it was used, in more letters and in more relationships, the easier the job of the potential codebreaker was, who would have more materials to identify breaking points. One would expect the expert cipher users of the early modern period to do all they could to avoid this danger.

It is surprising, however, that the issue of replacing a cipher is rarely mentioned in the letters. Updating it in order to prevent enemy eavesdropping seems to have been of little interest to early modern Hungarian political actors. Security was surprisingly neglected in this respect. Correspondents were not careful to use a clavis with one particular person only, and they did not aim at replacing the claves at least yearly, either.

For example, Ferenc Rákóczi II's envoys to Constantinople, János Pápai and Ferenc Horváth, had written several dozen almost completely enciphered letters to the prince during the year 1706.[37] For these, they had used a table that was so important that it has survived in several copies both in the secret archives of the prince and in the Ráday Archives.[38] If one looks at this pack of letters closely, one sees that three of them begin with similar combinations of numbers.[39] The two following letters, almost completely enciphered, are particularly long, more than ten pages.[40] Had a Turkish codebreaker captured the

35   MTT III/5. 291–292. 42.
36   MNL OL P 658, Fasc. 2, 367, and Teleki 6. 110–112.
37   MNL OL G 15 Caps. C. Fasc 36, fol. 1–29 and MNL OL G 15 Caps. C. Fasc 36, fol. 1–2—fol. 80–82.
38   Ráday Archives C64-4d2-25, 12, no., MNL OL G 15 Caps. C. Fasc 43.
39   MNL OL G 15 Caps. C. Fasc 36, fol. 9–10; 11–12, 13–15.
40   MNL OL G 15 Caps. C. Fasc 36, fol. 13–22.

package, he would have found ample resources to use the appropriate analyses and locate regularities that would aid codebreaking. Pápai even used the same table when writing to another correspondent, Ádám Vay.[41] What is more, the envoys were still using this key–not once or twice, but dozens of times–in the following three years from Belgrade and Constantinople, despite the change in the diplomatic circumstances.[42]

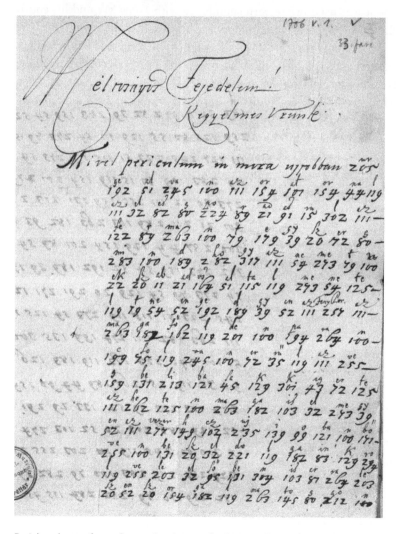

Enciphered report from a Constantinople envoy for the Prince from 1 May 1706[43]

41  MNL OL G 15 Caps. C. Fasc 33, fol 35–38.
42  MNL OL G 15 Caps. D. Fasc 80; Caps. E. Fasc 109; Caps. F. Fasc 160; Caps. H. Fasc 226.
43  MNL OL G 15 Caps. C. Fasc 33. fol. 19–20

This clavis was undoubtedly one of the most important ones in the eight-year-long freedom fight. This can be known not only from the fact that Rákóczi's diplomatic relationship with Constantinople was a high-lighted relation, but also because only three tables survived the freedom fight that were copied onto parchment, Pápai's table being one of these.[44] The other such table signals Rákóczi's most distinguished diplomatic goal, because it was used in the correspondence with Louis XIV and his court, and the third one, bearing no name, was not used for political purposes, rather with Rákóczi's secret love in Poland (to be discussed below). How-ever central Pápai's table could have been in the prince's correspondence, it was still highly dangerous to use it for five long years in several cities and with several partners. With this knowledge in hand, we should hardly be surprised to learn that after his freedom fight terminated and he was forced to leave the country for Poland, the fleeing prince took this key out once again, when he was hard pressed without ciphers that the addressees would also have a copy of. Wanting to share private information in letter, he suddenly remembered that he could start using Pápai's table again in his correspondence with Ádám Vay, too: "Although I would have liked to inform You *circumstantialiter*, I did not dare to write without a clavis, but then I was reminded by Pápai's letter that we can use his old clavis from Constantinople, which I am using right now; and since I do not doubt his faithfulness, he could decipher this message himself."[45]

Pápai's clavis was undeniably overused, even though several other tables were available and efforts were made not to overcharge this or any other clavis. András Bay, envoy to Constantinople in 1706,[46] Mihály Henter, envoy to Constantinople from Transylvania in 1707,[47] and Ferenc Ládonyi Horváth, another envoy to Constantinople in 1708 all used different claves – in fact, three different ones,[48] despite being at the same place, in the same period, in the similar function as János Pápai. Pápai himself used another different cipher method in 1707, when writing to József Voy-novich.[49] In cases, attitudes towards ciphers were cautious, in other cases not the least.

44  MNL OL G 15 Caps. C. Fasc 43.

45  MNL OL G 15. Caps. H. Fasc. 253, published in Béla Köpeczi, ed. *II. Rákóczi Ferenc válogatott levelei* (Selected letters of Ferenc Rákóczi II) (Budapest: Bibliotheca Kiadó, 1958). 68

46  MNL OL G 15 Caps. D. Fasc 81.

47  MNL OL G 15 Caps. D. Fasc 80. fols. 38, 40, 46.

48  MNL OL G 15 Caps. E. Fasc 109.

49  MNL OL G 15 Caps. D. Fasc 80. fol. 28.

A good example for irresponsible behavior is described in the 1706–1707 correspondence[50] of László Vetési Kökényesdi, who was Rákóczi's advocate at the Bavarian prince elector and who sometimes wrote under the pseudonym Casimirius de Miloftzky. Kökényesdi used the same clavis[51] with Ráday and Rákóczi in Hungarian[52] that he used with Chamillard, secretary of the French ambassador Des Alleurs in Latin[53] and in French.[54] Even Jakab Kray, another supporter of Rákóczi, applied this very cipher to write to Ráday.[55]

## 6.3.    The tiresome work of enciphering

In a particularly long letter Prince Rákóczi apologizes to Marquis Bonnac, "I am going to make my letter shorter so you are not as bored reading it as your secretary is when deciphering the clavis, because these are matters of seemingly low importance."[56]

Parties involved in enciphered correspondences often complained that encryption and decryption were time-consuming and tedious tasks. It is easy to experience what they meant with a simple encoding exercise involving an average homophonic table of about three to four hundred items, and a message of average length (made up of four or five paragraphs) waiting to be encrypted. Looking up and noting the corresponding numbers to every and each letter and one by one is a monotonous job that can take a long time even with a shorter letter. Decryption is an even longer process, most of all because the clavis usually lists the letters of the open text in alphabetical order, aiding the encryption but not so much the decryption. This is the reason why certain writers only encrypted some of the words or parts of the sentences.

Mihály Teleki wrote: "I had no time to decipher our lord's letter since I only received it in the evening and I had to leave early at dawn."[57] Rákóczi writes to his general, Bercsényi: "I could hardly wade through all these claves."[58] And in another letter: "I realized at last that you must have found

50  Ráday Archives C64-4d2-10.
51  Ráday Archives C64-4d2-25. 6.
52  Ibid. 27.
53  Ibid. 23.
54  Ibid. 24.
55  Ibid. 44.
56  Köpeczi, *II. Rákóczi Ferenc*, no. 39.
57  Teleki 8. 228–229, 195.
58  AR I. vol. 3. 113–114.

deciphering these letters very boring, since even their summary is annoy-
ingly long for me to read."[59] A month later Bercsényi laments the lack of
time needed for decryption, "Having finished my letter, an honest captain
has just arrived who has brought the golden lamb for His Majesty the Prince,
and he has also brought long ciphered letters that take a long time to decipher, especially since they are in French which I am not familiar with,
so I am rather sending out this letter to you now."[60] Rákóczi asks Sándor
Nedeczky, his envoy to Russia, in vain to use the clavis properly and not to
mix coded and un-coded letters in the same word.[61] Without a secretary,
Nedeczky finds this work too tiresome and asks his partners not to "ruin
him in the future", and "only encipher *secretum*, leaving the rest as open
text."[62] This angry request was aimed at Ráday, who knew precisely that the
partial use of a cipher saves a lot of time for the addressee, since he had
written this to Prince Rákóczi in a previous letter, "I did not wish to burden
Your Majesty by enciphering all of my humble letter, I only used that for the
secret parts and I am writing about the other things explicitly."[63]

Many years earlier Simon Kemény makes a similar request to Teleki: "By
God, I am asking Your Lordship to write only what is important, and only
*breviter*, and not to write such horribly long *pandechta*, enciphered, and
with a lot of mistakes, because with the ambassador being here we have
so much to do we can hardly get any sleep.[64] György Udvarhely, summa-
rizing the content of other enciphered letters for Teleki, closes his letter:
"I was working all night on the claves."[65] The leader of the anti-Habsburg
uprising, Imre Thököly, writes in his diary: "I have spent most of the night
deciphering texts, and when I have finished revising them, I called for the
French lord."[66] Deciphering required a long night's work more than once.

## 6.4.    The cryptologist

This last example is informative not only because it contains the usual
complaint about the tiresome work of enciphering, but also because of

59   AR I. vol. 3. 19–20.
60   AR I. vol. 8. 208–209, 32.
61   Gyula Benda, *Ráday Pál iratai* (Writings of Pál Ráday) (Budapest: Akadémiai, 1961) vol. 2, 227.
62   Benda, *Ráday Pál iratai* vol. 2.,313.
63   Benda, Ráday Pál iratai Vol. II. 265.
64   Teleki, 2.271–272.
65   Teleki 3, 227–229. 181.
66   Nagy Iván, ed., *Késmárki Thököly Imre naplója, 1693—1694* (Thököly Imre's diary) (Pest:
Eggenberger Ferdinánd, 1863), 43.

its (lack of) reference to the cryptologist. Normally, decryption was a skill practiced by a specialist, a servant or a secretary. Dániel Esterházy writes to Rákóczi in 1711, "Please forgive me that I did not write myself, I have been very sick for the last eleven days, but my servant who wrote this letter and who assists in all my secret *communicatio*, is a true Hungarian, I trust him very much because I have known him for a long time, this is why I share all my private matters with him."[67] Sometimes the name of the specialist who, as it is said in the sources, "translates" the clavis,[68] is revealed within the correspondence. Ferenc Rákóczi warns István Sennyei: "do the *clavisatio* yourself, if your illness allows, if it does not, trust it to Butler György Körösy."[69] Miklós Bercsényi, in his letter to the prince, makes a reference to a person deciphering the secret signs, a certain Jánoki, who seems not only a secretary decoding the ciphers with the clavis, but also a codebreaker expert.[70]

All in all, one cannot quite expect powerful politicians to labor for hours on the arduous job of deciphering. It is all the more surprising to read that noble leaders of different anti-Habsburg movements, such as Imre Thököly and Ferenc Rákóczi II, regularly did so.

Thököly mentions claves and ciphering a lot in his diary, they seemed to have been laborious part of his everyday life: "My Polish mail has arrived from Drinápoly, big packets of letters, and I spent the whole day looking through them, yet I could not finish with them, because they contained so many claves."[71] Similarly, though Rákóczi had several trusted secretaries assisting his extensive correspondence and the ciphering work involved, still, his letters quoted above obviously imply that the prince considered ciphering tiresome because he often did it himself. This is confirmed by what Gáspár Beniczky wrote in his diary, "His Majesty, having had the mail delivered to him, retreated to his room privately, and was diligently working on deciphering the letters containing a clavis."[72]

## 6.5. Cautious and reckless encryption

A general experience of the history of cryptography is that cipher systems are broken successfully not because they are weak but because they have

---

67  MNL OL G 15. Caps. H. Fasc. 237.
68  Teleki 4. 296–297.; AR I. vol. 3. 602.; AR I. vol. 5. 280–283.
69  AR I. vol. 3. 602, 22.
70  AR I. vol. 5. 280–283, 141.
71  Nagy, *Késmárki Thököly Imre naplója*, 298.
72  Révay, *II. Rákóczi Ferenc rejtjelezése*, 60.

not been used properly. The options they offer are not exploited fully, and they are used carelessly or incorrectly.[73] The Hungarian sources contain a number of direct and indirect information about how clerks were aware of the danger threatening ciphered content, how they tried to protect their ciphers from being found out, or how they made them withstand the attempts of the codebreakers. However, such information from the sources is highly ambiguous: there are many signs implying that cipherers were careful, and there are also signs that they did not have the faintest idea how they were making their ciphered texts vulnerable.

Some of the signs of carefulness have already been noted. A number of homophonic tables assigned a special sign for the numbers and the names of the months. This was wise because almost every message contains dates, which are in a special place (at the end or beginning of the letter), and if a codebreaker finds several letters, regularities can be identified as easy breaking points. If information had been also gained from traffic analysis (showing which letter was mailed in which month), the codebreaker would have had a reliable anchor with which to identify the months. If, however, the names of the months are not coded letter by letter, but each month gets a number code, then the codebreaker cannot use this as a breaking point. The same goes for salutations, greetings, or the name of the addressee, all of which can be easily identified by traffic analysis. Assigning separate characters to these in the code table is a sign of cautious and wise behavior. A similarly conscious cipher use is when the numbers are not in alphabetical order in the nomenclature tables, but are positioned vertically – as was described above.

For example, Mihály Teleki enciphered his letter to Mihály Apafi completely, but left the date as an open text.[74] Why bother enciphering the date and the signature when a potential codebreaker knows who had sent the letter and when? There is no danger in giving the reader information already known, but it would be unwise to offer a part of the text that would be easy to guess because that would also open a path into identifying certain characters. Teleki realized the paradox: leaving certain parts open actually increases the level of security.

Besides such indirect references showing the users' level of awareness when it comes to danger, explicit comments about their cautiousness can also be found. They were trying to protect the code key, often burning them

73  David Kahn, *The Reader of Gentlemen's Mail: Herbert O. Yardley and the Birth of American Codebreaking* (New Haven, CT: Yale, 2004), xvi.
74  Teleki 8, 240–241, 212.

upon reading. Dénes Bánffy asked Teleki in 1660 if he is allowed to give a copy of his clavis to someone else, "I have not yet seen one note from Your Lordship, although I have learned that you have sent one, but it was intercepted by Lord Gáspár Barcsai and he still has it. He asked for the clavis, but I did not give it to him because I did not know what Your Lordship was writing about in this note. So please let me know what was written in it, because they are suspicious about it."[75] Two years later, in a richly ciphered letter between the same people, Bánffy notes that Captain István Ébeni asked him to burn the letters that were with him for security reasons.[76] Two weeks later they exchange letters again, and Bánffy talks about the vulnerability of the information that the letters contain, "Please send my letter to Lord Ébeni with proper securitas, it would be bad if Germans or others had found it because I had written about these things a lot, and did not always use a clavis."[77]

While there are numerous examples of ciphering with a careful attitude, there are also as many signs of reckless and senseless behavior. Hungarian fugitives writing to Teleki for example acted quite inconsistently. It is typical of them to code only a small part of their letters. In the following case they only enciphered the words in italics, "He also completely destroyed places *under Turkish rule around* Dévény and Torna". What does the enemy see of this? "He also completely destroyed places xxxx xxxx xxxx xxxx Dévény and Torna" Some information is lost, but not much, and if someone is familiar with the recent military events, he may even know exactly what places the writer of the message had in mind.[78]

Dániel Absolon is characterized by frequent but economical cipher use. He does try to pick wisely what he will cover from prying eyes, which may be a clever thing in itself, if well applied. The following excerpt shows an unlucky choice of ciphered text from 1678, "I have humbly received Your Lordship's 12. letter praesentis from Kővár, and I have *sorrowfully* taken the *reproach* to my *heart*. If I wanted to excuse myself, there would be many words in this letter. I need to make this reply short, the *disconsolate spirit* indeed does not allow me to be longer."[79] One should try reading the text leaving the italicized words out and see that hardly any crucial information is lost.

75   Teleki 1, 555–556, 475.
76   Teleki 2, 398–399, 295.
77   Teleki 2, 398–399, 295.
78   Teleki 8, 428–429.
79   Teleki 8, 179–186. 154. and MTT III/6. 6–13.

The following paragraph from the same letter is not much better: "What *deficiencies* and numerous peculiar obstacles there have been on this part, I have written to you. To go on specificatio I have judged to be neither good nor necessary. Rather, whatever *deficiencies* there had been, I endeavoured to repair and mend – thinking that to frighten away minds with *defects* that are to be repaired is contra rationem status et interesse publicum, I was about to build, not to destroy." He consistently codes the words "deficiencies" and "defects", but not "peculiar obstacles", which is their synonym, as one can clearly see from the sentence structure. It seems that in this case Absalon had a hard time thinking with the head of his possible adversaries.[80]

János Pápai, Rákóczi's ambassador in Istanbul – a center partly, but not entirely in alliance with the fighting Hungarian prince – changed the key of his letters to Rákóczi dangerously seldom – as we have seen above. However, he wrote quite a lot to the prince with abundant ciphering. It would not have been the least surprising if the Turkish secretaries had stopped and copied his letters. Had they compared only three successive letters, which the key indicates all begin with the greeting "Your Lordship," they would surely have discovered that the number sequences at the beginning of the letters are always almost the same, and it would not have been a difficult task to guess what they mean.

Ke. gy. el. me. s. Ur. am.
133. 39. 32. 273. 80. 205. 61[81]

Ke. gy. el. me. s. Ur. am.
133. 39. 364. 32. 273. 308. 205. 61[82]

Ke. gy. el. me. s. Ur. am.
133. 39. 32. 273. 80. 205. 61[83]

Ke. gy. el. me. s. Ur. am.
133. 39. 32. 273. 80. 205. 61[84]

---

80   Ibid.
81   MNL OL G 15 Caps. C. Fasc 36, fol. 3–4.
82   MNL OL G 15 Caps. C. Fasc 36, fol. 9–10.
83   MNL OL G 15 Caps. C. Fasc 36, fol. 11–12.
84   MNL OL G 15 Caps. C. Fasc 36, fol. 13–15.

As this example shows, the danger was not that readers would figure out who the addressee was (which was known well in advance), but that the broken passage is a promising clue with which one can attack the remaining, more valuable and more private parts of the ciphered message.

The same danger threatens when one thoroughly compares letters from the rich correspondence of Rákóczi with his Polish partners. The two hundred and fourteen folios of the National Archives of Hungary G 15 Caps. C Fasc. 39 contain about a hundred coded and fifteen un-coded letters in French from the years 1704–1706. This was done by the same table that the prince used with the French envoys. Containing 450 codes, this encryption was the most elaborate table of the freedom fight.[85] But the sophisticated method is useless, as forty of the letters start with the encoded form of the same phrase: "a Danzik, le 20 Février, Monsieur" (where, of course, the date varies). As the key is homophonic, the particular number sequences differ; however, the corpus is large enough for a skillful adverse agent to correctly identify the numbers corresponding to the same syllables and letters. Even nullities do not pose much difficulty, because the writer of the letters always inserted them at the end of the rows. With such recklessness neither the homophonic system, nor the use of pseudonyms (Nathanaél Sylver or Pompeio Cesoni), makes Rákóczi's messages difficult to uncover.

## 6.6.    Sand in the machine

When many different people use a technology for different purposes, often under difficult circumstances, hitches do happen.

The most frequent and practical problem is the absence of the key for the enciphered message. Such questions often arise: "Your letters written with clavis have arrived to my hands, my lord, but I could not proceed with them happily, as the clavis you used was not given or sent, thus I am blind in their many terms to this day."[86] "A letter came from Incédi in Canea. He writes he is close to the Turkish vizier, but his letter being written with a clavis it is still untranslated, because neither my lords János and Miklós Bethlen has the copy of the clavis. Now they have taken it to Baló, hoping that he has the clavis."[87] "I have opened your letter, too, but I had no use of

85   MNL OL G 15 Caps. C. Fasc 44.
86   Teleki 6, 394–398.
87   Teleki 4, 278–279, 206.

it, as I do not know its clavis."[88] Thököly wrote to Teleki: "Lord Ubrisi's clavis being lost, God knows what 88 means, I do not."[89]

The problem of the absent clavis remained quite persistent in the case of Teleki's letter, full of numbers, to Mária Széchy dated 6 July 1666.[90] Széchy writes back three weeks later at the end of her letter, on a separate sheet, "My dear Lord Teleki, I could not answer your letter of numbers, you have not sent me its clavis, but I am asking you kindly, please send it."[91] The key has never been found, and the letter was published in ciphers.

Another woman having problems with Teleki's claves, his sister, Kata Bornemissza asked him, "My dear Lord Brother, I was unable to read the whole letter which you have recently sent by post, since it is not written in that note which you have left here. These are the unknown words: 020, 550207, 4y04, 9100, 1, I do not have these."[92]

In other cases the problem is not the absence of a clavis but that the sender or the addressee is unsure which one to use. Imre Thököly in 1679 was well aware of the problems of handling the ciphers in a secure way: "Regarding the question of the clavis I have no clue, my lord; for I have written using two different claves to You, and I do not know which one you understand." The writer continues, explaining that the "clavis of mine which was with you I am going to tear up and destroy completely; I have written this letter with the clavis of Lord Fajgel. It would not be secure to send the ciphered letter together with the clavis. Please make a new one, let us use that from now on."[93]

And again: "My Lord Bocskai had sent the letter included here. Although I tried eight or nine different claves, I was unable to read it. Please send it back from my Lord Gyulafi, maybe you can decipher it, or perhaps it is written using that big old clavis of which I have no copy."[94]

In the letter of Gáspár Pápai sent to Rákóczi in 1706 it is really difficult to follow the path of some claves, "I have passed on Your Majesty's honorable letter to my Lord Vajovics, however, since the included ciphers did not harmonize, he could not read any of Your Majesty's letter, and since the time he left Your Majesty he received two letters from Your Majesty, but he understands the meaning of none, for which reason he sent back the cipher

88   Teleki 8, 400, 376.
89   Teleki 8, 401–402, 378.
90   Teleki 3, 582–583, 432.
91   Teleki 3, 592–593, 441.
92   Teleki 1. 220–221, 191.
93   Teleki 8, 543–547, 526.
94   Teleki 4.176–178, 134.

and the letters, keeping a copy of the cipher, so that Your Majesty should use this cipher and it should not be changed as it happened now as a result of forgetfulness; now he has written his own letter to Your Majesty using my cipher."[95]

Prince Rákóczi gets similarly lost occasionally when he does not find the proper key. He writes Pál Ráday: "Since your departure from Moldova we have not received more than one letter of yours which, however short it be, we could not translate, although we even tried with the clavis we had given to Pápai when he left to Nándorfehérvár. Therefore we had to use the clavis of Lord Károlyi, which you may even know memoriter, we have once given a similar one to Dániel Eszterház."[96] Ten days later Rákóczi brings up the case again, but now in possession of the solution, "Although recently, being in Munkács, we were unable to translate your letter dated 3 September despite trying numerous claves, and therefore we had to use Lord Károlyi's clavis, when we received your letter written two days ago, on the 21, translating it we laboriously found the clavis, that is why we are writing this letter using that one, and you can safely use it too from now on."[97]

Even in the background of these complications, it must have been an exceptional case when Prince Rákóczi was unable to decide if some "suspicious" letters were written "with clavis or simply in Polish".[98]

Occasionally, the addressee writes back to a letter – with some amount of reproach – that he is unable to read the ciphered message: "Lord Szepesi wrote the clavis full of mistakes; especially the part about Lord Szalai I was unable to make out, and the end of the parchment which you had written. The rest I could figure out."[99] Pál Szepesi himself, in a similar situation with Teleki, acts more proactively when he reports, "I cannot figure out that capital D, and the [graphic symbol] in your letter, although I can make a good explanation for them."[100]

Such reproaches often do not lack humor: "What kind of gold did you write about in the postscript, with nice things about it, I could not penetrate your writing. At such times I wish that you were writing to me without clavis."[101] Correspondents of Teleki are less courteous: "Your witchlike writing caused us awful puzzlement. You wrote about so many things, as we

95   Benda *Ráday Pál iratai*, vol. 1, 728.
96   AR I. vol. 2. 582–583. 125.
97   AR I. vol. 2. 591–594. 135.
98   AR I., vol. 3, 75–78, 46.
99   Teleki 8, 310–312, 288.
100  Teleki 7, 158–159, 118.
101  Teleki 5, 126–127, 79.

spell out one, we forget the other. It has a start somehow, yet in the end it becomes like the bulls of Kővár let loose on the hillside."[102]

Miklós Bethlen also does not shy away from reproaching Teleki, "The Palatine's wife could never read your letter, neither could I, and if you write to me more in this way, I will still not be able to, not even if I put twelve glasses on my nose. It was a cipher indeed – maybe you could not have read it yourself. Next time be sure to write more orderly, if you want anyone to make out a word of it."[103]

Sometimes it happens that the addressee has the clavis, but it is faulty, or had not been followed correctly. Dániel Absolon simply confuses the nomenclator numbers in a letter, and writes 241 (Polish king) instead of 240 (French king).[104] Funnily, in another letter two weeks later he makes the same error the other way round, and writes French king instead of Polish, as if making some sort of compensation: "I wonder if now and in the future the *Hungarian nation* can live without the *French* and the *French kings*."[105]

We also find an example of a subtle sense of humor in the following, where Rákóczi asks his envoy János Pápai in a letter from Miskolc to refer to the Porte for permission to invade Szeged.[106] However, the Prince's chancellor must have made a mistake in ciphering the name of Szeged, as Pápai, in his coded answer, jokes about it. Despite the incorrect encoding he perfectly knows which city the message refers to, but he still writes: "Your Majesty commands that we petition the vizier to ... allow Your Majesty to invade Szrülavár. We were really curious to find this place on the map, but we have not found such fortification, we do not know anything similar under the Hungarian crown, so we cannot act accordingly. If, however, Your Majesty wishes to have permission to invade Szeged, since it is not yet under Your Majesty's protection, we judged it to be unnecessary to ask permission from the Turks.[107]

Sometimes it is not evident which party makes (more) mistakes. In such cases the correspondents can mutually blame one another. Here, Dénes Bánffy blames Teleki: "You are writing about the deficiencies in my usage of the clavis – perhaps there were a few, but in fact it is the blind laughing

---

102  Teleki 7, 140–142, 104.

103  Teleki 3, 594–596, 442.

104  Teleki 8, 188–191, 157.

105  Teleki 8, 195–198, 162.

106  Benda, *Ráday Pál iratai*, 502.

107  Quoted in Benda, *Ráday Pál iratai*, 505. Pápai's answer: G. 15. Caps. C. Fasc 36 (fol. 27v).

at the sightless. *Turpe est doctori.*[108] It is through such examples that the difference between the theory of cryptology and its meticulous everyday application can be grasped.

## 6.7. Breaking the code

Cryptography users in early modern Hungary did not always take the necessary precautions to avoid the secret message coming to light. Did the enemy take advantage of their carelessness? What kind of code-breaking professionals and offices were formed in the past to break the cipher texts of the enemy, and what tools did they use? My book has thus far focused on the process of decryption by the intended reader, but attention should also be paid to the tools applied by the enemy, who does not have the key and wants to reconstruct it. What did the science of cryptanalysis[109] and code-breaking look like in Hungary in the early modern period? This topic is inherently more discreet, so there are obviously fewer sources, data, or notes related to it than other areas of cryptography.

Code-breaking handbooks of the age available for average readers did not contain the most up-to-date decryption methods. The top-notch handbooks were only available by a privileged few among the political elite. It may sound odd today that J.P. Devos cryptography historian complained in 1967 about the fact that there was virtually no accessible information on the ciphers of WWII,[110] but this in fact had been true for all ages.

A large part of the code-breaking methods available in the early modern handbooks could only have been used for analyzing monoalphabetic ciphers. The 1474 collection of rules *Regule ad extrahendum litteras ziferatas sine exemplo* of Cicco Simonetta is one such cryptological resource.[111] Simonetta, as a statesman of Milan, worked with ciphered texts on an everyday basis for thirty years. Interestingly enough, his book was outdated even in his own time, because it exclusively dealt with cryptograms indicating word boundaries and having no homophones, nullities or nomenclatures,

---

108  Teleki 2, 244–247. 182.

109  Cryptanalysis is a modern word invented by William Friedman, codebreaker of the first half of the 20th century.

110  Devos and Seligman, *L'Art de Deschiffrer*, viii.

111  Meister, *Die Anfänge der modernen diplomatischen Geheimschrift*, 61–63; Augusto Buonafalce, "Cicco Simonetta's Cipher-Breaking Rules", *Cryptologia* 32 (2008): 62–70. See also: Marcello Simonetta, *The Montefeltro Conspiracy: A Renaissance Mystery Decoded* (London: Doubleday Books, 2008).

in a period when these had already been applied for decades in the diplomacy of the Italian cities.[112]

Another handbook from 1641 was written by Antonio Maria Cospi, secretary of the prince of Tuscany. Cospi admits that his expertise is limited to decrypting simple monoalphabetic ciphers and he clearly stays away from dealing with homophonic systems that he calls complex ciphers (*chiffres composés*), declaring these to be basically impossible to decrypt.[113] He then goes on to offer a detailed methodology on how to solve monoalphabetic ciphers, how to identify vowels, and he also presents frequency charts for syllables in French, Spanish and Latin.

Luckily, there were more adventurous codebreakers. The famous François Viète, a French lawyer and nonprofessional mathematician (1540–1603) who became known as "the father of algebra" after having used letters symbolizing mathematical quantities consistently for the first time in history. It is a little-known fact that he was also a genial codebreaker in service of the French King Henry IV, and he regularly assisted his king by cryptanalyzing messages of the hostile Spanish king. In a secret letter to the Prince of Sully, King Henry's minister, Viète describes an infallible codebreaking method (*infallible rule*).[114] This helps identify the place of vowels by analyzing the frequency of the combination of double and triple characters of the ciphertext. Since languages have fewer vowels than consonants, and since their places identify the structure of a word clearly, vowel-analysis is a necessary part of every codebreaking process. Viète's analysis begins with the typical code signs of the Spanish court, the most significant rival of France. He points it out that the Spanish codes of his age usually used three or four symbols for each letter, one or two for each syllable, several series of characters for the most frequent words and proper names, and special signs for double letters. He discusses frequency analysis, not so much of a novelty at the time; and then analyzes the triads and diads, or trigrams and bigrams of a text, so the hidden vowels can be discovered.

This method is effective indeed in breaking monoalphabetic secret writings where every character stands for a given letter. Homophonic ciphers, nevertheless, are a great deal more complicated, particularly

112  Buonafalce, "Cicco Simonetta" 67–69.

113  Antonio Maria Cospi, *L'interpretation des chiffres ou reigle pour bien entendre et expliquer facilement toutes sortes de chiffres simples* (Paris: Courbes, 1641), 3: "Or comme il y a deux sortes de chiffres, les uns simples, et les autres composez, laissant à part ces derniers comme presques impossibles à rencontrer et deschiffrer, nous ne parlerons que des premiers quie sont les simples."

114  Peter Pesic, "François Viète, Father of Modern Cryptanalysis = Two New Manuscripts," *Cryptologia* 21/1 (1997): 1–29.

when they encode syllables as well. Despite what the author suggests, his method may only be applied for homophonic ciphers with any chance of success if the text is strongly formalized, with a well-identifiable addressing, greeting, signature, date and other parts. Applying the "infallible rule" will be especially complicated if nomenclatures are extensively used and they are not easily distinguishable from the symbols of letters and syllables. One may reasonably suppose that Viète, the talented mathematician and experienced codebreaker, could successfully find vowels in homophonic ciphertexts too, and thus break a given code. This public description of the infallible rule, however, does not lead the reader into the depths of his method and does not provide them with really useful tools. It would seem more interesting to see what this writing does not tell us than what it does.

The most detailed and most didactic cryptological handbook survived from the early modern period is by an anonymous (supposedly Spanish) author, *The Art of Deciphering (Art de deschiffrer)*.[115] This 136-page manuscript has come to us in seventeenth century French translation. Not offering "infallible" solutions, it does describe a number of observations, maxims, rules and recipes that can help identify the language of the plain text, identify which signs stand for letters and which for syllables, recognize nullities, analyze letter frequency, and so on. The author, of course, distinguishes between simple (monoalphabetic) and complex (homophonic) ciphers, gives a detailed analysis of both, and introduces a case study for each, where he breaks a ciphertext step by step, applying his own maxims and recipes. As for the theory, it does not provide more than Viète's secret advices. What makes this handbook more helpful is that it is more detailed and practical, describing specific examples that illustrate the application of principles. Following the step-by-step analyses of the anonymous author and learning these skills one can successfully attack a cipher created in this period.

There is no indication in the early modern Hungarian sources that these four, or any other cryptanalytic handbooks were used. One can plausibly suppose, however, that practicing codebreakers had at most similar, if not more limited tools in solving the cipher messages of the enemy. Some sources imply a preference towards torturing the messenger or stealing the key instead of intellectually reconstructing it.

---

115   Devos and Seligman, eds. *L'Art de Deschiffrer*; see also H. Seligman, "Un traité de déchiffrement du XVIIe siècle," *Revue des Bibliothèques et Archives de Belgique* 6 (1908): 1–19.

Many of the claves used in the anti-Habsburg Wesselényi movement, for example, were outdated monoalphabetic ciphers[116] that the Habsburg court could easily have broken. Still, there is no source indicating that anyone bothered with code-breaking. It seems from the documents that they focused solely on intercepting the keys as the main method of mopping up the organization.[117]

The physical and not so much the intellectual way seemed to have been more rewarding and more practical in other cases too. Messengers or spies were tormented, executed, their letters and keys confiscated. The 1709 diary of the Edirne legation of two Hungarian envoys tells how concerned they were about securing the lines of information during the negotiations with the pasha. They were wondering about what kind of information they can send enciphered, what they can send only via special secret envoys, and whether that messenger would be tortured.[118]

The military regulations of Rákóczi are specifically keen on intercepting the enemy's letters.[119] "*The punishment for knowing about the enemy's correspondentia and not reporting it*: Whoever may hear about such correspondentia and does not capture it, does not report it to the officers, does not send it or give it to the officers, or hears about spies and messengers and does not report it, does not capture them and does not bring them and all their belongings to us or our generalissi, is sentenced to death." Moreover, "*The enemy's letters should not be delivered:* No one should deliver the letters of the enemy, but upon finding them, should hand them to us or the general nearby them, otherwise the person who knows about someone who has such letters or delivers them and does not report it is considered a traitor and will be punished as such."

Attempts were made on both sides to intercept the enemy's letters. István Ébeni mentions a systematic hunt for Hungarian letters twice in his messages to Mihály Teleki, the first time saying that the claves can be found out with the help of the captured letters.[120] Teleki's wife, Judit Véér attaches

---

116   ÖStA HHStA Ungarische Akten Specialia Verschwörerakten VII. Varia, Fasc. 327. Konv. D. Chiffres 1664–1668, fol. 1–61. See also MNL OL E 199.

117   Pauler Gyula, *Wesselényi Ferencz nádor és társainak összeesküvése: 1664–1671*, vols. 2. (Palatine Wesselényi Ferenc's conspiracy, *1664–1671*) (Budapest: Akadémia, 1876), 133–34 and 165–66.

118   Thaly *Kálmán*, ed., *Gr. Teleki Mihály és Pápai János Nándorfejérvári követségének diariuma* (Diary of the embassy of Mihály Teleki és János Pápai) 1709. (Budapest, 1875), 240–241.

119   *Regulamentum universale, inclytorum confoederati regni Hungariae statuum ac ordinum, tam militarium, quam et ex parte inclytorum comitatuum, liberarum item ac regiarum civitatum, aliorumque quorumvis, observandum* (Nagyszombat, 1707), quoted by Révay, *II Rákóczi Ferenc*, 14–15. See also Benda, *Ráday Pál iratai*, 415–6.

120   Teleki 2. 396–397, 293. and 436–437, 320.

a completely enciphered postscript to her undeciphered short letter mentioning a captured and hanged messenger, "If you had left this place earlier you would have been captured by the men with a rifle. The peasant from Szelnicze who was taking a letter to Szamosujvár (Gherla, Romania) was captured, taken to Apafi and the Turks had him hanged."[121]

Dénes Bánffy confesses to opening the letters of both the emperor and the bishop only in a ciphered part of the letter, here typeset in italics: *"... and all of these things I have learned when I cut open the letter to the bishop, and took out from the envelope the letter to the emperor also, and forwarded these letters* enciphered to Your Lordship."[122]

It seems that for these people the only possible way of reading an encrypted text was to get or own a copy of the key, the possibility of breaking a cipher by means of mathematical methods was hardly ever considered. János Kemény was writing to György Rákóczi I. in 1644, "I was brought some letters from Poland, I opened them, hoping to make sense of them, but since they are ciphered, I cannot read them. I am asking Your Majesty to let us know what they are writing."[123] In 1678, István Koháry reports to palatine Pál Esterházy the capturing of Thököli's letters, but, again, he seemed to have lacked tools for breaking the ciphered letters, "I would like to humbly report to Your Majesty that my soldiers have intercepted a lot of letters and I have torn these open. (They were sent from the camp of Count Tököli to Kővár and from Kővár to Count Tököli.) Unfortunately, almost all of them are written in numeric ciphers so I could not learn anything from them. They must be really important. (...) Among these are letters of Teleki and some other important French people and these cannot be read without a clavis."[124]

There are only a few references that suggest that someone did not sit around idly until they get hold of the proper key, but the cipher itself was also investigated. In 1706, Rákóczi reports in his confessions that he had learnt about the emperor's instructions to Rabutin through a ciphered letter that he had broken himself.[125] He also mentions the capture of a secretary of the enemy in 1708, who happened to carry a cipher key to General Heister. Miklós Bercsényi, in his letters to the prince, mentions several intercepted ciphered letters during the years 1705 and 1706 that he was trying

121  Teleki 2, 294–295. 223.
122  Teleki 2, 309–311.
123  MTT III. 3. vol. 45–46, 5.
124  Lajos Merényi, "Kohary István levelei Eszterházy Pál nádorhoz. 1670 — 1682." (Letters of István Koháry to palatine Pál Eszterházy) MTT IV. vol. 4. 67–82, particularly: 81–82.
125  Révay, *II. Rákóczi Ferenc,* 14 and 98.

to break.[126] And finally, there remained in the archives of the freedom fight at least ten German claves written in Gothic letters (including one from Rabutin to the emperor, and others to various captains and generals) that must have contained secret information from the Habsburg Court, and that were probably reconstructed by the prince's secretaries through intercepted letters.[127] Logical codeberaking practice had few followers in the area, Prince Rákóczi being the most famous among them.

## 6.8.     Advanced or outdated?

The question arises: how sophisticated was Hungarian cipher use compared to the cryptologic technology of Europe at the given time? The first impression might be positive. Comparing the best tables of the Rákóczi freedom fight to those of the chancellery of the Habsburg court, for example,[128] of the papal diplomacy,[129] or the French court,[130] one sees that they are not inferior in quantity (of numbers assigned to letters, syllables, and nomenclatures), nor in structure (since they were carefully designed homophonic systems complemented by nullities). It is also worth noting, however, that the most advanced practices of the prince's diplomatic correspondence were influenced by the French. It was the tables sent by the French court that helped Rákóczi catch up with the rest of Europe in this respect. In the seventeenth century, Antoine Rossignol, mathematician-cryptographer of Richelieu and then of Louis XIV, developed an enormous homophonic system of 590 items that coded syllables. The "Grand Chiffre," as it later became to be known, was a puzzle to everyone for the next two centuries, until Étienne Bazeries (1846–1931) came along and solved it.[131] The 'Sun King' of course did not offer this unbeatable system to his Eastern ally, but he shared their second most advanced one, which was still considered one of the most sophisticated tables of the time.

---

126  AR I. vol. 4. 374–375, 61. and AR I. vol. 5. 100–104, 38; 120–122, 53.

127  MNL OL G 15 Caps. C. Fasc 43, published in: Révay, *II. Rákóczi Ferenc*, 90–95.

128  ÖStA HHStA Staatskanzlei Interiora Kt. 13–16. Chiffrenschlüssel.

129  Meister, *Die Geheimschrift*. David Alvarez, "The Papal Cipher Section in the Early Nineteenth Century," *Cryptologia* 17 (1993): 219–24.

130  Edmond Lerville, *Les Cahiers secrets de la cryptographie* (Paris: Rocher, 1972); L. Sacco, *Manuel de Cryptographie* (Paris: Payot, 1951).

131  Lerville, *Les Cahiers secrets*, 64–74; Commandant Bazeries, *Les Chiffres secrets dévoilés, étude historique sur les chiffres appuyée de documents inédits tirés des différents dépôts d'archives* (Paris, E. Fasquelle, 1901); Kahn, "The Man with the Iron Mask."

In Rákóczi's environment, many envoys received claves that were developed according to the French system, just like the table of Pápai discussed above, but the locally used codes of the freedom fight remained surprisingly primitive. The 1705 clavis of General Sándor Károlyi and general Miklós Bercsényi, for example, was not only monoalphabetic; it also used graphic signs. Using these obviously did not help fast and clear communication on the battlefield. It is wearisome to draw a square instead of the letter 'a', a triangle instead of a 'b', an 'm' sign with a cross at the end instead of the letter 'e', but one should also consider how much more difficult it is to look up those signs from a table that cannot be ordered logically in any way, as opposed to consecutive numbers.[132] Still, there are a number of letters proving that this very impractical table was indeed used.[133] Similarly monoalphabetic and consisting of signs are the clavis of Rákóczi and Bercsényi from 1704,[134] as well as the 1707 key of Mihály Hentér, Rákóczi's ambassador in Constantinople.[135] The enciphering practice of the prince's diplomacy was not uniformly developed: higher-level ciphers were used internationally, less advanced ones internally.

Another feature of Hungarian cryptographic practice was that it advanced more slowly than in Western Europe, and even towards the middle and end of the seventeenth century, shockingly simple methods were used to cover information in life-and-death situations. In 1637, Prince György Rákóczi I was jovially writing to his envoy: "We would like to write more, but we cannot put it down in writing, so we are sending you a clavis that we are going to use in the future. Basically you only have to write down the above 12 letters with those of the bottom row, the bottom 12 letters with those of the top row."[136] In other words, the prince is offering a cipher that mutually assigns the second half of the alphabet to the first half. No nomenclatures, no nullities, no syllables, no homophones. And the prince of Transylvania actually used the system which could have been broken by a school-aged child.[137]

Staying in the Transylvanian area, a similarly odd case happened a few years later. Jónás Mednyánszky, in correspondence with the prince, György

---

132  War History Archives E. 1705/18.

133  War History Archives of Budapest E. 1705/5, 6, 03, 16, 17.

134  The key reconstructed in AR I. Vol. 4. köt. Appendix. The letters: AR I. vol. 2. 163–167, 10, 13, 28, etc.

135  MNL OL G 15 Caps. D. Fasc 80. fols. 38, 40, 46. MNL OL G 15 Caps. E. Fasc 109.

136  Beke and Barabás Samu *I. Rákóczi György*, 340–41.

137  Ötvös, *Rejtelmes levelek*, Révay, *Titkosírások*, 76–86.

Rákóczi II, used a decent homophonic system in his letters.[138] In this system (the table of which is extant in several copies) three numbers are assigned to each letter, syllables have their distinct numbers, and all this is extended with a couple of nomenclators (191 – Rex Hung or King, 346 – Moldavia, 294 – Roman Catholic, 347 – Transalpina, 366 – Russia, 192 – Palatinus, 194 – Primas, 204 – Svecus, 193 – judex curiae).[139] However, in 1658 they replaced this advanced homophonic clavis with a simpler, monoalphabetic key comprised of graphic symbols, letters and numbers.[140] In this latter one, there are no codes for syllables, only six nomenclators stand at the end of the list (4 – Nádasdy, X – Archbishop, 10 – Porta ottomanica, Z – Rákóczy, W – Chancellor, 271 – King, N – Palatinus).[141] What could have been the reason to drop the more advanced clavis in favor of a more primitive and laborious one? This is just as perplexing as those messages[142] and tables[143] of the mid-seventeenth century Wesselényi movement that were monoalphabetic.

Of course, it would be misleading to make the impression that in contrast with Hungary, Western Europe had a consistently high standard of ciphering. On the contrary, while the majority of the claves were certainly of a high standard, readers can find surprising exceptions. In 1621, Ferdinand II, Holy Roman Emperor, exchanged letters with Jacobus Curtis (Jakob Kurtz), his Polish trustee, using a monoalphabetic clavis.[144] In 1628–1629, Johann Ludwig Kuefstein, ambassador at the Porte, wrote to Emperor Ferdinand III with a cipher of graphic symbols (and he did so using a weak homophonic, practically monoalphabetic system).[145] Likewise, in 1632, the Emperor's secret reporters, or spies, coded their Italian letters with a clavis of graphic symbols.[146] Sixty years prior to this, it was a common method in the Imperial administration to use graphic symbols (see Carolus Rym's letters from

138  MNL OL E 190, Arch Fam. Rákóczi, 43, 5: 794, 802. 816. 821. 872. 875. 886.
139  MNL OL P 497 Mednyánszky Family, fasc. 3. Keys for the correspondence of György Rákóczy II and Jónás Mednyánszky, fol. 13, 5, 2, 4.
140  MNL OL E 190, Arch Fam. Rákóczi, 44. 5: 891–893, 897–8, 901, 904, 909, 924, 926.
141  MNL OL P 497 Mednyánszky Family, fasc. 3. Keys for the correspondence of György Rákóczy II and Jónás Mednyánszky, fol. 11–12.
142  MNL OL E 199 fasc. 8, pallium 1.
143  ÖStA HHStA Ungarische Akten Specialia Verschwöreakten VII. Varia, fasc. 327. Konv. D. Chiffres 1664–1668, fol. 17, fol. 32, fol. 39, fol. 54, fol. 55.
144  HHStA, Ung Akt. Misc Fasc 422 Conv 1 fol. 72–79.
145  ELTE University Library, G. 4. Fol. Tom. V. 469–958.
146  ÖStA HHStA Staatenabteilungen Türkei I. Kt. 112. Konv. 5. fol. 1–9 and fol. 17–28. I thank Dóra Kerekes for calling my attention to these sources.

Constantinople around 1571),[147] but the seventeenth century is dominated by the use of the more comfortable numbers. One could make a long list of similar exceptions that prove that development was not linear (from simple monoalphabetic substitutions to the more complex homophonic methods) in the Court of the Habsburg Emperor either, and that historical figures had different meanings for the terms "improved" and "practical" when it comes to ciphering.

By the end of the early modern period, the usage of ciphers in Hungary had generally caught up with the Central and Western European standard. This, however, was mainly influenced by Western practice itself. The letters from the correspondence of Transylvanian princes reveal that by the middle of the seventeenth century, ciphering practices in the Principality of Transylvania were on a less complex level (using simple monoalphabetic ciphers) than those of the envoys of the Habsburg (who primarily employed homophonic methods); even Mihály Teleki had only a few tables of Western quality, many of his claves remained monoalphabetic ones.[148] In addition, the fact that the Princes tended to do the coding themselves – something that György Rákóczi I, Imre Thököly and Ferenc Rákóczi II felt so natural – is not a practical usage of ciphering. Even a developed method can be used in an undeveloped way.

147  ÖStA HHStA Türkei I. Karton 28. Konv. 1. 1571. fol. 33–87, 44–47, 52–54, 65–66.
148  MNL OL P 1238 Mihály Teleki Collection, Miscellenous documents, Cipher keys.

# 7. Ways of knowledge transfer

Royals, princes, ambassadors and delegates in the sixteenth and seventeenth centuries in Central Europe used ciphers, code words, and signs for the syllables when exchanging diplomatic and political information with each other. Ferenc Rákóczi II applied a complex homophonic system when discussing his love affair in French with his political ally and lover, Elżbieta Helena Sieniawska (1669–1729), wife of a Polish palatine.[1] His generals, Sándor Károlyi and Miklós Bercsényi, used a vulnerable monoalphabetic system of graphic symbols to arrange military business.[2] An even simpler method was applied by the poet Bálint Balassi a hundred years earlier to conceal intimate family business, a cipher that assigned the first half of the alphabet to the letters of the second half and vice versa.[3] The would be palatine István Illésházy only enciphered the vowels in his private letter to his wife, Katalin Pálfy in his exile in 1605, and even those in a well-recognizable fashion.[4] The merchant Zsigmond Szaniszló also coded private affairs – financial details, names of certain people, a few liberal comments, his wife's extramarital affair – in his lengthy diary between 1682 and 1711. Like Illésházy, he only coded the vowels, so this ciphertext can be decoded at first reading.[5] The Transylvanian politician, Gábor Haller covered up his private secrets in his diary from between 1630 and 1644 – his alcoholism, marriage plans, details of his bedtime fantasies – using two different ciphering methods, one similar to the pigpen method of the Freemasons, consisting of dots and squares, and another one based on letter transposition.[6]

The question is inescapable: where did these people acquire their knowledge on cryptography, their practical skills on the use of ciphers?

Research in the past two decades in the history of science has increasingly focused on the ways and methods of knowledge transfer, especially

---

1  On this case, see more below.

2  The key: War History Archives E. 1705/18; the letters: E. 1705/5, 6, 03, 16, 17, Bercsényi's key with Rákóczi: AR I. vol. 4. Appendix

3  Révay, *Titkosírások*, 69–73; Révay, *II. Rákóczi Ferenc*, 41–46. Béla Stoll, ed. Balassi Bálint, Összes versei (Poems of Bálint Balassi) (Budapest, Helikon, 1974): 260–271; 391–394.

4  István Vadai, "Két XVII. századi titkosírás megfejtése."

5  Károly Torma, ed. *Történelmi Tár* (Historical documents), 1889 (12). 230–269, 503–522, 708–727, (13), 1890. 77–101, 307–327, 493–510, 757–770, (14), 1891. 267–295.

6  Károly Szabó, ed. *Erdélyi Történelmi Adatok* (Historical data from Transylvania) 4 (Kolozsvár: Erdélyi Múzeum Egyesület, 1862): 1—103

of passing on technological skills.[7] Which channels were primarily used: written, by means of books and letters, or personal, by means of schools and master-student relationships? Is the transfer of technological skills collective, based on the mobility of groups of artisans, or individual, based on the mobility and migration of particular experts, engineers, technological professionals? How is knowledge transferred in those areas where the details of theory and practice can be easily and explicitly expressed in writing, and how is it passed on in areas where a skill can only be learned implicitly, through practice and training?[8] Is it possible to follow the spread of a technology in the past across diverse geographical areas and across various knowledge-transfer communities, institutions and markets? How did these communities interact with the given technological information and how did they change it in the process of interpreting and applying the given knowledge to their local needs? How was circulation affected by the unavoidable translation processes?[9]

Can these ways of knowledge transfer be reconstructed at all? What sources provide reliable information on the circulation of such techniques that were hardly recorded and codified in their own times? And what about those crafts that were secretive both in their techniques and in their field of application?[10]

There were several possible sources of cryptographic knowledge in early modern Hungary. Up-to-date handbooks were available in libraries in the following three fields:

1) secret writings in the strictest sense in reference books on cryptography and steganography,

---

7   On the issue of knowledge transfer in history of technology, see: Liliane Hilaire-Pérez and Catherine Verna, "Dissemination of Technical Knowledge in the Middle Ages and the Early Modern Era: New Approaches and Methodological Issues," *Technology and Culture* 47 (2006): 536–565; Liliane Hilaire-Pérez and Anne-Francoise Garcon eds., *Les chemins de la nouveauté: Inventer, innover au regard de l'histoire* (Paris, 2004).

8   Ricardo Cordoba, ed., *Craft Treatises and Handbooks: The Dissemination of Technical Knowledge in the Middle Ages* (Turnhout: Brepols, 2013).

9   Josef Ehmer, "Worlds of Mobility: Migration Patterns of Viennese Artisans in the Eighteenth Century," in Geoffrey Crossick, ed., *The Artisan and the European Town, 1500–1900* (Aldershot, U.K., 1997), 172–99; Stephan R. Epstein, "Journeymen, Mobility, and the Circulation of Technical Knowledge, XIVth-XVIIIth Centuries," in Liliane Hilaire-Pérez and Anne-Francoise Garcon eds., *Les chemins de la nouveauté: Inventer, innover au regard de l'histoire* (Paris, 2004): 1–30, Michel Cotte ed. *Les circulations techniques: En amont de l'innovation – hommes, objets et idées en mouvement* (Belfort/ Besancon, France, 2004).

10   John R. Harris, *Industrial Espionage and Technology Transfer: Britain and France in the 18th-Century* (Aldershot, U.K., 1998).

2) artificial languages, which had a flourishing literature in this period,
3) the systems of speedwriting, stenography.

Two further possible sources should also be analysed

4) the Arabic written knowledge due to the Turkish neighborhood, because the practice of cryptography and codebreaking were a good five hundred years older in the Arab world than in Europe,
5) and finally, the proximity and effect of the everyday diplomatic practice should also be considered.


## 7.1.    Handbooks of cryptography

People interested in the technology of ciphers could have found a variety of printed handbooks in the libraries of the early modern period: the *Polygraphia* and *Steganographia* of Johannes Trithemius,[11] *De occultis literarum notis* by Giambattista Della Porta,[12] *Cryptomenytices et cryptographiae libri IX* of Gustavus Selenus, the famous library founder, Prince August of Braunschweig,[13] and *Traicte des Chiffres* by Blaise Vigenère[14] were all available in print by the beginning of the seventeenth century. These were followed by the *Polygraphia* of Athanasius Kircher,[15] and the *Rules for explaining and deciphering all manner of secret writing* by Englishman John Falconer.[16] These reference books, especially those five by Trithemius, Porta, Vigenère, Selenus and Kircher must have been the crown jewels in the libraries of every fan of cryptology, offering a wide range of methods from monoalphabetic substitution through transpositional to polyalphabetic and other highly advanced methods.

It makes sense to suggest – as historians Zoltán Révay[17] and Ágnes R. Várkonyi[18] did – that one of these early modern monographs, that by Athanasius Kircher could have been an important source of Hungarian

---

11   Johannes Trithemius, *Polygraphiae libri sex* (Oppenheim: Haselberg de Aia, 1518), *Steganographia: ars per occultam scripturam* (Frankfurt: Becker, 1606).

12   Giambattista Della Porta, *De furtivis literarum notis vulgo de ziferis liber quinque* (Naples: Johannes Baptista, 1602), *De occultis literarum notis, seu artis animi sensa occulte aliis significandi* (Starssbourg: Zetzner, 1606).

13   Gustavus Selenus, *Cryptomenytices et cryptographiae libri IX* (Luneburg, Sternen, 1624).

14   Blaise de Vigenère, *Traicte des Chiffres* (Paris: Abel l'Angelier, 1586).

15   Athanasius Kircher, *Polygraphia nova et universalis* (Roma: Typographia Varesij, 1664).

16   J. Falconer, *Rules for explaining and deciphering all manner of secret writing* (London: Printed for Dan. Brown ... and Sam. Manship, 1692).

17   Révay, *Titkosírások*, 89 and 110.

18   R. Várkonyi Ágnes, *A rejtőzködő murányi Vénusz* (Budapest: Helikon, 1987), 213.

cipher use. To confirm this, one should look at first how easily accessible these or similar handbooks on cryptology were in the private libraries and church collections. But the results of a methodical investigation into early modern library catalogues will be disappointing. There is no proof that early cryptologists were acquiring their methods from these handbooks. While noblemen applied cryptographic methods relatively frequently, there is hardly any reference literature of it in their libraries.

Pál Ráday, the head of the chancellery of the Rákóczi freedom fight is one example. There are few people in Hungarian history who have seen more ciphered messages than he did, he had separate cipher keys with a number of ambassadors and European rulers. There are thirty-one extant tables from the period of the freedom fight in the family archives of the Rádays,[19] and ninety-nine in the secret archive of Rákóczi.[20] Even if the number of double copies is subtracted from the sum of these two, there are still several dozens of different cipher techniques that were employed by him (or his secretaries) on a daily basis.

What about his library? Thorough research has adequately reconstructed it.[21] Ráday built up his collection through careful choices, it reflects his good taste (and that of his son, Gedeon). He had borrowed the help of academics to guide him in increasing his collection,[22] and had enriched it with encyclopaedic completeness in more than one field, such as history, law or politics.[23] The literature of cryptography, however, is completely missing from the library.

A similar example is that of András Dudith from over a century before Ráday, who had used cipher keys extensively in his numerous envoy's reports to the court in Vienna.[24] His library has not totally been reconstructed, yet research has found no trace of a handbook on cryptography in his library yet.[25]

19   Ráday Archives C64-4d2-25.

20   MNL OL G 15 Caps. C. Fasc 43. and Fasc. 44.

21   Györgyi Borvölgyi, *Ráday Pál (1677–1733) könyvtára* (Library of Ráday Pál (1677–1733)) (Budapest, OSzK, 2004).

22   Ibid. 63.

23   Ibid. 80–84.

24   ÖStA HHStA Staatskanzlei Interiora Ceremonie und courtoisie und Chiffren schlüssel: Kt. 12. Nr. 172, published: Lech Szczucki, Szepessy Tibor, eds. *Epistulae / Andreas Dudithius*, vol. 1, 40–41, see also vol. 2, 22–23; vol. 3, 16–17; vol. 4, 18–22.

25   József Jankovics, István Monok, eds., *Dudith András könyvtára* (Library of Andreas Dudith) (Szeged: Scriptum, 1993).

Johann Heinrich Bisterfeld sent a high number of enciphered messages to Zsigmond Rákóczi.[26] If the Ráday library was said to have been carefully selected, this is even more true for the library of Bisterfeld. He was one of the major encyclopedic minds of his age. As a professor at Herborn and later Alba Iulia (Gyulafehérvár), he built a well-structured library and even had a lasting influence on the book-collecting practice of Zsigmond Rákóczi.[27] And although some books of Giambattista Della Porta and Athanasius Kircher were undeniably there in his library, not the ones on cryptography, as any other books on cryptography are not there either.[28] One can assume, of course, that Bisterfeld had gained his cryptographic knowledge from his colleague and father-in-law, the other famous encyclopedist, Johann Heinrich Alsted.[29] Alsted's *Encyclopaedia* does indeed contain a chapter entitled *Polygraphia*, in the last, seventh, volume, among the "miscellaneous sciences", in the section called *"Farragines disciplinarum, seu disciplinas compositas"*, under *"Mnemonica"*, following the part on the combinatorial method of Raimundus Lullus, called *"Ars lulliana"*.[30] This little section, however, only makes up one page, while tobacco is discussed in two pages under *Tabacologia*. Alsted's short section on *Polygraphia* explains the polyalphabetic table of Trithemius in a period when the polyalphabetic methods were way too complex to be applied in actual practice – theory and practice were not in touch. Homophonic ciphers are not even mentioned.

No cryptographic handbook was found in the reconstructed family libraries of the Rákóczis[31] or Telekis[32] either, despite the fact that Prince György Rákóczi I had used ciphers extensively, and Mihály Teleki's ciphered messages had survived in the hundreds, some of which he had even

26   Sándor Szilágyi, "Herceg Rákóczy Zsigmond levelezése," (Correspondence of Prince Zsigmond Rákóczy) MTT III/10. 654–676.; MTT III/11. 289–300.; MTT III/13. 229–257.

27   Noémi Viskolcz, ed., *Johann Heinrich Bisterfeld (1605–1655). Bibliográfia, A Bisterfeld könyvtár (Johann Heinrich Bisterfeld (1605–1655). Bibliography, The Bisterfeld library)* (Budapest – Szeged: OSZK, Scriptum, 2003.), 91.

28   Ibid.

29   Howard Hotson, *Johann Heinrich Alsted 1588–1638: Between Renaissance, Reformation, and Universal Reform* (Oxford: Clarendon Press. 2000); idem, *Paradise postponed. Johann Heinrich Alsted and the Birth of Calvinist Millenarianism* (Dordrecht-Boston-London: Springer, 2001).

30   Ioan. Henrici Alstedii, *Encyclopaedia septem tomis distincta* (Herbornae: 1630. and Lugd. Batav: 1640.) Repr: Wilhelm Schmidt Biggemann, ed., *Johann Heinrich Alsted: Encyclopaedia septem tomis distincta.* Stuttgart-Bad Cannstatt, 1989–1990).

31   István Monok, ed., *A Rákóczi-család könyvtárai, 1588–1660* (Libraries of the Rákóczi family) (Szeged: Scriptum, 1996).

32   István Monok, Noémi Németh, András Varga, eds. *Erdélyi Könyvesházak III. 1563—1757: A Bethlen–család és környezete, Az Apafi–család és környezete, A Teleki–család és környezete, Vegyes források* (Transylvanian libraries, the Bethlen, Apafi and Teleki libraries) (Szeged, Scriptum, 1994).

written in his own hand. The reconstruction of these libraries is not complete, so this result is not final either. It is still significant that the research has not found many things so far. One of the few exceptions is one item of the 1638 description of Máté Csanaki's library: *De occultis literarum Notis Johanne Baptista Porta Neapolithano Authore.*[33] Csanaki (1594–1636) was the court physician of György Rákóczi I and a rector at Cluj Napoca, Romania (Kolozsvár). On returning from abroad, he left his books in Gdansk and after his death it was the prince who bought them and had them delivered to Sárospatak. Since the Sárospatak library already had many of these books, they were finally taken to Alba Iulia, (Gyulafehérvár) in Transylvania.[34] Bisterfeld himself was excited at the prospect of receiving the collection. One can therefore assume that György Rákóczi I must have had a copy of Della Porta's book, although no influence of it can be detected on the ciphering practice of the prince (he used many monoalphabetic ciphers and few homophonic ones.)[35]

Another of the few cryptographic resources that have been found is the 1678 Viennese booklist of Ferenc Nádasdy. An item here is the 1608 Frankfurt edition of Trithemius's *Steganographia.*[36] One is inclined to suppose that the magnate Nádasdy, Judge Royal and a participant of the Wesselényi movement, applied in his cryptographic practice whatever he had learned from Trithemius, but there is no evidence for it. His enciphered messages either use a monoalphabetic system[37] with code words, nomenclatures, or a homophonic,[38] which was more up-to-date in that time, bearing no sign of the complex methods suggested by Trithemius. It is important to note, however, that research in this field has not yet been completed and might still bring up further evidence.

The rest of the cryptographic relevant books were found in collections whose owner – or the church establishment behind them – are not known for applying ciphers. Though we cannot exclude the possibility, there is no

---

33  Ibid., 183.
34  István Monok, "Csanaki Máté könyvjegyzéke" (Booklist of Máté Csanaki) *Magyar Könyvszemle* (1983): 256–262.
35  Ágoston Ötvös, *Rejtelmes levelek első Rákóczy György korából.*
36  Gábor Farkas, András Varga, Tünde Katona, Miklós Latzkovits, István Monok, eds., *Magyarországi magánkönyvtárak II. 1588–1721* (Hungarian private libraries II. 1588–1721) (Szeged: Scriptum, 1992.), 103. See also Rita Bajáki, Hajnalka Bujdosó, István Monok, Noémi Viskolcz, eds., Magyarországi magánkönyvtárak IV. 1552–1740. (Hungarian private libraries IV. 1552–1740 (Budapest: OSZK, 2009).
37  HHStA, Ung Akt. Spec Verschwörerakten IV. Nádasdysche Akten Fasc. 314. Konv. B. 1671. I-III. fol. 76–78.
38  HHStA, Ung Akt. Spec Verschwörerakten IV. Fasc. 312. Konv. A. fol. 4.

indication that these books were ever used as handbooks. One such find is the item *De occultis literarum notis* by Della Porta that is listed twice in the 1632 catalog of the Jesuit library in Trnava (Nagyszombat, Slovakia), and another is *Poligraphia, octavo, Argentorati, 1600* by "Trithemij Abbatij" in the 1690 catalog, also listed twice (perhaps once existing in two volumes), in the section *Scriptura sacra, et patres* (presumably by mistake).[39] The *Polygraphia* of Trithemius (*Polygraphie libri sex* and *Clavis polygraphiae*, 1518) could be found in the collection of Hans Dernschwam,[40] the humanist scholar who died in Hungary in 1568, as well as in the library of Sárospatak,[41] and, according to the list of 1679–1680, in the school library of Nagyenyed.[42]

Previous literature has supported the claim that the works of Athanasius Kircher (1602–1660) had had a lasting influence on Hungarian cryptographic practice. This statement should be investigated carefully. Kircher, the pride of the Jesuit order, was one of the most prolific authors of his time. A professor of Eastern languages and mathematics in Avignon, he later went to Rome to become professor of the Collegium Romanum. He might have been the first person to realize the opportunities involved in the mass printing of books. With the help of a publishing company in Amsterdam, he compiled several encyclopediae covering every possible aspect of classic and modern knowledge, chockablock with linguistic, paleographic, historic and scientific data. During the fifty years of his career he had written almost thirty books. He was in correspondence with all of Europe, and even the transcontinental parts of the world. He was the friend of popes and princes. Bishops, archbishops and aristocrats supported him, borrowed books from him and provided him with academic information. Relying on the resources of the Jesuit order, he created an information network that covered the whole world from China to South America. His correspondents delivered him data on everything from local volcanoes to magnetic fields, and to writing systems.[43]

39   Farkas Gábor Farkas, ed. Magyarországi jezsuita könyvtárak 1711-ig, II, Nagyszombat 1632–1690 (Hungarian Jesuit libraries til 1711, II, Nagyszombat 1632–1690) (Szeged, Scriptum, 1997.), 96–97 and 321.

40   Jenő Berlász, Katalin Kevekázi, István Monok, András Varga, eds., *A Dernschwam-könyvtár: Egy magyarországi humanista könyvjegyzéke* (The Dernwchwam library, booklist of a humanist from Hungary) (Szeged: JATE, 1984), 19.

41   Róbert Oláh, ed. *Protestáns Intézményi Könyvtárak Magyarországon, 1530–1750* (Protestant institutional libraries in Hungary, 1530–1750) (Budapest: OSZK, 2009), 281.

42   István Monok, ed., *Erdélyi Könyvesházak II: Kolozsvár, Marosvásárhely, Nagyenyed, Szászváros, Székelyudvarhely* (Transylvanian Libraries II: Kolozsvár, Marosvásárhely, Nagyenyed, Szászváros, Székelyudvarhely) (Szeged: Scriptum, 1991), 151.

43   John Edward Fletcher, *Athanasius Kircher und seine Beziehungen zum gelehrten Europa seiner Zeit* (Wiesbaden: Otto Harrassowitz, 1988); Paula Findlen, *Athanasius Kircher: The Last Man Who*

Kircher was enthralled by automata and impressed a many rulers with the clever devices he had designed. He had a grand collection in Rome that attracted scientifically minded visitors from faraway lands. Kircher guided his visitors around this exceptional collection of various oddities himself: machines, wooden obelisks, children's skeletons, dissected animals, Roman burial pots, Chinese objects, mosaics or coins.

He was also a renown codebreaker, sending cryptographic puzzles to his correspondents and also receiving some undeciphered texts. At one point his library included perhaps the most enigmatic book of all times, the manuscript that was later named Voynich after the person who rediscovers it almost two hundred and fifty years later (Wilfrid Voynich, 1865–1930). Kircher examined the book famous for its drawings on botanics and astronomy, naked bathing ladies and a special writing system, and wisely decided to put it aside instead of being put to shame with an incorrect bluff of a solution. And right he was. Not even elite WWII codebreakers had success with the manuscript, despite their much richer resources, and the text has not been broken to this day.[44]

Kircher's 1663 book on cryptography, entitled *Polygraphia Nova et Universalis*, was printed in limited numbers, in accordance with the author's intention. It was then sent to a limited number of royals and other dignitaries, accompanied by a private letter. Most if it is not even on ciphers, it is rather a *Polygraphia* following the track of Trithemius, i. e. a means of communication that is meant to override the linguistic chaos of Babel. It creates an extensive multilingual dictionary by assigning the same number to the words of different languages with the same meaning. This way, if a scribe writes down the numbers corresponding to the words of a German sentence, a reader who does not even speak German may still be able to read it, for example in Italian. A seventeenth century translating software. The system is designed to ease communication, but book three of the volume also gives advice on how to conceal the content of a text. Here a description of the letter substitution and permutational methods by Trithemius and Vigenère are described. Artificial languages and cryptography walked hand in hand.[45]

*Knew Everything* (New York: Routledge, 2004); Joscelyn Godwin, *Athanasius Kircher's Theatre of the World: The Life and Work of the Last Man to Search for Universal Knowledge.* (Rochester, Vt.: Inner Traditions, 2009).

44  Gerry Kennedy, Rob Churchill, *The Voynich Manuscript: The Mysterious Code That Has Defied Interpretation for Centuries* (Rochester, VT; 2006).

45  On Kircher's Polygraphia: Nick Wilding, "'If you have a secret, either keep it, or reveal it'": Cryptography and Universal Language' in Daniel Stolzenberg, ed., *The Great Art of Knowing – The Baroque Encyclopedia of Athanasius Kircher* (Fiesole: Stanford University Libraries, Edizioni

Kircher had contacts in Hungary – friends, correspondents, followers.[46] He dedicated a chapter to Ferenc Nádasdy and Archbishop György Lippay, respectively, in his book on Egypt. Many aristocrats, including counts Batthyány and Erdődy had visited him in Rome. The topic of his correspondence with Nádasdy was the design of telescopes, he even sent him an astronomical telescope. He received mining information from the Jesuits in Nagyszombat for his book on the underground world regarding various ores, underground waters, and cave dwarfs. Several of his books could be found in the Zrínyi library too, including *Oedipus Aegyptiacus,* a book that contained his solutions of the hieroglyph, and *De Magnetica Arte libri tres* on the phenomenon of magnetism.[47] Lippay had read several of his books, including a few that the Jesuit scholar himself had sent to him. Imre Jakusith, lord of Oroszlánkő, who also collected Kircher's books, was corresponding with the scholar, who had sent him the complete list of his books in response. Today, altogether ninety-six copies of thirty different works of Kircher can be found or identified in libraries in Hungary.[48]

This means that Kircher was well-known among the circles of the Hungarian literati. But could he have become a source of the local knowledge on cryptography? Only one of his books, and only one part of that, dealt explicitly with the field of cryptography. The topic of code does emerge in his other books too, but never in such depth that would allow a reader to learn the actual practices of ciphering from it. However, this only book, the *Polygraphia* was among the least known volumes of Kircher in Hungary. To our best knowledge, it was not part of the Zrínyi library. A note by Jakusith says that this book was missing from his collection. Only one copy of it can be identified in Hungary, the one sent by Kircher to Archbishop Lippai. This copy has been in the Library of the Esztergom Primate since then.[49]

Cadmo, 2001), 93 – 103; idem, "Publishing the Polygraphy: Manuscript, Instrument, and Print in the Work of Athanasius Kircher' in Paula Findlen, ed. *Athanasius Kircher,* 283 –296; Daniel Stolzenberg, "The Universal History of the Characters of Letters and Languages: An Unknown Manuscript by Athanasius Kircher," *Memoirs of the American Academy in Rome* 56/57 (2011/2012): 305–321.

46   Gábor Kiss Farkas "'Difficiles Nugae' Athanasius Kircher magyarországi kapcsolatai" ('Difficiles Nugae' Kircher's contacts in Hungary), *Irodalomtörténeti Közlemények* 109 (2005): 436–463.

47   Gábor Hausner, Tibor Klaniczay, Sándor Iván Kovács, István Monok, Géza Orlovszky, eds., *A Bibliotheca Zriniana története* (History of the Bibliotheca Zriniana) (Budapest: Argumentum Kiadó, 1992,) 324–326. Kircher's books in the library: *Oedipus Aegyptiacus* (1652), *Jesu Magnes, sive de Magnetica Arte libri tres* (1654) *Ars magna lucis* (1646) *Scrutinium Physico-medicum* (1658).

48   Kiss Farkas, "Difficiles Nugae" 457.

49   Esztergomi Főszékesegyházi Könyvtár (Archiepiscopal Library of Esztergom) Ms 28879: Kiss Farkas "Difficiles Nugae" 443.

All in all, Selenus and Vigenère were hardly known, whereas Della Porta, Trithemius and Kircher were rather familiar names in seventeenth-century Hungary. Their works could quite easily be found. Porta and Kircher, however, were not famous in Hungary for their cryptographic works. Porta was better known by his *Magia naturalis* (Antwerpen: 1560), while Kircher by his *Oedipus Aegyptiacus* (I–II, Rome, 1652–54). In addition, all these authors were rather interested in the more sophisticated and advanced technologies of cryptography: combinatorial polyalphabetic ciphers consisting of several alphabets and requiring a great deal of intellectual capacity. Diplomatic, political, military or private ciphers of the time, however, did not use these complex technologies but stayed on the level of monoalphabetic and the more progressive homophonic cipher. But the homophonic ciphers used, among others, by Miklós Zrínyi[50] and György Lippay,[51] were not covered in these handbooks, while those monoalphabetic methods that assigned the first half of the alphabet to the second half, or that only exchanged vowels for code signs were considered so outdated that they were not even mentioned. Certain cipher users might possibly have seen Trithemius' or Kircher's *Polygraphia* or perhaps *De occultis literarum notis* by Della Porta, but there is no sign that they developed or modified their earlier methods on the basis of their readings. Quite clearly, the source of their cryptological knowledge is to be found elsewhere.

## 7.2.    Artificial languages

Several authors created universal, perfect, philosophical or artificial languages for a number of purposes in the mid-seventeenth century (Kircher being one of them).[52] This is roughly the same group of intellectuals who

50    Károly Széchy, *Gróf Zrínyi Miklós* (Count Miklós Zrínyi) (Budapest: Franklin, 1896–1902) vol. 3. 335–338, vol. 4. 252–268.

51    Antal Beke, ed., "Pázmány, Lippay és Eszterházy levelezése I. Rákóczy Györgygyel [1629–1637]. 1–3." ("The correspondence of Pázmány, Lippay and Eszterházy with György Rákóczy I [1629–1637]. 1–3." *Magyar Történelmi Tár* (1881): 641–674, (1882): 134–148, 279–325, the key: 144–146.

52    Louis Couturat, Leopold Leau, *Histoire de la langue universelle* (Hachette, Paris, 1903); *Les nouvelles langues internationales* (Hachette, Paris, 1907); Arno Borst, *Der Turmbau von Babel: Geschichte der Meinungen über den Ursprung und Vielfalt der Sprachen und Völker* (Hiersemann, Stuttgart, 1957–1963); Paolo Rossi, *Clavis universalis: arti della memoria e logica combinatoria da Lullo a Leibniz* (Bologna: il Mulino, 1983), James Knowlson, *Universal Language Schemes in England and France, 1600–1800* (Toronto, University of Toronto Press, 1975), Roberto Pellerey, *Le lingue perfette nel secolo dell'utopia* (Roma-Bari: Laterza, 1992), Mary M. Slaughter, *Universal languages and scientific taxonomy in the 17th century* (Cambridge: Cambridge University Press, 1982), Umberto Eco, *La ricerca della lingua perfetta nella cultura europea* (Bari: Laterza, 1993).

have authored the major works on cryptography, almost all belonging to the leading literati of the early modern era: Johannes Trithemius, Athanasius Kircher, René Descartes, Isaac Newton, Gottfried Wilhelm Leibniz, Marin Mersenne, George Dalgarno, Joseph de Maimieux, Francis Lodwick, Cave Beck, John Wilkins, or the Hungarian György Kalmár.[53] Their purposes might have differed. One of them wanted to design a practical, user-friendly common language, while the other wished to create a logically structured tool suitable for establishing human knowledge philosophically. One of them was looking for Adam's lost language, and others, like Kircher or Cave Beck, designed a common writing system that everybody could read in their own language.

All of these designs aimed at making language available and accessible, they were open projects, by nature not secretive, fundamentally different from secret writing designs.[54] Still, the two seemingly opposite trends contained many common elements. The authors are often identical, who found the creation of a useful artificial language as thrilling as the secrecy offered by more practical ciphers.[55] Another similarity is that an artificial language without its structural description and vocabulary is pretty much like an unbroken cipher.

There is a third reason to consider the impact of artificial language designs. While most cipher tables assign code symbols to letters, syllables or to code words, there are a few cipher keys where grammatical elements also appear, such as the sign for accusativus, genitivus, dativus and ablativus, or for plural. These often appear as graphic symbols in a table consisting otherwise of number codes. There are two examples for such symbols among Mihály Teleki's tables.[56] These grammatical categories are widespread in artificial languages, for example in those of Wilkins, Della Porta, Kircher and others. Theirs are, of course, more complex systems than the cipher keys: Kircher's *Polygraphia* for instance applies graphic signs for declination and conjugation too.[57] I have yet to find any trace of conjugation in code keys, just as there is no direct evidence that the appearance of declination items in cipher keys in the second half of the seventeenth century can be directly

53  See more details: Benedek Láng, *The Rohonc codex*, forthcoming.

54  Cave Beck, *The Universal Character by which all the Nations in the World may Understand one anothers conceptions, Reading out of one Common Writing their own mother tongues* (London: Thomas Maxey, 1657); Athanasius Kircher, *Polygraphia Nova et universalis ex combinatoria arte detecta* (Rome: Varesius, 1663).

55  On the common history of artificial languages and cryptography, see Strasser, *Lingua Universalis*.

56  MNL OL P 1238 Mihály Teleki Collection. Miscallenous documents. Cipher keys.

57  Kircher, *Polygraphia nova*, 15.

linked to artificial languages. One can entertain the idea of such relationship, but one also needs further evidence supporting such assumptions.
Whether the designers of cipher keys had read artificial language schemes
is a question that cannot be decided without further evidence.


## 7.3.    Stenography

The connection between Hungarian cryptographic practice and stenography, i.e. shorthand has been recognized as early as in the nineteen thir-
ties.[58] The same secretaries were recording the political speeches and the
drafts of the letters with speedwriting, who were encrypting the classified
information according to a particular code key – creating an obvious link
between the two areas. The father of one of the earliest stenographic methods, John Willis himself underlines the fact that his method could in fact
be used as a cryptologic method, as it hides information well from those
who are unfamiliar with it.[59] Several books covered the two fields together
in the nineteenth, and in the twentieth century too.[60] Examples testify that
a stenographic note without its character table might become a real secret
writing, either in accordance with, or contrary to, the intentions of its author.[61] But was there any actual relationship between the two areas in the
sixteenth and seventeenth centuries?

These two centuries constitute a blind spot in the Hungarian history
of stenography. Shorthand symbols, in other words, Tironian notes (*notae
Tironianae*) were most widespread during the late antique and early medieval periods, when letter-writing was especially laborious. The system
became more sophisticated by the twelfth century when it had several
thousand signs, including signs concepts. By the later medieval period,
however, normal Latin writing became fluent enough, abbreviations and
truncations were becoming more general, making Tironian notes less

---

58  László Siklóssy, *Az országgyűlési beszéd útja* (Budapest: Királyi Magyar Egyetemi Nyomda,
1939), 30–45.

59  John Willis, *The Art of Stenographie, teaching by plaine and certaine rules, to the capacitie of
the meanest, and for the use of all professions, the way of compendious writing* (London, Cuthbert
Burbie, 1602.) Bibliothèque Nationale de France, Réserve, V 30834.

60  E.g. Giorgio Costamagna, *Tachiografia notarile e scritture segrete medioevali in Italia* (Rome:
ANAI, 1968).

61  E.g. James J. Gillogly, "Breaking an Eighteenth Century Shorthand System", *Cryptologia*
11/2 (1987): 93–98 and Emanuele Viterbo, "The Ciphered Autobiography of a 19th Century
Egyptologist," *Cryptologia*, 22/3 (1998): 231–243; Géza Gárdonyi, *Titkosnapló* (Secert diary)
(Budapest: Szépirodalmi, 1974).

indispensable. Shorthand symbols practically disappeared. There is a gap in the history of stenography for the next couple of centuries, until it was rediscovered in the sixteenth century. Fifteenth-century Italian scribes developed their own shorthand methods to record official speeches, mostly sermons, still, we consider three early modern authors the new founding fathers of shorthand: Timothy Bright (*Characterie; An Arte of Shorte, Swifte and Secrete Writing by Character*, 1588), John Willis (*Art of Stenography*, 1602), and Thomas Shelton (*Short-Writing*, 1626, in later editions: *Tachygraphy*). Their systems often only had individual signs for the consonants. Vowels were only indirectly indicated, by the position of the following consonant, its width, or the surrounding dots, for example. Roughly one hundred and fifty to two hundred signs were used in these systems, making them similar in size to an average homophonic cipher.

While modern shorthand systems were born in England around 1600, the first Hungarian handbooks only appeared a hundred and fifty to two hundred years later, it seems. The early centuries of Hungarian stenography lack a reliable overview, but as of present, there is no sign that there was such a complex system of shorthand for recording political speeches that could have had a lasting influence on the encryption methods. On the contrary, ciphering seems to have been more developed than stenography.

## 7.4.    The Turkish factor

Chapter 4.2 faithfully tracked down the development of medieval Arabic cryptology, both the science of secret writing and the different code-breaking techniques offered by scholars, poets and linguists from Damascus and Cairo. The five-hundred-year-old vantage point of Arabs is documented in the series *Arabic Origins of Cryptology*.[62] It has been also pointed out, how Western cryptology developed independently from the Arabic developments, as a result of the flourishing Italian diplomacy. In other fields of science, Western culture happily profited from Arabic culture (mainly through the translation movement going on in the Iberian Peninsula and Sicily), yet it could not access the fundamental cryptographic works by the Arabs.

The place where the works of Al-Kindi, ibn 'Adlan, ibn Dunaynir, ibn ad-Durayhim, al-Qualquasandi, and a few others actually survived was right there, in the Istanbul collections. The question arises: could the

---

62   See above, in chapter 4.2.

Central-European expansion of the Ottoman Empire have opened a new channel of knowledge transfer? Could the Turkish presence in Hungary have introduced cryptographic techniques that were later used in Western practice? Could Hungary in the sixteenth and seventeenth centuries be a place where cryptographic methods were passed on from author to author, just like Spain and Southern-Italy were places where other fields of science were passed on in the eleventh to thirteenth centuries? Could the spies, writers of secret letters or particularly the double agents have been the means of knowledge transfer?

Recent decades have seen extensive studies on early modern Habsburg[63] and Ottoman[64] espionage in the Hungarian territories that were divided into three parts.[65] The spies' network spread to all of the areas under Turkish rule, besides the territory of the Hungarian Kingdom under Habsburg control, and the Principality of Transylvania. These agents regularly employed ciphers in their messages. It can be plausibly supposed that they were part of knowledge transfer, especially if they were double

---

63  Josip Žontar, *Obveščevalna služba in diplomacija avstrijskih Habsburžanov v boju proti Turkom v 16. stoleju. Der Kundschafterdinst und die Diplomatie der österreichischen Habsburger im Kampf gegen die Türken im 16. Jahrhundert.* (Ljubljana: Slovenska Akademija Znanosti i Umetnosti, 1973). Pál Fodor, "Kémkedés a török korban," (Espionage in the Ottoman era) *Keletkutatás* 1995: 121–126. Ferenc Szakály, "Egy végvári kapitány hétköznapjai" (Everydays of a fortress captain) in József Kanyar, eds., *Somogy Megye Múltjából* (From the past of Somogy county) 18 (1987): 45–126. Tivadar Petercsák and Mátyás Berecz, eds., *Információáramlás a magyar és török végvári rendszerben* (Information flow in the Hungarian and Ottoman fortress systems) (Eger: Dobó István Vármúzeum, 1999), particularly the articles of Géza Pálffy and István Hiller. See also: Dóra Kerekes, "Kémek Konstantinápolyban: A Habsburg információszerzés szervezete és működése a magyarországi visszafoglaló háborúk idején (1683–1699)," (Spies in Constantinople, the organization and functioning of the Habsburg intelligence, 1683–1699) *Századok* 141 (2007): 1217–1258; eadem, "Hírszerzés a XVI-XVII. században," (Intelligence in the 16th-17th centuries) *Irodalomismeret* 13 (2003): 63–70; eadem, *Diplomaták és kémek Konstantinápolyban* (Diplomats and spies in Constantinople (Budapest: L'Harmattan, 2010).

64  Emrah Safa Gürkan, "The efficacy of ottoman counter-intelligence in the 16th century" *Acta Orientalia Academiae Scientiarum Hung.* 65 (2012): 1–38, Géza Dávid – Pál Fodor, "Oszmán hírszerzés Magyarországon," (Ottoman intelligence in Hungary) in Petercsák–Berecz, *Információáramlás,* 197–207; Gábor Ágoston, "Információszerzés és kémkedés az Oszmán Birodalomban a 15–17. században," (Intelligence and espionage in the Ottoman Empire in the 15th -17th centuries) in Petercsák–Berecz, *Információáramlás,* 129–157. Dejanirah Couto, "Spying in the Ottoman Empire: Sixteenth-Century Encrypted Correspondence," in Francisco Bethencourt and Florike Egmond, eds. *Cultural Exchange in Early Modern Europe (Volume III) - Correspondence and Cultural Exchange in Europe, 1400–1700* (Cambridge: Cambridge University Press, 2007) 274–312.

65  A helpful historiographical overview: Zoltán Péter Bagi, "A 16–17. századi határvidéki és diplomáciai kémkedés magyar nyelvű irodalmának áttekintése" (Overview on the Hungarian secondary literature on the 16th – 17th century espionage along the borders and in diplomacy) *Aetas* 27 (2012): 176–188.

agents. It is also possible that the cryptographic offices of the enemy, working on the codebreaking of captivated messages, learned from these solved cipher systems.

Some well-known double agents (János Trombitás,[66] David Passi,[67] and others)[68] and their stories constitute an especially intriguing chapter of the history of espionage. There has been a significant research on the central and peripheral intelligence organizations: the ways of contact, social status, profession, fate, life and death of spies, and also the content of the acquired information, the enciphered messages, and the effect of the transfer of information. The picture of this area is much more detailed and accurate now than it was two decades ago, but many more hours of archival research is needed to make a complete overview of the intelligence systems in the whole of the early modern era, and to have a clear view of the cipher use of the time. For example, little is known of how the spies had received their code tables that they then had to memorize for the sake of security,[69] and equally little is known on how frequently they were changing their codes. The first part of these questions could be clarified by further research of the archives, but the second part is not that easily accessible. Ciphered letters were often destroyed, and only the "translated" or plain text versions survived.

On the basis of the presently available information, it seems quite impossible that any cryptologic knowledge was passed on between the Turkish (Arabic) and Western (Hungarian-Habsburg) worlds. What is even more unlikely is that this happened exactly via ciphered correspondence.

First of all, unfortunately it is uncertain whether the above-mentioned Arabic cryptographic handbooks ever got out of the archives of the Ottoman capital. In other words, it is not clear whether any knowledge was passed on between Arabic (of Damascus and Cairo) and Turkish-Ottoman

---

66  Ferenc Szakály, *Mezőváros és reformáció. Tanulmányok a korai magyar polgárosodás kérdéséhez*. (Oppidum and Reformation: studies on the early Hungarian formation of bourgeoisie) Budapest, 1995. 225–290.

67  Elif Özgen, "The connected world of intrigues: the disgrace of Murad III's favourite David Passi in 1591", *Leidschrift* 27 (2012): 75–100; Pál Fodor, "An anti-Semite Grand Vizier? The crisis in Ottoman-Jewish Relations in 1589–91 and its Consequences," in idem, ed., *In Quest of the Golden Apple: Imperial Ideology, Politics, and Military Administration in the Ottoman Empire* (Istanbul 2000) 191–206.

68  Gürkan, "The efficacy of ottoman counter-intelligence, 28–31.

69  Dóra Kerekes, "Titkosszolgálat volt-e a Habsburgok titkos levelezői intézménye?" (Was the 16-17th Century Habsburg "Secret Correspondence" a Secret Service?) in Csaba Katona, ed. *Kémek, ügynökök, besúgók. Az ókortól Mata Hariig.* (Szombathely: Magyar Nemzeti Levéltár Vas Megyei Levéltára, 2014): 97–137.

context. Despite the source publications that are based on thorough background investigations, the provenience of the manuscripts is dubious: the editors did not find the relevant details, or might have not even looked for them. What happened to these manuscripts, where they were kept, whether they were consulted by anyone in the last six or eight centuries remains unclear. In several cases, only one surviving copy is identified anyway, and therefore a likely scenario is that the books were lying on the shelves in Istanbul untouched.

There is further data indicating the lack of knowledge transfer. In 1551 the Turks could not decipher the letters of Johann Malvezzi, the Habsburgs' envoy who had been temporarily captured. The code was too difficult for them.[70] The Ottoman Turks were so much concerned about the messages that they could not read that between 1560 and 1570 they tried several times to ban the ambassadors of Venice and other cities in Constantinople from sending ciphered messages home. On one occasion, not without any irony, they even ordered the ambassador to teach them the codes, which the ambassador politely refused.[71] Professional codebreaking was seldom applied, instead they preferred physical aggression towards the people carrying enciphered messages. The Turks also repeatedly asked their French allies to help them decipher a key used by some other nation.[72]

On the one hand, there is no proof then that the Ottoman Turks were in possession of the advanced cryptographic knowledge of the Arabs. On the other hand, there is no sign that the secret agents (double or not) used a technology that was more advanced or newer than the average ciphers of that age. In fact, the secret reports sent to the Habsburg court in the 1630s are full of outdated graphic symbols instead of the more easily manageable numbers.[73]

The archival research done so far is far from being complete, yet no correlation can be seen at present between the level of cryptographic advancement and the proximity to the Turkish ciphers. The obvious correlation is rather between the development of cryptography and the diplomatic practice.

70  Lajos Kropf, "Malvezzi elfogattatása," (Malvezzi's detention) Századok 30 (1896): 389–393.

71  Gürkan, "The efficacy of ottoman counter-intelligence," 22–23.

72  Communication of Dóra Kerekes.

73  ÖStA HHStA Staatenabteilungen Türkei I. Kt. 112. Konv. 5. fol. 1–9; fol. 17–28. I thank Dóra Kerekes for calling my attention to these sources.

## 7.5.    Distance from diplomacy

The examples quoted at the beginning of this chapter show that "average users" tended to employ monoalphabetic – in a technological sense: outdated – ciphers. The poet Balassi and the merchant Szaniszló were way outside the circles of professional diplomacy. Though with some effort, they could have taken hold of cryptographic handbooks, they saw no need to do so. The savant Johann Heinrich Bisterfeld had easier access to such books, he could probably have just reached for the shelf and opened the *Encyclopaedia* of his father-in-law, Alsted, to select from the various polyalphabetic methods. Bisterfeld, nevertheless, chose to apply the homophonic methods that were so widespread in the diplomatic practice of the age. A further example is Rákóczi, who used homophonic codes in his correspondence with the French court or his Polish allies, but a more outdated cipher in writing to his generals, just as they (Bercsényi and Károlyi) also used simple graphic and monoalphabetic signs to write to each other that were difficult to use but easy to misunderstand.

However tempting it is to trace early modern Hungarian encrypting practice back to some book-based knowledge, there is no indication that any books from Hungarian collections like Trithemius, Della Porta, and Kircher, or manuscripts hidden in faraway Istanbul like al-Kindi's were actually used in the region. There is ample proof, nevertheless, that the closer someone stood to diplomatic practice, the more likely he was to use advanced, homophonic codes. And the other way around: the further someone was from diplomatic circles, the more likely he was to use less advanced monoalphabetic codes, regardless of his education and experience. The sophisticated ciphers from Della Porta, Vigenère, Selenus, or the Arabic writers were simply and completely disregarded. Early modern cipher users showed no academic interest in the science of cryptography.

# 8.    Scenes of secrecy

## 8.1.    Dissimulation and the secret

"Dear Lord Nemessány, I know what I owe you, but *for a while* I need to *dissimulate*," writes Dániel Absolon to Bálint Nemessányi in a long letter on the Christmas of 1678.[1] He enciphers the word dissimulation, becoming a showcase example for present-day research literature that considers the sixteenth and seventeenth centuries the *par excellence* age of dissimulation.[2]

In the early modern period, „dissimulation" named not merely an ad hoc behavior, as it always had in Latin, but a cultivated courtly practice, which had rules of etiquette that could be systematized – an „art," as can be seen from Torqueto Acceto's 1641 book, the *Della dissimulazione honesta*. Courtiers and royals, officers and politicians, spies and ambassadors, philosophers and scientists always covered up their real motives and intentions in order to survive and step up on the career ladder. People necessarily concealed their true motives, emotions, intentions and thoughts in diplomatic and commercial meetings, in wartime and at peace treaty negotiations, in discussing heritage and property issues, often showing something different to all of their communication partners at the same time. One needed to be able to control his emotions and behavior in order to play a proper role in his social or private life. In the big game of dissimulation at court the real emotions and thoughts were hidden behind the rituals of power, etiquette and conversation rules. In grand-scale politics the *raison d'état* was the cause for the diverse usage of dissimulation as the absolutist states were being established. However, such events happened not only in politics and court intrigue, but they were also part of other areas of life.

Dissimulation and secrecy were intertwined in practice. Faking is concealing the real thought, emotion or intention in such a way that makes even the act of faking secret and unknown. So does dissimulation have a similarly close relationship with the main written tool of secrecy, cryptography?

---

1    MTT III. vol. 22. 443–446, 7.

2    Brief selection from the literature of dissimulation: Perez Zagorin, *Ways of Lying: Dissimulation, Persecution and Conformity in Early Modern Europe* (Cambridge, MA, 1990) 1–14; Jon R. Snyder, *Dissimulation and the Culture of Secrecy in Early Modern Europe* (Berkeley: University of California Press, 2012); Carlo Ginzburg, *Il Nicodemismo: Simulazione e dissimulazione nell'Europa del '500* (Turin: Einaudi, 1970), Vígh Éva, *Barocco etico-retorico nella letteratura italiana*, (Szeged: JATE Press, 2001).

Can any conclusions be drawn from the fact that the only enciphered word in Absolon's letter is "dissimulation"? I am not aware of any studies on this problem, although it seems to me a crucial issue in the two hundred years between 1500 and 1700, a period that was the heyday not only of dissimulation but also of cryptography.

Jon Snyder, a historian studying the early modern "art" of dissimulation, contrasts it with wearing a mask. If you put on a mask, you are being honest about covering your real face. Anyone looking at you will know that they do not see you as you really are. If you dissimulate, however, you act as if you were not hiding anything, as if wearing an invisible mask that still covers you.[3] This is what made life difficult for those who lived in the age of dissimulation: they did not know what was underneath the masks, and they did not know who was actually wearing a mask and who was not.

In this way cryptography seems to be rather different: it does not cover up its ruse, but in fact advertises it. It is not cryptography (the concealing of messages in an obviously secret code), but rather steganography (the concealing of the existence of messages altogether, or the hiding of secret messages in apparently non-secret text) that corresponds to this activity. Cryptography transforms an accessible text into a code that is no longer legible to everyone, but which is self-evidently a cipher. Seeing an encrypted message motivates one to break the code, whereas in contrast, by hiding the fact that a message is present, steganography yields no such motivation. While enciphering results in a message that is clearly wearing a mask, steganography dissimulates (so to speak) even the mask. It is thus more effective if real hiddenness is a concern.

Technically speaking, steganography may be done in various ways. Ancient messengers were said to have written messages on their scalp, which was then hidden behind their growing hair (although this may be an altogether unlikely scenario). Another more widespread technique was to use invisible ink or miniaturized letters, or in a way that the cognoscenti would know that they must read the first letters of every word in an innocuous open document to make up the true secret message. One might also write characters in bold, flagging the secret message in an otherwise non-secret text. An exciting Hungarian case of steganography is quoted by Miklós Bethlen in 1667 from a letter in which ciphers are not numbers, whole words stand for nomenclators. The result is a text which seems meaningful yet irrelevant, but with the aid of the key one could substitute the political and geographical names, and unfold the real message. Bethlen lengthily

---

3     Snyder, *Dissimulation*, xiii.

quotes the original letter, then tries to give meaning to it himself: "I scarcely understand Bory's letter. He writes, 'There was no hope concerning Palatinus's life, and if he dies, it is a major change, but it does not derogate the great power of the holy majesty of God. I judge it to be worthless to start trade from Moldova and Wallachia, and I hope it will have no development. Where does the poor landlord's fortune lie? Should they never bring a horse for a rider from there, you would not believe what pretty herds the good husbandmen raise here. It is different; I am not sure if You have understood; trade has started from Vienna as far as Constantinople. Whoever has the inclination and the funds, with this commodity one can afford horses and everything.' – These are the words of Bory which I cannot understand, for I do not have the clavis. By trade from Moldova and Wallachia, I suspect, he means the support of the Turks whom he does not like – in fact I have never liked them either; while I had been out there, they had not been thinking that way. By trade from Vienna he must have meant the status of France – maybe that if we cannot help him, they may still agree with them. But this is just a guess, what he really meant by it, I do not know. Whatever is the case, we have done according to their resolutio written with clavis: we have called for Lord Baló today."[4]

This puzzlement of the author clearly shows that steganography is real dissimulation, pretending to be nothing, or something else. Cryptography by comparison is an honest genre: visible, if not legible. Dissimulation and cryptography are two faces of (the act of) secrecy.

## 8.2.    Communication in politics

Secretiveness and secrecy are the inalienable parts of political communication, and should not be considered special or outstanding phenomena. Politics do not work without secretiveness. Private diplomatic correspondence, parallel negotiations carried out with different partners at the same time, espionage, envoy's messages sent from hostile, or even from allied, territories – none of these can be carried out without the different practices of secret. As we have seen at the beginning of this book, retaining, hiding or restricting information is power, power that forms a hierarchy, power that is the lifting and excluding tool of authority.[5]

---

4    Teleki 4, 78–80, 63.

5    Michael Jucker, "Secrets and Politics: Methodological and Communicational Aspects of Late Medieval Diplomacy," in Paravacini Bagliani, ed. *Il Segreto / The Secret*, 275–309; idem, "Trust

The need to apply ciphers in political communication is indicated by a number of sources where 'clavis' and 'secret' are mentioned in the same sentence, or where a secret is said to be only shared with a cipher: "I have used a clavis to make this more secret. We pray to God that it would remain secret."[6] "If I had a clavis to use in corresponding with Your Lordship, I could write about things that you would all need to know. You would be amazed at these things".[7] Dénes Bánffy does not even feel the need to explain the reason for using a clavis:, "When writing about us, please use a clavis, because, etc., etc."[8] The association of the two notions can be seen in this letter, in which almost every second word is encrypted (in italics). "...although *Lords Béldi and Csáki were really accusing His Lordship,* do not be afraid, for *I have good will for you* and *I am saying it to you* in summo secreto, but please *do not tell this* to anyone, quia totum negotium *perdes,* quia jam est in summo *secreto determinatum,* sed *mihi* interdictum, neque *vobis* adhuc *revellem,* per amorem Dei rogo, *sit* in *secreto.* (...) Nevertheless, I am asking Your Lordship *to report secretum about Your Lordship* only to your trusted people lest they would gossip about the secret *annuentia too soon,* quia magnum esset *periculum.*"[9]

To be sure, enciphered correspondence was not the only tool applied in political secrecy, nevertheless, our analysis below will be limited to one issue: to what extent are cryptographic sources (cipher keys, enciphered letters, and other sources about the use of ciphers) informative about the secret concept and practices of secrecy of the past.

An overwhelming majority, at least ninety-five percent of the cryptographic sources is political in nature. Private, scientific, magical and other kinds of cipher uses have also survived, but their mass quantity is negligible compared to that of political ciphers. Ferdinand I in Vienna, Rudolf II in Prague, György Rákóczi I and II in the Principality of Transylvania, and Imre Thököly in Northern Hungary used the same type of substitutions when corresponding with their generals, ambassadors and

and Mistrust in Letters: Late Medieval Diplomacy and Its Communication Practices," in Marco Mostert, Petra Schulte, Irene van Renswoude, eds., *Strategies of Writing. Studies on Text and Trust in de Middle Ages* (Utrecht 2008), 213–236; Jonathan Elukin, "Keeping Secrets in Medieval and Early Modern English Government," in Gisela Engel, Brita Rang, Klaus Reichert and Heide Wunder, eds. *Das Geheimnis am Beginn der europäischen Moderne* (Frankfurt am Main: Klostermann, 2002), 111–129.

6    Teleki 8, 78, 68.
7    MTT II/3. 109, 91.
8    Teleki 5, 121, 74.
9    Teleki 8, 169–171, 146.

agents as their Western European colleagues. Besides official diplomacy, the private correspondence of political nature among the aristocracy also exploited the opportunities that cryptography offered. In the letters of magnates and primates in the sixteenth-seventeenth centuries, Miklós Zrínyi, Mihály Teleki, Zsigmond Kemény, Ákos Barcsay, Mihály Apafi, Mihály Teleki, György Lippay, Péter Pázmány it was not uncommon to have a word, sentence chunk or complete sentence coded in the homophonic system.

Because of the high quantity and variety of sources, it is worth making distinctions between various categories: grand politics and interstate diplomacy, powerful barons' correspondence on internal affairs, the aristocracy's movements that sometimes resulted in a conspiracy or revolt, the generals' military correspondence, the envoys' reports, and espionage. There are no strict boundaries, though, and the numerous borderline cases prevent the historian from being strict in applying these categories. Does the enciphered letter of Miklós Zrínyi, ban of Croatia to György Rákóczi II, prince of Transylvania, fall in the category of interstate diplomacy, correspondence by the aristocracy, or a conspiracy against the Habsburgs? When Archbishop Péter Pázmány is writing to C. H. Motmann, his Italian trustee, or when György Rákóczi II is writing to Jónás Mednyánszky, his trustee in Vienna, do these fall in the same category as envoy János Pápai sending his report to Ferenc Rákóczi, or rather in the category of a Serbian secret correspondent reporting to the court in Vienna? Due to the existence of the many unclear cases, diplomatic-political correspondence is going to be discussed as one category, while a careful attempt will be made at treating intelligence and military sources separately.

Though the majority of all historic ciphers belong to this category, it may seem at first that it is rather monotonous in its use of secrecy and in its motivation. Most of political ciphers obviously hide secrets of diplomatic and political nature, the reason for encryption being, even more obviously, the effort to make a message inaccessible for political enemies. This is especially true for the envoys' messages: this kind of text happens to be less varied concerning its concept of secret.

It seems more relevant to study however (as has been done above), the advancement of the code systems, and one can conclude, among other things, that the differences are not only chronological by nature (the earlier systems being less improved), but also geographical. The envoy to Constantinople often received a more advanced clavis than his colleagues from other regions. Johann Malvezzi, envoy of Ferdinand I to the Porte, used a homophonic key with nomenclatures, nullities and misleading

Latin words with different meanings as early as 1548–1549,[10] while Jacobus Curtis, Ferdinand II's agent in Poland, applied a monoalphabetic cipher even seventy years later – at least with numbers instead of graphic signs.[11] The importance of foreign affairs influenced the level of technological development in other cases too. Ferdinand I used a homophonic clavis with his brother, Charles V,[12] but a monoalphabetic one with the voivode of Moldova.[13]

Geography, however, was not only relevant as the area where a cipher was being used, but also as its place of origin. The beginnings the history of Hungarian cryptography fall around the time of Matthias Corvinus' reign (1458–1490). In a letter book by Matthias Corvinus that contained the letters by the royal chancellery in the 1460s and 1470s a very simple cipher grid in the shape of a square was to be found (unfortunately, the binding of the codex perished together with the cipher, so it is no longer extant). It is a so-called pigpen cipher, next to which there was also an encrypted text of three Latin words, in which (supposedly Bishop Janus Pannonius, the first Hungarian poet) illustrated how the system worked. It read MATIAS SEX HUNGARIAE (correctly: Matias rex Hungarie).[14]

| a | b | c | k. | l. | m. | t | v | x |
|---|---|---|----|----|----|---|---|---|
| d | e | f | n. | o. | p. | y | z | 9 |
| g | h | i | q. | r. | s. |   |   |   |

The cipher key of the letterbook[15]

10   War History Archives, 1548/3, Révay *Titkosírások*, 64–65; OSZK Quart. Lat 2254. 15.

11   HHStA, Ung Akt. Misc Fasc 422 Conv 1 fol 75 and fol 72–79.

12   OSZK Quart. Lat 2254. 8 and 9.

13   OSZK Quart. Lat 2254. 17.

14   Décsényi Gyula, "Mátyás király leveleskönyve a gróf Khuen-Héderváry család könyvtárában" (King Matthias' letterbook in the library of the Khuen-Héderváry family) *Magyar Könyvszemle* 19 (1891): 169–175; Rácz György, A Héderváry-kódex hasonmás kiadása (The fac-simile editon of the Héderváry codex), in Héderváry-kódex. Mátyás király leveleskönyve a Héderváry család egykori könyvtárából (Héderváry-codex. Letter book of King Matthias from the late library of the Héderváry family) (Budapest: Magyar Országos Levéltár, 2008).

15   Décsényi, "Mátyás király leveleskönyve" 173.

More serious encrypting methods were also in use in Corvinus' court as the letters of Matthias' wife, Beatrix of Aragon with his sister Eleanor,[16] a 1491 note, also written by Beatrix in a book from the Corvinian library about Vladislaus arriving at Eger,[17] and the cipher key of the ambassadors to Milan testify.[18] All of these, however, were coming from Italy. Origin did play a major part in the quality of encryption.

This correlation can also be seen in the following centuries. Early modern cryptology in Hungary reached its zenith by the end of the period, in Rákóczi's time. Although high-quality ciphers can be found even from before that, these are again with Italian background, the homophonic system of Cornelius Heinrich Motmann from the 1630s being an example.[19] Motmann provided Archbishop Péter Pázmány with information from Rome. The archbishop and his Italian correspondent used number bigrams (such as 24) to code the letters of the plain text: usually two bigrams were assigned to a letter, but some vowels got three, just like in an advanced homophonic clavis. They used a combination of one consonant and one number for syllables and a trigram of three numerals for code words, which were basically nomenclatures. These combinations were systematically assigned to letters, syllables or code words in numeric or alphabetical order. This kind of structure is easy to use but it is also vulnerable, although it only helps the codebreaker when a part of the key is already broken and the structure is recognizable enough. In this cipher, Motmann informs the archbishop of issues that are too private to be included in the official reports from Rome, or even in the plain texts of Motmann's letters: current events of Rome, diplomatic and legal problems related to Hungary. The high level of the encryption that was still rare in Hungary at the time was most probably due to the fact that Motmann was an experienced figure in Italian church diplomacy who acted as the agent for many a German high priest and ruler throughout the course of his life in Rome.[20] Presumably

16  There are dozens of enciphered letters of Hungarian interest in the State Archives of Modena, a few of which have a microfilm copy in Budapest: MNL OL Microfilm 8620. For the letters, see the results of the Vestigia project: http://vestigia.hu/; and György Domokos, Norbert Mátyus, Armando Nuzzo, *Vestigia - Mohács előtti magyar források olasz könyvtárakban* (Pre-Mohács Hungarian sources in Italian libraries) (PPKE BTK 2015, Piliscsaba).

17  Miklós Vértesy, "Titkos írás egy Corvinában," (Secret writing in a Corvina) *Magyar Könyvszemle*, 77 (1961): 167–169.

18  Péter E. Kovács, "Corvin János házassága és a magyar diplomácia," (The marriage of János Corvin and the Hungarian diplomacy) *Századok* 137 (2003): 955–971.

19  Péter Tusor, "Pázmány bíboros olasz rejtjelkulcsa." Archives of the Archbishop AEV n. 148/3 and n. 159

20  On Mottmann, see: Tusor, "Pázmány bíboros olasz rejtjelkulcsa," 538–542.

he did not receive the structure of his key from the Hungarian archbishop. More likely, he copied the structure of other highly developed Italian keys.

It is not an exaggeration to argue that the closer the origin of a cipher was to Italy, and the closer its intended place of use was to Constantinople, the more advanced its system was. An example for this rule is the big 1560 homophonic key of Baile Vettore Bragadin, delegate of Venice in Constantinople.[21]

But what happens when the classification of ciphers is made not only on the basis their level of development but also according to their content? It may seem that the messages studied so far say nothing new as for the concept of secret these historic figures had. The informant simply describes the news he has heard, the negotiations he has done, whereupon the addressee gives him coded instructions. A more careful analysis, however, shows a sophisticated picture concerning both the content and the reason for using a cipher. Practices of secrecy can be examined following two procedures related to each other: first a study of the geographical and political names and the most frequent concepts in the ciphers, in other words, some research into the nomenclatures, and second, a close reading of the enciphered content.

In her book, *A rejtőzködő murányi Vénus* (*The Hiding Venus of Murány*) historian Ágnes R. Várkonyi emphasized the conclusions that can be drawn from the nature of nomenclatures. She called attention to the fact that some items of the code tables captured from the members of the Wesselényi movement illustrate well the members' political concepts, main goal and greatest needs: "against the Pagans=1576", "getting money=1615," "we are gaining money=1616".[22]

Name nomenclatures seem to be the most convenient in this respect. They show who counted as relevant political figures for the corresponding partners. More than once, secret communication started with changing the names in an otherwise plain text, and sometimes it did not even go further. As Ferenc Rákóczi is writing to the vice general in Kassa (Kosice, Slovakia), "We are sure you have received our letter about how to change the names in the communication with Poland in the future."[23]

---

21   Christiane Villain-Gandossi, "Les Dépêches chiffrées de Vettore Bragadin, baile de Constantinople (12 juillet 1564-15 juin 1566)," in eadem, *La Méditerranée aux XIIe-XVIe siècles: relations maritimes, diplomatiques et commerciales* (London: Ashgate Publishing, Limited, 1983), 52–106.

22   Várkonyi, *A rejtőzködő*, 214.

23   AR I. vol. 1. 664–66, 4.

Both the political realities of a historical situation, and the expected frequency of a particular word in a given correspondence can be sensed on a cipher table: palatine Pál Esterházy and Mihány Apafi put "mining towns" and "frontier militia" in their keys,[24] the only fifteen nomenclatures that Ferdinand I and Charles V used in a cipher included: "madame nostre tante" and "lutherien",[25] whereas "tartari" is one of the twenty-three nomenclatures on the clavis of Ferenc Rákóczi and the envoy of the Russian tsar.[26]

Good example is another of Rákóczi's tables. Its few nomenclatures nicely map up the main foreign relations during the freedom fight: Imperator, Rex. Rom, Pr. Ragozi, Turca, Bavarus, Rex Prussiae, Sveciae, Poloniae, Galliae, Angliae, Belgium, Hungaria, Austria, and Transylvania.[27] A thorough comparatistic research into the tables of the freedom fight would vividly show the way the prince was maneuvering and looking for allies and how his tactic changed in space and time.[28] The sophistication of the nomenclatures and the quality of the claves also mark the importance of a particular diplomatic relation. The prince used a much more primitive code table with the Russian tsar than with his other allies, as if it had been more than satisfactory to use graphic signs in a monoalphabetic system in this direction.[29]

A close look at the encrypted content yields in some cases results similar to the study of the nomenclatures. One letter from Dominique Reverend to Mihály Teleki for example only encrypts the key names: *Dominus Nalassi, Rex Galliae* and *Marchionis de Béthune.*[30] Similarly, an extensive study of Teleki's letters shows that the most frequently ciphered items are key words, places, names of people, money and time, and in general, political figures, exactly what can usually be seen in a nomenclature table. The fact that the enciphered parts are similar to nomenclatures is obviously the result of the users often restricting their encryption activity to the nomenclatures. It saved them time and characters to only replace a couple of names with numbers. Arriving to a partial encryption of a given text, there seemed to be no need for the arduous job of encrypting the other words character by character. This negligence of the scribes sometimes resulted in the

24  MNL OL P 125 No. 119775,
25  OSZK Quart. Lat 2254. 8
26  Ráday Archives C64-4d2-25. 16.
27  Ráday Archives C64-4d2-25. 3.
28  Ferenc Tóth, *Correspondance diplomatique relative à la guerre d'indépendance du prince François II Rákóczi (1703–1711)* (Paris-Genève: Honoré Champion, 2012).
29  MNL OL G 15 Caps. C. Fasc 43. and Ráday Archives C64-4d2-25, and the back of Ráday Levéltár C64-4d2-25. 8.
30  Teleki 8, 121, 112.

fact that even the encrypted nomenclators were easy to reconstruct based on the rest of the plain text. This is rather intellectual than technical carelessness – the scribe does not make the effort to step into the shoes of his adversary, and does not examine what could be understood from the letter without the help of a key.

This limited use of enciphering, nevertheless, was not typical. There were great variations as to the quantity and quality of cipher being used, according to the person of the author or his situation. They can be observed in the correspondence of Dániel Absolon and Mihály Teleki. Absolon is very economical in all his letters, encrypting only the key concepts either with nomenclatures, or by concisely spelling it (*"the Polish king", "prince of Transylvania", "His Majesty" "business of Hungary", "on his part", "Lord Mac-* skássi (...) *is ready* per *occultos canales* to help *his lordship's business",* etc.)[31] Teleki, by contrast, uses ciphers a lot more frequently. Beside the names of politicians, he encrypts complete sentences, descriptions, characterizations, so the result is a letter in which one third or even half of the text is enciphered.[32] Imre Thököly – this time in a letter to Teleki – acts similarly. He does encrypt a lot of text: complete paragraphs, or just a couple of sentence fragments, but so many of them that no one has any chance to understand the letter without the key.[33]

Are these differences a matter of personal taste in ciphering strategy? Or are these connected to the fact that major political figures such as Thököly and Teleki employed a secretary, while simpler correspondents like Absolon did the encryption themselves. Not quite so. It has been already shown that being high on the social ladder did not necessarily exempt one from the manual tasks of cryptography. Thököly, too, often did the job himself. It seems rather likely that they were more sensitive in secret matters than Absolon. Why Teleki used a more advanced cipher when writing to Absolon than to Apafi probably has political reasons and must be answered by the nature of each letter's content. He must have found his own secret he shared with Absolon more valuable than the future prince's secret to which he refers in writing to Apafi.

The ciphering ratios are similar in the correspondence of Prince György Rákóczi I and his envoys. The envoys are economical with the encryption,

31   Teleki 7, 371–373, 272. On the correspondence of Absolon and Teleki, see: Lajos Hopp, "Sobieski és a 'magyar malkontentusok' a barokk politikai irodalmi hagyományban (Bécs, 1683)" (Sobieski and the 'Hungarian malcontents' in the baroque literary tradition) *Filológiai Közlöny* 30 (1984): 1–24.

32   Teleki 8, 202–206, 168.

33   Teleki 8, 143–144, 127.

trying to limit it to place names, peoples' names, numbers, and data concerning military power. The prince, in contrast, uses his code tables more often, more extensively and more cleverly, though he does not encipher complete letters or paragraphs either.[34] The smartest cryptologist, nonetheless, is Archbishop Péter Pázmány, who uses a combination of good-quality clavis and carefully selected parts of the text. While Rákóczi relies on four different equally outdated monoalphabetic keys, Archbishop Pázmány only has one, but that is a tough homophonic one.[35]

Encrypting critical statements, concepts and names in the main body of a letter was just one widely-used method. Another strategy involved leaving the full body of a letter as a plain text, and only putting the post scriptum in cipher. Political actors of the late seventeenth century, Dénes Bánffy,[36] Imre Thököly[37] and Simon Kemény,[38] all have letters following this procedure. The post-scriptum in these cases involves various topics: the trustworthiness of a third party, the space and time coordinates of a meeting, or just information that does not even seem to be sensitive today. The relationship of the plain text of a message and the encrypted note is especially interesting in a letter by Simon Kemény. There is a mysterious sentence in the short letter ("No doubt that you should not be bothered by the Fox on the sides of the fortress, but if I were you, I would surely set up that trap.") which becomes meaningful when one reads the encrypted post-scriptum: *"By the name of the Fox you should mean Sigmond Bánfi."*[39]

The encrypted secret – as also seen in the previous example – often warns about an untrustworthy figure, a supposedly malicious and possibly dangerous person: a warning goes in this way: "As for you, my lord, you surely *have a great many adversaries,"*[40] and like this: "let us be very careful about these three: 1. *Veselényi*, because he is evil, 2. *the Porte*, 3. the peace we have with the Turks now."[41]

---

34  Ötvös, *Rejtelmes levelek*, 27–156, Révay, *Titkosírások*, 76–86. For Rákóczi, see Gábor Kármán, *Erdélyi külpolitika a vesztfáliai béke után* (Transylvanian foreign policy after the peace of Westphalia) (Budapest: L'Harmattan, 2011), 33–118.

35  Ötvös, *Rejtelmes levelek*, 1–4, Révay, *Titkosírások*, 87–107.

36  Teleki 2, 323–324, 244.

37  Teleki 8, 173–175, 150.

38  Teleki 2, 266–268. 196.

39  Teleki 2, 262, 192.

40  Teleki 8, 114–115, 106.

41  Sándor Szilágyi, "Herczeg Rákóczy Zsigmond Levelezése," (Correspondence of Prince Zsigmond Rákóczi) MTT III/11. 288–289, 102. For the distrust between the prince and Wesselényi, see also Kármán, *Erdélyi külpolitika*, 214–215.

In many cases the secret writing is not used to cover up a secret as much as to defend oneself or others. It is a tool that prevents the writer (or the person he names) from getting into a delicate situation in case the letter got into the hands of illegitimate readers. Scribes often encrypt those names that they share sensitive information about.[42] The following sentence from Mihály Teleki is an illustration of approaching authority carefully and self-defensively: *"The prince is mortal too, if he happens to die, there is a new prince."*[43] Similarly, he writes in another letter, "Believe me, *this aforementioned princess* if she finds a way, as she already started, *will steal this captainship from me."*[44]

The relationship of the cipher and the concept of secret is particularly relevant in the case of a major statesman, poet and military leader of the mid-seventeenth century, Miklós Zrínyi (1620–1664). Although his agent from Sopron, the lawyer István Vitnyédi asked a clavis from him more than once,[45] and did correspond with a clavis himself,[46] no trace survived that Zrínyi, ban of Croatia ever answered him using a cipher. Most probably these letters were lost. All of the half dozen extant enciphered letters by the ban were addressed to the same person, György Rákóczi II, prince of Transylvania.

This correspondence of Zrínyi, ban of Croatia and Rákóczi, prince of Transylvania is among the most carefully studied chapters of Hungarian history.[47] Although theirs obviously must have been a two-way communication, none of the princes' letters to Zrínyi have yet been found. All of the ban's enciphered letters used the same code key,[48] a then-up-to-date homophonic clavis of Latin letters. It assigned three numerals to almost all of the letters and used some thirty nomenclatures, making it a table of nearly ninety code signs. This could be adequately safe were it not for three things.

42   MTT III. vol. 22. 441–442, 5, and Teleki 8, 175–176. 151.

43   Teleki 2, 578–579, 394.

44   Teleki 2, 586–589. 400.

45   András Fabó, "Vitnyédi István levelei," (Letters of István Vitnyédi) MTT II/3. 237–239, 229. MTT II/4. 37–41, 261. See also Gergely Sárközi, "Álhírek és valóság."

46   Fabó, "Vitnyédi István levelei," MTT II/3. 256–257, 245; MTT II/4. 64, 285; MTT II/4. 63–64, 284; MTT II/4. 65, 286.

47   Katalin Péter, "Zrinyi Miklós terve II. Rákóczi György magyar királyságáról," (Mikós Zrinyi's plan on György Rákóczi's Hungarian reign) *Századok* 106 (1972): 653–666, Levente Nagy, *Zrínyi és Erdély. A költő Zrínyi Miklós irodalmi és politikai kapcsolatai Erdéllyel* (Zrinyi and Transylvania: the poet Zrinyi's literary and political relations to Transylvania) (Budapest: 2003); Kármán, *Erdélyi külpolitika*, 276–295; Révay, *Titkosírások*, 109–123.

48   Károly Széchy, *Gróf Zrínyi Miklós 1620–1654* (Count Miklós Zrínyi 1620–1654) vols. I-V kötet (Budapest: Magyar Történelmi Társulat, 1896–1902).

First, the homophones assigned to one particular letter are obviously related, ending in the same numeral. (A: 1, 11, 21, E: 5, 15, 25, 35). Second, the numbers are assigned to the letters in a predictable order. Third, nomenclatures are three-digit number and are consequently easily discernible from one or two-digit letter signs.[49] Still, we must give credit for the nomenclatures – some of the numbers are still left unbroken, leaving the identity of the person behind it unknown.

Zrínyi was fully aware that his rival, in his case his direct superior, the Habsburg court, will not be confused by the cipher, as traffic analysis in itself could be used against him. The mere fact that he exchanges enciphered letters with the prince of Transylvania, ruler of an adversary country, could have been perilous to him. He does discuss this danger twice. Once in a postscript in 1654: "Dear lord, do not be offended that I am not writing very frequently, I would be in great danger if my correspondentia with you was revealed. I can serve you better if my service to you is kept secret." And again in 1655: "I would be lucky if I could tell you my sensus in person. I cannot trust this to a letter or any kind of character. I must wait for God, time and good luck."

Zrínyi was economical and strategic in his ciphering. He wrote his letters himself (they all survived in his own handwriting except for one). He mainly used nomenclatures, and assigned several of them to the names of the most important persons of the actual confused political situation: Archbishop Lippay – 219 and 450, Puchaim 217 and 400, his own name, Miklós Zrínyi – 270, 515, his addressee, the prince of Transylvania – 260, 310 and 510. The number 375 is still left unbroken from one of his letters.

When necessary, he makes use of the code alphabet to translate the most sensitive parts of the plain text character by character. Some of these are negative remarks about the Habsburg court, "All of Europe is watching the debility of *the house of Austria*" (...) *"The emperor is sickly and weak and everybody thinks he will die soon."*[50] There are also remarks about members of the aristocracy that happen to be on the other side of an internal conflict, *"Archbishop, Puchám* are plotting something, we shall see, quid parturiunt, both are with great exhibito towards me, as I am to them. I don't suppose that they believe me, but I don't believe them either. Trust me, the *cancellarius* is very deceitful, he has made us all believe that the *prince of Transylvania* listens to him and that he can control him."[51] Elsewhere he warns

49  Révay, *Titkosírások*, 110.
50  Széchy, *Gróf Zrínyi Miklós*, vol 4, 262.
51  Széchy, *Gróf Zrínyi Miklós*, vol. 3. 338.

the prince that the Judge Royal had shown the court what the prince had written to him, "The *letter you had written to Nádasdi* he had immediately *sent to the court,* I do not know what is in it but there is much ado about it and they are *afraid.*"[52] In general, he only hides information that is of high relevance politically.

A special case is the so-called "memorandum on the palatine" that is a highly ambiguous letter. No manuscript of it survived, it is only known from the publication of the nineteenth century historian, Kálmán Thaly.[53] In this lengthy letter Zrínyi allegedly offers cooperation to the prince of Transylvania, an offer that would have been equal to a death sentence if it had been found out either by the Habsburgs. One would expect the whole letter to be encrypted, yet we find a surprising method of encryption, one that Zrínyi never used elsewhere.[54] The letter begins in the usual way, with three-digit numbers substituting the names of the major political figures. These numbers look as if they had been taken from the nomenclature table that Zrínyi was using in his authentic letters. Yet, the names of the prince of Transylvania and Zrínyi appear as plain text, while they are coded in all the other letters we have. Certain code numbers appear here that none of the other letters contain,[55] their meaning is revealed in Thaly's publication as if they had been given in the manuscript. The most important number, 445, the code for the person who would be – in Zrínyi's opinion – the only suitable person for the position of palatine, is not given. Beside the nomenclatures, some other parts of the text are spelled letter by letter, following a procedure familiar from the other letters of Zrínyi, but oddities occur. There is no reason, for example, in only coding the letter *v* at the beginning of the word *venné* (he would buy). Beside the code *ooooo* (Puchaim), often used in the other letters, in the "memorandum on the palatine" the code *ooo* (emperor) also appears,

---

52   Széchy, *Gróf Zrínyi Miklós,* vol. 4. 268

53   Kálmán Thaly, "Gr. Zrínyi Miklós emlékirata." (The memorandum of Count Miklós Zrinyi), *Századok* 1868, 633–648.

54   Ágnes R. Várkonyi, "Az elveszett idő: Zrínyi Miklós nádori emlékirata?" (The time lost: a memorandum of Palatine Miklós Zrínyi?) *Hadtörténeti Közlemények* 113 (2000): 269–328, particularly: 291. See also eadem, "Navigare necesse est: A Nádori emlékirat az újabb kutatások koordinátáján," (Navigare necesse est: The memorandum on the palatine in the coordinates of the most recent research) in eadem, *Európa Zrínyije* (Europe's Zrinyi) (Budapest, 2010), 346–283; Gábor Várkonyi, "Emlékirat a nádorság ügyében," (Memorandum in the issue of palatineship" *Irodalomismeret* VI (1995): 40–47.

55   Historian Ágnes R. Várkonyi has made a complete list of these: Várkonyi, "Az elveszett idő," 290.

which in quite arbitrary and confusing. While Zrínyi had written the other five partially enciphered letters with his own hand, here there is no sign that he had done the same, all the more so as the letter names him in third person singular.

Use of secrecy is even more shocking in this memorandum than these technical details. The most sensitive parts of the letter, including the names of Zrínyi and Rákóczi, are left as plain text. In contrast, there is a diligently encrypted note about the marriage of a nobleman's daughter that any contemporary could easily have learned about. The servile attitude that characterizes all of the letter would have been so compromising for the ban, had the letter been captured that hiding the details of the royal family's marriage customs (that is also enciphered) was a totally unnecessary precaution. One also wonders why the two long enciphered parts of a lengthy letter full of internal politics are on the topic of marriage. And the list of problems goes on, as historian Várkonyi has compiled it in a long study: the suspicious lack of the original source, the suspicious historian, and known fabricator, Kálmán Thaly's central role in "finding" the letter, the unusually submissive role Zrínyi seems to play, the illogical structure of the letter that is so atypical of the ban, and so on. When adding all of these to the analysis of the cipher and of the author's concept of secrecy, one can be convinced that this letter is of dubious origin, to put it mildly. It could, nevertheless, have been 'stitched together' by Kálmán Thaly from several other texts by Zrínyi in order to serve as an argument for the historian in a late 19th century scholarly debate.[56]

Zrínyi's clavis had only been known in a reconstructed form until very recently the original table of letters was found (in the course of my own archival research), unfortunately without the nomenclature table. It is a great loss because it could help identify the reference for 375, and it would clarify whether the nomenclatures only existing in the memorandum such as the mysterious 445 had really been part of the original clavis or whether they had been made up by Thaly.[57]

---

56  On Thaly's literary fabricates and unreliable and dubious historical scholarship, see Ágnes R. Várkonyi, *Thaly Kálmán és történetírása* (Kálmán Thaly and his history writing) (Budapest, Akadémiai Kiadó, 1961).

57  ÖStA HHStA Ungarische Akten Specialia Verschwörerakten VII. Varia Fasc. 327. Konv. D. Chiffres 1664–1668, fol 15.

## 8.3.    Military operations and espionage

Secrecy concepts of generals sending encrypted messages to each other from stormy battle zones seem as monotonous as those of the diplomatic sources seemed at first sight. Rákóczi's generals for example restricted their correspondence to the size of the enemy's army, to coordinates of their passage, to military news to be verified and to details of discipline issues in the army.[58] Taking a closer look, however, soon reveals a few interesting details, just as it did in the case of political letters. The method is similar, too. First, nomenclatures are studied, then the ratio and length of enciphered and plain text paragraphs.

The results are intriguing. In politics, the recurrent motivations were– beside forwarding a specific diplomatic message–warning, carefulness and avoiding danger. In military communication, the main themes are–beside passing on data of technical nature–fear, being threatened, and covering up weakness, sickness or cowardice on the writers' part.

Ciphers often become crucial when the enemy encircles the letter writer and his troops. Ferenc Palkovics, inspector writes to General Bottyán, "In case the enemy will encircle us, make claves and use them to write to us." (The envelope reads, "Judge of Madocsa, pass this letter on secretly today or you will die. Cito, cito, cito, cito. Citissime, citissime, citissime, citissime.")[59] In the spring of 1710 the increasingly threatened Rákóczi instructs the commanders of Érsekújvár to use claves too.[60]

Danger engenders fear. Fear generates stiff, enforced and abundant encryption. There are only one or two plain text words in the one-page handwritten letter of Kata Bornemissza, who has every reason to worry in the year characterized by political and military turmoil, and often called the most tragic year of the history of Transylvania. In her letter sent to her older brother, Mihály Teleki, almost everything is coded, for example, "*I fear that your help will never arrive.*"[61] The same person, in contrast, will only encrypt one or two words in normal circumstances.[62]

58   War History Archives E. 1705/4–17.

59   AR I. vol. 9. 714–715, 538.

60   Kálmán Thaly, "Érsekújvár utolsó magyar várparancsnokainak utasítása," (Orders to the last Hungarian commanders of the fortress of Érsekújvár) *Hadtörténelmi Közlemények* 1889, 44–45, no. 20.

61   Teleki 1, 402–403, 354.

62   Teleki 1, 220–221, 191.

In a threatening warlike situation, particularly when someone is sur-
rounded by the enemy, it is a question of life and death not to disclose
information on his weakness and beaten-up state. In a long letter that
the Hungarian "fugitives" wrote to Mihály Teleki, relatively little (military) information is encrypted, but the following words are: *"although,
according to a bad Hungarian tradition, only one third of the army came
out of the camp."*[63] Towards the end of his long freedom fight, Rákóczi is
writing in 1710: *"the enemy is pushing us down from that territory".*[64] During
the next month the prince sends several similar letters, most of which
are plain texts, but those few sentences that are encrypted all describe
their own military weaknesses, "The praesidium *has left Huszt," "we* won't
*help Újvár,"*[65] *"not more than 33 has been left at camp," "do not expect any
more help from me," "no armies are left anywhere," "the dragoons are secretly leaving," "Kassa deperierit,* there are not more *than 500 soldiers left."*[66] In
this final, doomed phase of the freedom fight it was important to conceal
the details on the fighters' weaknesses not only from the enemy but also
from the personal messenger of the prince in order to prevent disparag-
ing talks from spreading among the militia.

The best-known example of concealing one's own weakness is the
oft-quoted last letter of the famous general János Bottyán sent from the
fortress of Szentlőrinckáta, dated 18 September 1709. There is only one enciphered sentence in this letter: *"I am sick and cannot get out of bed because
of an illness that hit me a couple days ago: if the barbers had not bled me, I
might even have died."*[67] The sickness did indeed prove fatal in his case six
days after the letter was written.

The spies' reports reveal another kind of secret concept, though fear
is not missing from these letters either. History of intelligence services,
including espionage, used by early modern states, is fairly well documented. Charles Howard Carter wrote about the secret diplomacy of the
Spanish Habsburgs between 1598 and 1625,[68] while Paolo Preto revealed the
works of the spy agency of Venice.[69] In the last two decades considerable
research has been carried out concerning the intelligence activity of the

---

63   Teleki 8, 343–347, 316.
64   AR I. vol. 3. 152–154, 94.
65   AR I. vol. 3. 160–162, 99.
66   AR I. vol. 3. 169–172, 104.
67   AR I. vol. 10. 51–52, 22.
68   Charles Howard Carter, *The Secret Diplomacy of the Habsburgs, 1598–1625* (New York:
Columbia University Press, 1964.)
69   Paolo Preto, *I servizi segreti di Venezia* (il Saggiatore, 1994).

Ottoman[70] and Habsburg[71] empires, a number of new sources have been studied, quickly making these areas well documented.[72]

Secret networks of spies, agents, and correspondents (*Geheimagent, secretarius explorator*) were enmeshed in the territories between the Habsburg and the Ottoman Empires, including the Kingdom of Hungary and Transylvania. When a new agent was roped into the system of correspondents, the encoding system was fixed.[73] The scope of espionage extended well beyond sheer diplomacy; it involved all strata of society – local doctors, merchants, soldiers, ambassadors' interpreters, that is, everyday people far from the diplomatic hierarchy – who risked their lives collecting and transferring information. Thanks to their professions, their frequent travels did not cause much suspicion (as opposed to someone like a farmer, who would have looked awkward if he had taken part in an extensive correspondence, many meetings and much traveling).

The spies in the region were most often people coming from the border regions of the European and Turkish cultures, most frequently of southern Slavic (Serbian, Bosnian) origin, in other cases they were Armenians, Sephardi Jewish doctors, or Christian renegades who fled to the Turks. Often the same families provided several generations of agents. Because one never knew if a letter had been successfully delivered, their reports were often sent in three to six copies. The spies from Constantinople regularly sent their reports via Venice, Ragusa or Split. There are signs that the Signoria of Venice took the opportunity to break the messages.

The reports most often included political information and were written in Italian. The authors wrote sparingly about themselves, partly self-defensively. Those few sentences that are there, however, help create a vivid picture of their fears, education or linguistic skills, knowledge of the Bible, history and geography, religious and cultural background, their fees, the threats surrounding them. It is also relevant, how seriously the

---

70   Gürkan, "The efficacy of ottoman counter-intelligence;" Dávid = Fodor, "Oszmán hírszerzés"; Ágoston, "Információszerzés és kémkedés az Oszmán Birodalomban," Dejanirah Couto, "Spying in the Ottoman Empire."

71   Žontar, *Obveščevalna služba in diplomacija avstrijskih Habsburžanov*; Fodor, "Kémkedés," Szakály, "Egy végvári kapitány. Petercsák and Berecz, eds., *Információáramlás*. Kerekes, "Kémek Konstantinápolyban."

72   Bagi, "Határvidéki és diplomáciai kémkedés."

73   Kerekes, "Hírszerzés a XVI-XVII században;" eadem, *Diplomaták és kémek*; Petercsák and Berecz, *Információáramlás*. One example for original and solved letters from 1632: ÖStA HHStA Staatenabteilungen Türkei I. Kt. 112. Konv. 5. fol. 1–9 and fol. 17–28.

information arriving with their help was taken by the Habsburg court and how urgently the Hofkriegsrat, the Court Council of War had them decoded.[74]

## 8.4. Love, politics and male bonding

The best-known European example of combining love, politics and cryptography is the encrypted correspondence of Anna of Austria, the queen regent of France and her minister, the cardinal in charge of the country, Mazarin in the years around 1651. Emotional secrets were just as important in their correspondence as political ones. Modern publishers realized early on that the authors used separate codes, nomenclatures to express their attachment, friendship and love. Most of the farewell parts are left open, but they used numbers to name themselves, and broad graphic signs for encoding their own emotions. It seems that both Mazarin and the queen had used professionals (the most famous of whom was Antoine Rossignol, the designer of the "Grand chiffre" of Louis XIV) to help them in their official ciphered correspondence, yet they did the encoding and decoding themselves when writing letters about their own covered-up emotions, making these a nice example of how to express gentle love with the help of nomenclatures.[75]

There is a similar secret love affair in Hungarian history. Two beautiful cipher tables survived from the archives of the Rákóczi freedom fight on parchment (as opposed to the much more common paper) and in colored ink. One of them, the famous flower-patterned clavis, a sophisticated homophonic system, was used for important negotiations with his main ally, the French king, Louis XIV.[76]

74 Kerekes, "Kémek Konstantinápolyban." The collection of deciphered spy report from Constantinople from the years 1684–1696: Archiepiscopal Library of Esztergom, Ms. II. 303. On microfilm: MTAK Mf. 5528–5529.

75 Claude Dulong-Sainteny, "Les signes cryptiques dans la correspondance d'Anne d'Autriche avec Mazarin, contribution à l'emblématique du XVIIe siècle," *Bibliothèque de l'école des chartes* 140 (1982): 61–83.

76 MNL OL G 15 Caps. C. Fasc 44, Révay, *II. Rákóczi Ferenc*, 68 and 84.

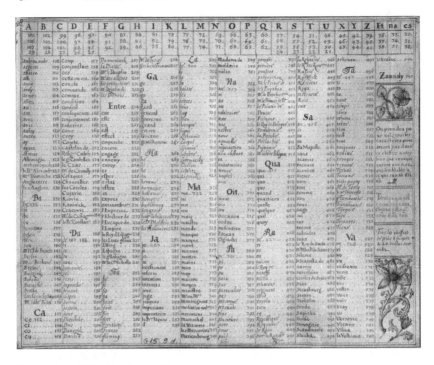

The code key of Rákóczi and Louis XIV

The other clavis under study is in French too, and it is nearly as beautiful. It is also copied on parchment, it is also homophonic, and it is almost as extensive as the previous one, containing circa three hundred fifty elements. Yet we find a few odd items among its nomenclatures. While the previous code table of the French king assigns number codes to geographical and political names, here only two cities belonging to the Polish-Lithuanian Commonwealth, Krakow and Warsaw appear as place names, and there are hardly any political figures named. In addition, there are a few unusual words among the frequently used nomenclatures, such as "abandonne", "adorable", "chagrin", "jaloux" "solicitude", "sentimans", "souvenir". There is no clue as to the recipient of these special letters encrypted with this code, but it must have been someone close to the prince's heart.[77]

<hr />

77  MNL OL G 15 Caps. C. Fasc 44.

The anonymous code key of Rákóczi on parchment

There is, however, in the same archive another version of this mysterious table copied on paper. It is similarly anonymous, but it has a love letter written on its back.[78]

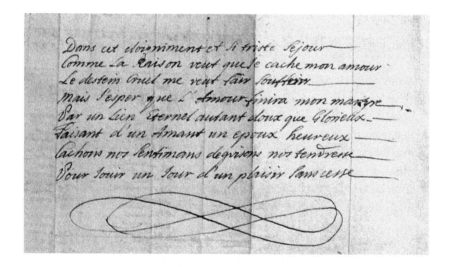

The poem, surviving in the prince's handwriting, looks very eloquent at first sight, yet it contains a number of metric mistakes that no native speaker

78   MNL OL G 15 Caps. C. Fasc 44.

could have made. The poet, for example, does not know that the normally silent *e* letters at the end of a line in French poems are always pronounced. It is well known that Rákóczi, partly due to the special circumstances of his education, considered French, along with Latin and Hungarian, as one of the most important languages in which he could express himself. French was the most important diplomatic language for him, and he used it to communicate with his sons, who did not speak Latin or Hungarian. But just as with Latin, in the case of French, Rákóczi was content with a relatively high level of knowledge, and he did not wish to achieve perfection.[79] All of these make it very likely that this imperfect yet expressive verse is not only copied by him, but it is Rákóczi's own poem:

> Dans cet eloigniment et sí triste Sejour
> Comme la Raison veut que je cache mon amour
> Le destein cruel me veut fair soufferir
> Mais J'esper que l'Amour finira mon martyre
> Par un lien Eternel autant doux que Glorieux
> Faisant d'un Amant un epoux heureux
> Cachons nos Sentimans deguisons nos tendresse
> Pour jouir un jour d'un plaisir sans cesse.

In an approximative English translation:

> *In this gloomy loneliness, in this sad journey*
> *When reason calls me to hide my love,*
> *Cruel destiny has sentenced me to suffer.*
> *But I hope that my martyrdom will end*
> *And the sweet, glorious eternal bond of love*
> *will make me a merry spouse at last.*
> *So let us wear our masks and disguise our desires*
> *And wait for the day when endless joy we receive.*

As a historian has pointed out long ago, the addressee of this poem and the recipient of the secret letters written in the special clavis must have been the Polish palatine's wife, a major politician of the times, Rákóczi's love, Elżbieta Helena Sieniawska (1669–1729).[80] It is worth noting that Rákóczi

---

79  On Rákóczi's knowledge in French: Ilona Kovács, "Exil et Littérature: La période 1711–1735 dans l'oeuvre de François II Rákóczi," *Cahiers d'études hongroises* 7 (1995): 20–28.

80  The authorship and addressee of the poem was identified by Árpád Markó: "A versíró Rákóczi" (The poet Rákóczi), *Magyar Könyvszemle* 26 (1936): 259–264.

usually wrote his letters to Sieniawska in French,[81] while he used German in his letters to his wife, with whom he also had a separate homophonic clavis, just as developed technically as the previous one, lacking, however, such emotionally loaded words.[82] Consequently, this second French clavis must have been used to protect the prince's intimacy, and not to help his diplomatic correspondence.

The next example is related to the relatively unknown historical actor, István Dalmády, and Mihály Teleki, his often quoted childhood friend, then would be Transylvanian politician. Dalmady's letters to Teleki, concealed another type of intimate relationship. A recurrent theme in these is that Dalmády assures his friend of his devotedness, and urges the twenty-odd-year-old Teleki to meet him. He even asks for a clavis in an early letter in 1659. "The synceritas you show towards me is a reality for me. I ask you to judge me similarly." And in the same letter, he goes, "If it is not inconvenient, please make a clavis of secret letters, so we could write to each other with bigger confidentia. But I am asking you to try and arrange a meeting as soon as possible, so we could meet in person. You are a very fast young lad, you could find a good way to get here, something that I would like very much, and you would not regret either."[83]

Then, already owning and frequently using the clavis, he repeatedly emphasizes the sincerity, specialness and stability of their relationship, all the while urging a personal meeting, "Believe me, I am assured about your true affectio towards me, that *I have no other friend in this whole world* like you."[84] (The enciphered words are marked in italics.) *"There is nothing I would not do for you,* and if you doubt it, *I will give you a reversalis about it."*[85] *"Trust me, I am y*ours. *I have no other, more secret and truer friend in the whole world, than* you."[86] *"For I think of You and love you as myself. May God help us talk to* each other *as soon as possible."*[87]

In these times there was nothing unusual about expressing such a high level of respect, faithfulness or friendship in personal letters. Yet the way Dalmády is devoted and the way he expressed it, are both extraordinary. He must have known that this is not becoming to male friends, so he used

81  Gábor Tüskés, Ilona Kovács, Béla Köpeczi, eds. *Correspondance de François II Rákóczi et de la palatine Elżbieta Sieniawska 1704–1727* (Budapest: Balassi, 2004).
82  Ráday Archives C64-4d2-25. 5. On the back of the table: Mme la Comtesse de Transylvanie.
83  Teleki 1, 311–312, 278.
84  Teleki 1, 320, 284.
85  Teleki 1, 336, 298.
86  Teleki 1, 350, 310.
87  Teleki 1, 386. 340.

ciphering (see in italics) every time he was writing about his emotions. His open letters or the parts that are left open, are considerably more restrained. This relationship must have looked strange in the eyes of the people surrounding them too, at least that is the way it sounds from the following quote, "*I wish I could talk* to you soon, *I would* truly *pour out all my heart, my secrets* to you. I wish to be face to face with you, twice as strongly as before (...) If I need to, *I will keep secret* any of the things you entrusted me with; *I will take* Your covenant *with me to my coffin.* I will regret that many know *our true friendship, because both of us have many people who envy us.* "[88]

In the following, he gets more enthusiastic, stressing his devotedness even more, all the time enciphering the emotionally loaded words, "Truly, since I have not seen you, *not one day has passed that I have not thought of you.*"[89] "I will confess to you that *I have no better friend than you.*"[90] At times he literally confesses his love to Teleki, "I am writing this to you with a good conscience, *my soul has not been drawn to anyone than you*; be sure about it, *I have no truer friend in this world than You.*"[91] As a true friend, he also gives him marriage advice,[92] and later comforts him on losing his wife, "but, my sweet lord, what can you do about it? she will not be raised from the dead (...) The Lord God gave her and the Lord God took her away."[93]

Then he considers his friend's marriage again, while emphasizing over and over again how much he misses his friend, evaluating their friendship, and then finally concluding by using the word *amanti* to describe themselves. "It is to my contentio that you have been assured about my perfect and sincere friendship to you. You are right, we should not trust every friendship. I have also been assured about you so much, *may the Lord God bless me, I regard* you *highly above all other friends* (...) it has been 17 full months since we have seen each other, I wish I had at least two hours to talk to you. *I am already thinking about your marriage.* I would be ready to assist you in love with all my talent, if I had the means. (...) My dear sweet brother, there should not be any problem between the two of us. Amanti enim nihil difficile. Still, I am begging you, let us make plans to meet each other as soon as possible, this would do both of us good."[94]

88   Teleki 1, 395–396, 346.
89   Teleki 1, 474–475, 410.
90   Teleki 1, 507–508, 433.
91   Teleki 1, 496–498, 426.
92   E.g. Teleki 1, 372–374, 331.
93   Teleki 1, 500–502, 428.
94   Teleki 1, 500–502, 428.

Teleki's answers are not known. He does sometimes mention Dalmády in letters written to others, but always in connection with some practical matter. What is known about Teleki is again from one of Dalmády's letters, namely, that he had dreamed about Dalmády once, "Your dream about me, my dear brother, is not in vain."[95] It is not known exactly how the meeting went, when they finally met, to the joy of Dalmády. His enthusiasm, however, somewhat abates in the coming years, or they may have agreed that their relationship is only a friendship after all. Dalmády, for sure, writes less in a clavis, and there are no more expressions of love like the ones quoted above.

What is common in the enciphered correspondences of Anna of Austria and Mazarin, Rákóczi and Sieniawska, or Dalmády and Teleki is that the encrypted content is personal relationship, love, devotion, desiring each other's company and friendship.

## 8.5.    Family secrets and privacy: ladies and ciphers

Dalmády has an – almost completely enciphered – postscript after one of his letters, which is entirely devoted to supporting the then twenty-five-year-old Mihály Teleki in his marriage plans, *"You might be asking my advice about an already arranged thing, because I have already heard from others about your plans to marry the young girl. I have heard good about the family of poor old Ferenc Pekri, I have also known him personally, but I do not know how wealthy he is, if he has any wealth at all. The girl loves you, you like her too, so I advise you to marry her, just be careful about the means, because I do not know where else you could find it. The princes are not very generous in handing out the gratia, even that Barcsai, You will see it now. For God's sake, do not tie yourself to him together with your marriage, because God's blessing will not rest on you; You might risk Your good reputation, name and consciencia. For me, the only hard thing that I often think of will be that our true friendship will get cooler in your absence."[96]*

The few enciphered sentences of the famous Hungarian poet, Bálint Balassi (1554–1594) also belong to the chapter on encrypted family secrets. The castellan, poet, soldier and great seducer lived in a never-ending inheritance dispute with his relatives. A number of towns were pursuing him in discipline issues because of his scandalous and pugnacious nature. He had

95    Ibid.
96    Teleki 1, 372–374, 331.

an endless number of love affairs to add to his problems. During his rough and tough life he was often forced to use encryption in private and financial letters too.[97] He used partial encryption, only enciphering certain names, most often names of people.[98] He had a monoalphabetic code, a very simple one. He assigned the first half of the alphabet to the second half, and vice versa. Once he enciphered his request to keep something secret in this way, "But if you are my lord and true friend, bq zcqucb [do not tell] gqbxubqx gqauh [anyone a word]".[99]

It is hard to figure out whom Balassi wanted to confuse with this simple method, but after all, the best codebreakers of the Habsburg court were not likely to be interested in his heritage and love secrets, and this method could have successfully protected his letters from nosy mailmen, or relatives. He wrote altogether four letters, where the encrypted text portions mainly to conceal his marriage plans. In one famous line, "I will be a great lord, if all else fails, by means of my cock," he refers to his plans to get rich by marrying. It reads like this, "bmsu if yqzqx, if all else fails, rmfxma ihmb."[100]

Women and family matters only serve in these letters as the *topic* of the encrypted parts. There are other cases, however, in which the corresponding *partners* are women: wives, relatives, female politicians. A study of the sources clearly reveals that enciphering in early modern Hungary was not a male privilege.

It was not even a male privilege in the late medieval times either. Beatrix of Aragon (1457–1508), wife of King Matthias Corvinus (1443–1490), corresponded with several Italian political figures, but she only used encrypting with a few partners. One of these was her sister, the princess of Ferrara, Eleanor of Aragon. The sisters used a simple monoalphabetic cipher with graphic signs. Their letters are kept in the State Archives of Modena,[101] including the one in which Beatrix is sending Eleanor the code key.[102]

---

97   Kőszeghy Péter, *Balassi Bálint, Magyar Alkibiadész* (Balint Balassi, the Hungarian Alcibiades) (Budapest: Balassi, 2008).

98   Révay, *Titkosírások*, 69–73; Sándor Eckhardt, *Balassi Bálint összes művei* (Complete Oeuvre of Bálint Balassi) (Budapest: Akadémiai Kiadó, 1951); Béla Stoll, ed. *Balassi Bálint, Összes versei* (All the poems of Bálint Balassi) (Budapest: Helikon, 1974) 260–264, no. 5; 264–267, no. 6.; 269–271, no. 8; 391–394, no. 87.

99   Stoll, *Balassi*, 394.

100  Stoll, *Balassi*, 394.

101  MNL OL Microfilm Reading Room Mf. 8620.

102  Nagy Iván and B. Nyáry Albert, eds. Magyar diplomácziai emlékek Mátyás király korából 1458–1490. (Hungarian diplomatic sources from the time of King Matthias, 1458–1490) vol. III. (Budapest, 1877.), 67: "Con la cyfra havemo antiquamente con Yostra Signoria con la quale la fara cavare, et accioche cla qua avante Yostra Signoria et suo consorte possa serivere ala Maesta de nostro marito et ad nuj, ne li mandamo qui alligata un altra nova, con la quale le Signorie Yostre

There are several examples when secret letters are exchanged with one's wife. One private letter sent by the count István Illésházy (1541–1609) from his temporary exile to his wife, Katalin Pálffy in 1605 is an easy-to-break cipher where only the vowels are coded, although this was not actually identified until very recently.[103] A stronger code was used by the count Sándor Károlyi to his wife, Krisztina Barkóczy[104] in one still unbroken line of a 1706 letter, and Mihály Teleki and his wife both used encryption in writing to each other in the military turmoil of those years, though mostly in the postscripts. In these encrypted sections politics mingles with marital affection and worrying about each other. This is what Teleki wrote to his wife *"Sweetheart, there will be enough Germans coming, do not worry, God will provide."*[105] In her already quoted response she answers: *"If you had left long ago this place, you would have been captured by the gunmen."*[106] She writes to him a few days later again in an encrypted postscript, *"Mihály Katona is your friend, but the court judge is evil. Lord Mihály Katona has quarreled a lot about some wretched cattle that, but I did not get involved."*[107] Teleki, by the way, also tried ciphered correspondence with Mária Széchy, the wife of the palatine,[108] but neither her, nor us could decode what he had enciphered.[109]

## 8.6.     Private sins – public morals: secrets of a diary and shame

Having read the previous sources, one can reach some noteworthy conclusions. The nature of the enciphered content changes along with the genre of the encrypted literature and the social category the author belongs to. In the latter sources, the covered information falls more in the category of privacy, rather than secrecy. It is even more typical of the genre of diary.

Early modern Hungarian history is rich in diaries.[110] Only a small portion of diary writers used encryption, and they enciphered only a limited

potrano serivere, che cossi fara nostro marito, et nuj ancora con essa medesimo seriveremo ad Yostra Ill-ma Signoria, ala quale le ce recommandamo, et si dignara Yostra Signoria da parte nostra basarerre tutti soi Ill-mi figlioli, li quali tutti salutamo."

103  Vadai, "Két XVII. századi titkosírás megfejtése."
104  MNL OL P. 398, The archives of the Károlyi family, the age of Rákóczi: no. 35409.
105  Teleki 2, 293–294, 220.
106  Teleki 2, 294–295, 223.
107  Teleki 2, 304–305, 229.
108  Teleki 3, 582–583, 432.
109  ibid., 593, appendix to letter 441.
110  Margit S. Sárdi, *Napló-könyv: magyar nyelvű naplók 1800 előtt* (Diary-book: diaries in Hungarian before 1800) (Budapest: Attraktor, 2014).

amount of their text. Their cryptographic practice and concept of secrecy is rather fascinating, nevertheless. In the following we are going to introduce writers whose political roles differ significantly, but whose encrypting practices are fairly similar.

The whereabouts of the manuscript of Gábor Haller's (1614–1663) diary written between 1630 and 1644 is unfortunately still not known, so it is only available in a source publication from a hundred and fifty years ago.[111] Haller was a major political figure in his times in Transylvania. As a teenager, he was the valet of Catherine of Brandenburg, princess of Transylvania and then of György I. Rákóczi, then he traveled, and studied military engineering and mathematics in Leiden. Later he worked for several subsequent Transylvanian princes, the third of whom lured him over to his service, and finally he headed the legation sent to the Turks in Timisoara, where he was captured and executed, as politics changed back in Transylvania.[112] His papers go missing then, but the already complete diary he had left home survived him – to disappear only later.

As many as twenty-two short sections are enciphered in this diary. Haller used two different methods. The first is a simple anagram that he explains in detail at the end of his diary, in case the reader failed to break it on his own.[113] The second is a version of the famous pigpen cipher, made up of a grid and dots, later also used by the Freemasons. This cipher appears to be graphic, but is indeed monoalphabetic and its logical setup (of an alphabet placed in a grid) makes it easy to decode even for those who are not familiar with this method.

Surprisingly, Haller, who studied mathematics in the West, and (could have) had access to the most up-to-date ciphers of his time, chose such a childish way of encryption. After all, he played a major role in the politics of Transylvania, facing constant threats in trying to make his way around four princes. One explanation could be that cryptologic knowledge was not transferred to Central Europe by means of Western cryptographic and mathematical handbooks, rather by diplomatic practice and personal contacts. If Haller had no major source with which to compare his ciphers other than the diplomacy of his own time and country, it is no surprise that he

111  Gábor Haller, *Napló, 1630–1644* (Diary, 1630–1644), in Károly, Szabó, ed. *Erdélyi Történelmi Adatok*, 4 (Kolozsvár: Erdélyi Múzeum Egyesület, 1862): 1–103.

112  András Péter Szabó, *Haller Gábor – egy 17. századi erdélyi arisztokrata életpályája*, (Gábor Haller, the career of a Transylvanian aristocrat) Doctoral dissertation, ELTE, http://doktori.btk. elte.hu/hist/szaboandras/diss.pdf last accessed: 2017.07.29.

113  Haller, *Napló*, 103.

stayed on the level of pigpen ciphers. Not even his lord, György Rákóczi I had used a better cipher with his own envoys.

There is another explanation for the simplistic ciphers he had used: he might simply have regarded encrypting as a playful activity. He seems to invite his readers for a game. He does not seem to mind that his reader finds a way to the encrypted parts too, that is exactly why he gives the key at the end of the diary. [114] In either way, nineteen of the twenty-two encrypted sentences can be found in the pre-1637 part of the diary, the times when Haller was not yet a significant figure in politics. He could, after all, have decided simply not to write down his truly important political secrets.

But what did he actually write down in cipher? Small secrets of politics, and details of various negotiations. More frequently, however, family issues (marriage plans the prince had for him),[115] remarks on his own feelings, and his struggle with alcohol. *"I was drunk and behaved in a way I should not have."* He makes a resolution, *"I promised not to drink wine for a month."* Two days later, *"This is how long I could go without wine."* Next he records on a two-day period, *"Drunk, feeling sick."*[116] He encrypts his record on how the prince had sarcastically noted that he would sooner find a cup of wine than a book. Once he covers up a dream in which he is punished for his sexual desires, *"In my dream I saw Moses come down from heaven to grab me and threaten me for my sins, at which I got scared and prayed to God and immediately stopped having sinful desires."*[117] He may have had other ciphered comments with a sexual topic because the bashful editor decides to leave out two ciphered parts, a behavior that is not quite worthy of a philologist.[118] All in all, the secret to be enciphered for Haller is related to his private life.

Zsigmond Szaniszló's (c. 1655 – c. 1721) enciphered diary records served similar purposes of hiding details of private life and personal secrets.[119] Szaniszló, a notary and later high judge of Torda County in Transylvania, made a record on almost every single day of the period between 1682 and 1711, making his diary a truthful, if somewhat monotonous summary of his life.

"November

5: Gave the belt maker denar 60 for rice porridge and linen.

---

114  See also the conclusion of Sárdi, *Napló-könyv* and Szabó, *Haller* (174).

115  Haller, *Napló*, 30.

116  Haller, *Napló*, 16, 25, 69.

117  Haller, *Napló*, 38.

118  Haller, *Napló*, 31, 44.

119  Zsigmond Szaniszló, *Napló, 1682–1711* (Diary 1682–1711), ed. Károly Torma, *Történelmi Tár* 1889 (12). 230–269, 503–522, 708–727, (13), 1890. 77–101, 307–327, 493–510, 757–770, (14), 1891. 267–295.

8. Sent Michael to Komjáczeg with the wagon. He brought the oat approx. metr. 61, also brought cabbage a(bout) two hundred.

11. Martin came on a white horse. I went to Komjáczeg.

13. I herded cattle from Polyan. Mss Miklós has brought some pots..."[120]

When he wished to hide something, he used a very simple transposition cipher but certain letters (f, h, k, l, z) are left unchanged.[121] The ciphered parts, usually only single words, are connected to the accounts (*"I have bought* hay *for 56 fl."*) to family (his daughter's marital problems), or unchaste acts ("I have caught *John* Váradi *with a woman last night*"). Some other records do also report a lewd act, but without encrypting ("I have had a prostitute tied up in that same place.") and he leaves a few curses as open texts too ("that motherfucker").[122]

The most appalling encrypted record of the diary reveals an amoral event connected to his family life. His wife, heavily pregnant with their daughter who is to be born 8 July, spends the night of 30 April 1693 in the company of their established guest, "I have understood that the *treasurer had spent the night with my wife*. Dear Lord, do not forsake me, for the sake of your holy son, help me! I could not help it."[123]

All of these details are only slightly better hidden than the secrets in Haller's diary, who directly provided the key to the code he had used. Szaniszló obviously did not expect determined codebreakers to work on his diary that he had always carried with himself. More likely he was only trying to defend the financial secrets and intimate details of his diary from people casually peeking into it. The dreams and alcoholism of Haller, the adventure of Szaniszló's wife, or even the vulgar comment of Balassi on his plan to get rich – all of these are cases that Georg Simmel's above quoted observation seems to apply to: secrecy is often not simply a hidden piece of information, but more like the mark of shame, the documentation of trespassing the boundaries of social norms

Not all enciphered diary records are connected to privacy, however. There is an entire chapter of early modern Hungarian diaries that are different: the daily records of envoys, the aim of which was to record data to be used later in an official report. Both Thököly and Rákóczi ordered their envoys to make detailed diary-like entries of delegations, Thököly even adding the use of clavis.[124] Thus, envoys produced lengthy diaries, and some

120  Szaniszló, *Napló*, 247.
121  Encrypted parts: 1889: 505, 506, 518, 715, 718; 1890: 85–86, 88; 1891: 290.
122  Ibid. 1891: 518, 505, 84, 270.
123  Szaniszló *Napló*, 1890: 85–86.
124  Benda, *Pápai János törökországi naplói*; Thaly, *Késmárki Thököly Imre*, 614.

among them used encryption.[125] These diaries are official documents, comments about personal life are missing from the enciphered parts of them, the occasionally encrypted paragraphs cover rather the confidential details of their negotiations.

## 8.7.    Science, chemistry and alchemy

Despite the fact that science is conventionally regarded as a public affair, there are long-standing traditions of encrypting scientific results.[126] One of the earliest and perhaps most publicized cases are the anagrams Galileo Galilei sent to the envoy of Prague in Florence (and indirectly to Kepler). The first message (smaismrmilmepoetaleumibunenugttauiras) preceded the 1610 appearance of Sidereus Nuncius, and documented the discovery of the moons of Saturn: *Altissimum planetam tergeminum observavi* (I have observed that the uppermost planet is a triplicity). The Florentine scientist acted in a similar way when announcing the moonlike that is, phase-having) behavior of Venus. But for the last two letters, this anagram was meaningful on its own: *Haec immatura a me iam frustra leguntur - o y* (these immature things are yet read by me in vain – o y). Its other form, using all the letters, *Cynthiae figuras aemulatur mater amorum*, (the Mother of Loves [Venus] imitates the forms of Cynthia [the moon]), documented Galileo's real discovery.[127]

Sixty years later similar anagrams were sent by the first scientists of the Royal Society, Christian Huygens, Robert Hooke, and even Isaac Newton to the Society's secretary, Henry Oldenburg, about discoveries that they had not had the opportunity to confirm, or simply had not published yet.[128]

125  Diary of Mihály Bay naplója: MNL OL G. 15. Caps A.1. Fasc 24. fol. 75- 124r. Diary of Gáspár Sándor: MNL OL G. 15. Caps A.1. Fasc 24. fol. 1–28. Published: Kálmán Thaly, ed., Késmárki Thököly Imre, Bay: 579–627, 646–650. Sándor: 651–708.

126  Ernan McMullin, "Openness and secrecy in science: some notes on early history," *Science, Technology and Human Values* 10 (1985): 14–23. David Hull, "Openness and secrecy in science: their origins and limitationism," *Science, Technology and Human Values* 10 (1985): 4–13;

127  Mario Biagioli, *Galileo's Instruments of Credit: Telescopes, Images, Secrecy*, Chicago: University Of Chicago Press, 2006); *idem*, "From ciphers to confidentiality: Secrecy, Opennes and Priority in Science," *The British Journal for the History of Science*, 45 (2012): 213–233.

128  Thomas Birch, *The History of the Royal Society of London for Improving of Natural Knowledge, From its First Rise* (London: Printed for A. Millar in the Strand 1756–57) Vol.2, 345-345, and vol. 3, 179 and 190. See also: Kristie Macrakis, "Confessing secrets: secret communication and the origins of modern science," *Intelligence and National Security* 25 (2010): 183–197. Biagioli, "From ciphers to confidentiality," Gábor Zemplén, "Newton's Strategic Manoeuvring with Simple Colours and

Nevertheless, anagrams are not ciphers. They are not based on the sub-stitution of letters, but on their transposition. The most important differ-ence is that anagrams often have several solutions. This is why Kepler could solve Galileo's first anagram in a completely different way, making sense of it in light of his own Mars-related theory. Anagrams cannot be broken as a cipher, and they are not meant to be channels of secret communication. The goal of these scientists was to document their own scientific hypothe-ses and the priority of their discovery in an age when the mechanisms of es-tablishing priority were not yet established. There existed patent office-like institutions, and publishing a discovery in a book or journal was also an available alternative, but a particular scientist never knew where the sys-tem leaked – which editor, patent specialist or assessor of a contest would pass on crucial information. We now know that the very idea of Galilei's telescope was also the result of such a leaking,[129] so we are not surprised that Tycho Brahe felt the need to have his own press operating on the island of Hven, the place of his astronomical discoveries. The process of printing a discovery, which meant to secure its priority, involved risking its very pri-ority. The use of anagrams did not aim at disguising, it was rather meant to provide protection from the risks inherent in the process of recognition and publication. It was a defense mechanism.[130]

The motivations of the astronomer Michael Van Langren might have been similar to those of Tycho Brahe, when he published a small book in 1644 in Spanish, with the title *La verdadera Longitud por mar y tierra*. The book puts forward a solution to one of the most urgent scientific problems of the age, the exact determination of longitude. This had become a burn-ing issue in navigation: based on the position of the Sun and the stars, it was relatively easy to determine the latitude of the position of one's ship in the open ocean, but for exactly determining the longitude (and thus, answering questions such as "How far is America from here?" or "Where do the continental shelves begin under the water?"), they would have needed more precise chronometers than were available at the time. Sovereigns rec-ognized the importance of the problem, and founded grants to encourage scientists to solve it. Van Langren finally found the solution. However, we

Diagrams: a Radical Historical Interpretation," in Tamás Demeter, Kathryn Murphy and Claus Zittel, eds. *Conflicting Values of Inquiry: Ideologies of Epistemology in Early Modern Europe* (Leiden: Brill, 2014): 221–245.

129 Mario Biagioli, "Venetian tech-transfer: how Galileo copied the telescope," in Albert van Helden, Sven Dupré, Rob van Gent and Huib Zuidervaart, eds., *The Origins of the Telescope* (Amsterdam: Amsterdam University Press, 2011): 203–230.

130 Biagioli, "From ciphers to confedentiality."

are not in the position to assess whether he was right or not, because he enciphered his proposition before he printed it, and this cipher text – not longer than a paragraph – still resists code breakers. The first solution that we can actually read was proposed a hundred years later, when, in the mid-eighteenth century, John Harrison developed such precise clocks that the determination of longitude on open sea finally became possible.[131]

Proper ciphers – that were not used to ensure priority, but rather concealed a longer text and could be actually solved – were used only to a limited extent in scientific and technological texts. A well-known case is that of the Renaissance engineer Giovanni Fontana (c.1395?-1455). Fontana used substitution ciphers in entire books, among them his *Bellicorum Instrumentorum Liber,* describing his complex military machinery, and his *Secretum de Thesauro,* on mnemotechnic devices. He used simple, monoalphabetic substitution ciphers.[132] What his motivations might have been we can only guess, but we are probably not very far from the solution if we suppose that he wished to add to the secrecy of the description of the technological devices as well as demonstrating how his substitution cipher itself functioned. As cracking Fontana's code was not hard, one could more properly call this procedure the rhetoric of secrecy than a real secretive technique.

The motivations of Robert Boyle were different. He relied more heavily on proper cryptographic methods, such as name substitution, code words, and monoalphabetic ciphers. He applied these in his private letters, not his published documents. The purpose of his secrecy was different from that of Huygens, Hooke, and Newton. It was not to secure the priority of a discovery; rather, he did not wish the results of his alchemical experiments to be found out. No professional codebreakers would have been stopped by his encryption, however. His purpose was, instead, to exclude his learned assistants from the communication of his secrets.[133]

131 Valero-Mora and Ibáñez Ulargui, "The First (Known Statistical Graph: Michael Florent van Langren and the 'Secret' of Longitude," 2010. http://www.datavis.ca/papers/langren-TAS09154.pdf (accessed July 27, 2017)

132 Lynn Thorndike, *History of Magic and Experimental Science* (New York: Columbia University Press, 1923–58), vol 4. 150–182; Alexander Birkenmajer, "Zur Lebensgeschichte und wissenschaftlichen Tätigkeit von Giovanni Fontana (1395?-1455?)" *Isis* 17 (1932): 34–54. *Bellicorum Instrumentorum Liber* (München, Bayerische Staatsbibiliothek, Cod. Icon. 242), *Secretum de thesauro experimentorum ymaginationis hominum* (Párizs, Bibliotheque Nationale, Cod. Lat. Nouv. Acq. 635). See also: Horst Kranz, Walter Oberschelp, eds., *Mechanisches Memorieren und Chiffrieren um 1430: Johannes Fontanas Tractatus de instrumentis artis memorie* (Stuttgart: Steinr, 2009).

133 Lawrence M. Principe, "Robert Boyle's Alchemical Secrecy: Codes, Ciphers and Concealments," *Ambix,* 39 (1992): 63–74.

Another completely enciphered book, which forms an entirely independent category, is the world-famous Voynich manuscript.[134] This book, with its unique drawings of biology, astronomy and bathing women, plus a writing system that is completely confusing, has kept myriads of codebreakers, information technologists and historians enthralled ever since a Polish antiquarian and bookdealer, Wilfrid Michael Voynich (1865–1930), had bought it in the 1910s from the Jesuits in Villa Mondragone, Italy. The book has created a whole subculture of codebreakers who have conferences and communicate via an email list. Apart from the groups of amateurs, a number of special historians and philologists have examined it, and the best cryptographers of WWII had tried to identify its code in vain, even William Friedman (1891–1969),[135] who had broken dozens of Japanese military codes. The illustrations help to distinguish three longer sections, one on astronomy, one on balneology, and one on botanics, but the script next to the pictures remain illegible. It is not even known whether the writing is a cipher text, a code, a constructed or an existing language.

One naturally has the lurking suspicion that the book is either a hoax or a counterfeit document. Several people have been suspected of having forged the codex, from the sixteenth-century medium and alchemist Edward Kelly to the twentieth-century collector, Wilfrid Voynich. Their motivation is thought to have been nothing else than to create a mystical and enthralling book that would sell for a fortune. This could have been the case with Kelly, whose main sources of income were the gullible John Dee, English mathematician and magus, and the generous Rudolf II, Holy Roman Emperor; but also with Voynich, who made a living by selling books to enthusiastic readers. Along with these historical arguments, the hoax hypothesis was also thought to be supported by statistical data based on the characteristics of the text.[136] A recent American laboratory study, nonetheless, revealed the pages to be from the fifteenth century, so the modern hoax theories seem to be ruled out.[137]

---

134  Two titles and three webpages from the rich bibliography: Mary E. D'Imperio, *The Voynich Manuscript - An Elegant Enigma* (Aegean Park Press, 1978); Gerry Kennedy, Rob Churchill, *The Voynich Manuscript* (London: Orion, 2004); http://www.voynich.nu/, http://www.world-mysteries. com/sar_13.htm, www.ciphermysteries.com.

135  Jim Reeds, "William F. Friedman's Transcription of the Voynich Manuscript" *Cryptologia* 19 (1995): 1–22.

136  Gordon Rugg, "An Elegant Hoax?"; Andreas Schinner, "The Voynich Manuscript: Evidence of the Hoax Hypothesis" *Cryptologia* 31 (2007): 95–107. See also: Gabriel Landini, "Evidence of Linguistic Structure in the Voynich Manuscript Using Spectral Analysis" *Cryptologia* 25 (2001): 275–295.

137  Paula Zyats, Erin Mysak, Jens Stenger, Marie-France Lemay, Anikó Bezur, and David D. Driscoll, "Physical Findings" in Raymond Clemens, ed. *The Voynich Manuscript.* New

Obviously, we cannot completely dismiss them until the code is broken. It is still not satisfactorily verified whether the manuscript is really an enciphered scientific work, or an example for an artificial language, or just some automatic writing.

In the old secrecy–openness dichotomy, alchemy was certainly on the secretive side, considered to rely on all kinds of methods that excluded uninvited readers from alchemical communications. In recent decades, however, historians have increasingly noticed that secrecy in alchemy is a more complex issue; in fact it was not in all cases more secretive than other occupations of the period.[138] To be sure, metals were represented by special graphic symbols, and many alchemic documents combine symbolic language use with chemistry. However, direct and intentional encryption, as seen in Boyle's letters, was rare; in any event only a few ciphers applied in alchemical texts from before 1600 are known. One of them is from the Beinecke library (just like the Voynich manuscript), the sixteenth-century Latin and German collection of alchemical (and partly medical) recipes of a certain Martin Roesel of Rosenthal from around 1586, in which some recipes are encrypted in a numeric monoalphabetic cipher.[139] Another one is from the national library of Madrid, the *Libro del Tesoro* attributed to Alfonso the Wise, a twenty-page text, which is almost entirely encrypted.[140] Both manuscripts have been identified and researched by the historian of alchemy Agnieszka Rec, who argues that the relative lack of cryptography in sixteenth century alchemy is due to the fact that the kind of secrecy guaranteed by ciphers do not actually fit the special needs of the alchemists. In fact, she writes: "ciphers represent an entirely different tool than that commonly wielded in the service of alchemical secrecy. Other methods alchemists relied on to conceal their ideas – *Decknamen*, allegories, and others – were meant to exclude the great mass of the unworthy, but they were by design legible to those with the appropriate knowledge, that is,

Haven and London: Bienecke Tate Book & Manuscript Library and Yale University Press, 2016, 23–37.

138  The traditional view contrasting secretive alchemy with open chemistry or public mining methods: Betty Jo Teeter Dobbs, "From the secrecy of alchemy to the openness of chemistry," in Tore Frängsmyr, ed., *Solomon's House Revisited,* (Canton: Science History Publications, 1990): 75–94; Long, *Openness, Secrecy, Authorship.* The criticism and reappraisal of this view: William Newman, "Alchemical symbolism and concealment," in Peter Galison and Emily Thompson, eds., *The Architecture of Science* (Cambridge, MA: MIT Press, 2000): 59–77; Tara Nummedal, *Alchemy and Authority in the Holy Roman Empire* (Chicago: The Chicago University Press, 2007).

139  MS Beinecke Mellon MS 27 (fol. 23r). Agnieszka Rec, "Ciphers and Secrecy Among the Alchemists: A Preliminary Report," *Societas Magica Newsletter,* 31 (2014): 1–6.

140  Madrid, Biblioteca Nacional, MS reservado 20.

other adepts. When a text instructed the alchemist to "take the green lion" (*recipe leonem viridem*), he would know to reach for his supply of antimony ore. Ciphers present an entirely different barrier to entry. Revealing their contents does not require a particular body of knowledge, but rather a single piece of information: the cipher key whether obtained directly or figured out. Any reader can recover the text if he can get the key. Acquiring that key becomes much easier when an earlier reader writes in the solution next to the cipher (....) With ciphers, then, being worthy is entirely beside the point, and the alchemist very quickly loses control of his readership. It is precisely this quality that makes ciphers uncommon in alchemical manuscripts, which, as books of secrets, were meant to be written in a particular language understood by a chosen group."[141]

A third, in many ways similar source survived from the region of Hungary, that is the diary of Johannes Cementes of Kolozsvár, a sixteenth-century jewelry maker who worked in the mint of Cluj (then part of Hungary: Kolozsvár) as a "cement guy": a refiner of precious metals. His diary, from the mid-16th century, consists of almost two hundred pages, and is basically a collection of recipes, including jewelry-making, gold refining and alchemy, written partly in Latin, partly in Hungarian.[142] The diary is entitled *The Book of Happiness*. More precisely, the title is "*The name of this book is happiness, if you live with it the way I do*," and the very title itself is enciphered. The author provides the code key right at the beginning on fol. 2v, which enables those few sentences that are encrypted to be read. Just as the two previous alchemical texts, this diary also uses a simple monoalphabetic method; as such, none of them constitute the highest achievement of cryptography available in their period:

The Cipher-key of János Cementes[143]

141  Rec, "Ciphers and Secrecy," 4–5.

142  I thank Dóra Bobory for calling my attention to this source. Herzfelder Armand Dezső, "Kolozsvári Czementes János könyve" (The book by Johannes Cementes of Kolozsvár) *Magyar Könyvszemle* (1896): 276–301, 351–373; Zolnai Gyula, "Jegyzetek Czementes János könyvéhez" (Notes to the book by Johannes Cementes), *Magyar Könyvszemle* (1896): 373–377.

143  Herzfelder, "Kolozsvári" 277.

Cementes often represents the metals with their alchemical symbols in the mining, minting and alchemic recipes, and occasionally he enciphers a few words in describing a procedure, like the use of the candle applied in treasure hunts:

"*Candela* bona, cum qua *thesaurus* inveniatur.

Rp. *ceram* virgineam *three parts* with four *part camphor and* with five *part myrrh* and six *part sulphurusstone et merc*urium sublimatum, quibus mixtis iterum *adde* seven *part sulphurus*stone. D*einde* virgo... litman de lana alba *that is w*ool ad longitudinem unius cubilis et perf*icias can*delam illam, incende et ardebit quiete et ubi f*aerit thesa*urus, mox extinquitur. Super quod adducta faerit sive in terra, sive in muro vel pariete."

In his practices of secrecy, Cementes did not distinguish between recipes of alchemy and treasure hunt, on the one hand, and jewel-making and gold refining descriptions, on the other. He did not encrypt consequently the first category and left as plain text the second. For example, his unencrypted recipes include many that are similar in nature to the one quoted above. Alchemy and gold refining for Cementes fall in the same category from the point of view of secrecy.

## 8.8.    Secret characters and magic

Magic, just like alchemy, had been represented in the traditional literature as secretive in contrast to science, which was supposed to be open.[144] However, as we have seen in the introductory chapters, this simplifying opposition has, fortunately, been lately modified.[145] Still, and most interestingly, learned magic and cryptography seem to have had an unusually close relationship in the sixteenth and seventeenth centuries. They share their major authors, to start with. Works of Cornelius Agrippa and John Dee contain secret alphabets, whereas Johannes Trithemius, Athanasius Kircher, and Gerolamo Cardano were all authors noted in both the history of magic and the history of cryptography.

In late medieval magical manuscripts, written or compiled by anonymous authors, accessible and popular in circles of students and the low clergy, cipher alphabets and shorter encrypted messages appear in considerable quantity. Some of these alphabets and messages were the inventions

144  Brian Vickers, ed., *Occult and Scientific Mentalities in the Renaissance* (Cambridge: Cambridge University Press, 1984).
145  Vermeir, "Opennes versus secrecy."

of the scribes, others appeared in such widespread and often copied texts as the *Picatrix*, the *Book of Runes*, and a number of short hermetic and Salomonic texts.[146] In the *Book of Runes* for example – a Latin talismanic text on manipulating planetary spirits – the spirits' names are to be engraved on metal plates in a runic alphabet associating the sacred aspect of the runes with the celestial forces. This was the most famous, but not the only, magical text featuring a runic script. In a German manuscript from the late fifteenth century, for example, runic characters were used for transcribing various names and notions of the divinatory, prognostic, and occasionally demonic material of the book. In a demonic invocation written in proper German, for example, the following terms are spelled in runes: *boes geist* (malign spirit), *diabolo diaboliczno, satana sataniczno,* and *kum her zuo mir* (come to me).[147]

Cipher alphabets in magical texts have two common traits. First of all, they all stay on a relatively simple level, not stepping beyond the usual monoalphabetic system, despite the fact that by this time, the turn of the fifteenth and the sixteenth century, homophonic systems complemented with nomenclatures were known. Furthermore, ciphers in magic manuscripts usually encrypt short fragments of texts, and more often than not, these text fragments function as names of planetary spirits, as characters to be inscribed in a planetary talisman used for benign and evil magical purposes, or simply as demonic invocations.[148]

Proceeding in time, and looking at early modern manuscripts of magic, the picture does not change substantially. The wide range of magic alphabets collected in the comprehensive book by Gilles le Pape (*Les écritures magiques*) are again without exception monoalphabetic, be they of Arabic, Hebraic, Irish, or Western European origin. Cornelius Agrippa's celestial alphabets, the many anonymous talismanic ciphers, and even the famous Freemason cipher belong to this simple category.[149]

146 Benedek Láng, *Unlocked Books, Manuscripts of Learned Magic in the Medieval Libraries of Central Europe* (University Park, PA: Penn State University Press, 2008), chaps. 3 and 9. MS Biblioteca Apostolica Vaticana, Pal. Lat. 1375, fol. 19r. about which, see also: Láng, *Unlocked Books,* 132. MS BAV Pal. lat. 1375 f. 270v, on which: Láng, *Unlocked Books,* 117.

147 Hartmut Beckers, "Eine spätmittelalterliche deutsche Anleitung zur Teufelsbeschwörung mit Runenschrift-verwendung," *Zeitschrift für deutsches Altertum und deutsche Literatur* 113 (1984): 136–145.

148 Dresden, Sächsische Landesbibliothek N. 100, fol. 198r-200v; BAV, Pal. lat. 1439, f. 346r-347v. Beckers, "Eine spätmittelalterliche deutsche Anleitung."

149 Gilles le Pape, *Les écritures magiques* (Milan: Arché, 2006).

Encrypting methods in these cases do not in the least seem to be used as means for hiding information. This is not only because these cipher alphabets are easy to break, but also because the accompanying text, which is left open, clearly reveals what the coded text is about. Ciphers make no content inaccessible. It seems very likely that the special characters used to denote or conjure up the magical content of the spiritual world in effect worked to call attention to the ritual of the text, rather than hide it. Their mysterious appearance worked more like a strategy of exposure, an advertisement by means of the rhetoric of secrecy. The purpose of using special letters was not so much to satisfy cryptographic needs as to provide a channel of communication with the spiritual world.

## 8.9.    Encrypting in religion

Cryptography and religious practice were rarely paired. Three examples will be introduced though, but none of them really fit the framework of this study in the strictest sense. The first example is from a period beyond the early modern era, the second is – most probably – from an area outside Hungary, and the third one cannot be clearly classified as cryptography. The reason for including them is rather that they all add important aspects to the relationship of secrecy, cryptography and religion.

The first is a rather unusual writing of Ladislaus Simandi (or László Simándi: 1655 – 1715). Simandi was a Pauline monk of Croatian origin who wrote in Hungarian and Latin. Selecting from an array of shaped poems, acrostics and other visually exciting short writings, he edited a volume for his students praising Saint Paul, the monk, and thus carving out his place in the early history of Hungarian and Croatian visual poetry.[150] Into the selection of his own visual poems he inserted a poem made by using a cipher, in which he assigned numbers to the letters of the alphabet in an increasing order.

150 I thank Szabolcs Serfőző for calling my attention to this source. Ladislaus Simándi, *Corvi albi eremitici nova Musa inconcinna* (Typ. Clari Montis Czestochoviensis, 1712). See also István Kilián, *A régi magyar képvers* (Old Hungarian Shaped Poetry) (Budapest, Felsőmagyarország Kiadó – Magyar Műhely Kiadó, 1998), 23.

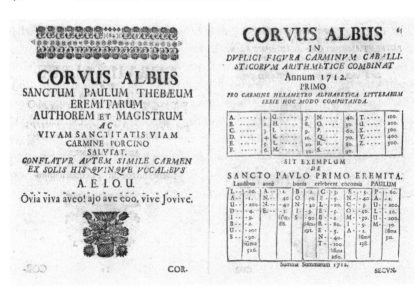

Versus cabalisticus: Ladislaus Simándi, *Corvi albi eremitici nova Musa inconcinna 65.*

The second example is from the letters of János Zakarjás (1720?–1772), a Jesuit priest,[151] written to his superior from Peru, where he was working as a missionary between 1749 and 1756, a few decades after our examined period.[152] He provides detailed accounts of the everyday problems and conflicts of missionary life on the South-American continent, including his life among the Amerindian people, their various healing, funeral and other practices, as well as of his breathtaking travels from Genoa through Cadiz, Cordoba and Panama to Lima. The generally decent and 'comme il faut' Latin text is interspersed with less appropriate Hungarian expressions. In certain places he toys with such insertions, showing his real self to be less official in Hungarian than the rest of the letters in Latin would make us believe: "We were crawling on all fours all day." In other places he writes about Hungarian-related things or his own emotions in Hungarian, "God knows, if I will ever see Hungary again." He calls a certain lady honorable in Latin, to which he adds in Hungarian "the old hag". Describing a greying Saracen he bashfully adds in Hungarian that he was "walking up and down

---

151 I thank Gábor Farkas Farkas for calling my attention to this source. Ödön Sztankovics, ed. "Zakarjás János és Fáy Dávid délamerikai jezsuita misszionáriusok úti levelei (1749–1756)" (Travel letters of missionaries János Zakarjás and Dávid Fáy), *Földrajzi Közlemények* 38 (1910): 115–128, 215–236. The manuscript of the diary: ELTE University Library, G. 689.

152 Letters of Zakarjás in Latin: Lajos Boglár, "The Ethnographic Legacy of Eighteenth Century Hungarian Travellers in South America", *Acta Ethnographica*, 1955, 313–358.

the seashore stark naked like Adam in Paradise." One of his comments, however, makes it clear that he uses the Hungarian language not only as a game but also as a tool for secrecy: here he shares his suspicion with his addressee that his letters are being captured.[153] A particular situation: the natural language of Hungary becomes a tool of cryptography in a remote part of the world, making the intimate content of the letters inaccessible for fellow missionaries.

Zakarjás goes deeper in cryptology: when he describes the cruelty of Brazilian slave merchants and fake missionaries, presumably fearing his own life too, he uses Hungarian Runic letters to write the Latin text, "Because malicious people have come over from Brazil, who have treated me too worse than you treat a tiger. *They were Christians, not even Indians* (he writes in Hungarian). They usually captured anyone whom they came across and took them to work in the *mines* (in runes), and other *miserable places* (in runes), they take the *lives* (in runes) of the *elderly* (in runes) to stop them from spreading word about them, they take the *fingers* (in runes) of others with which they would draw the archery bow, they take the *mothers* (in runes) more fit for travel by tearing their *babies from their breasts* (in runes) and *slamming* them at the first pole they find. And to deceive the careless people more, they sent one of their people ahead who pretended to be a *missionary* (in runes) in his clothes and appearance." He ends by giving his brother the key to the secret writing, specifying the well-known books where the Hungarian Runic alphabet is described. He uses a writing that he expects his addressee to be familiar with, but which is also completely inaccessible in South America.

This cannot be said of the third example for religious cryptography, the puzzling Rohonc codex, which got a membership in the elite club of unsolved ciphers.

This manuscript is a nearly 450-page long handwritten book filled with 9–14 lines of unknown sign strings on each page and more than 80 illustrations.[154] The first and last few dozen pages have been detached from the book itself, and the original order of these pages is not known. There is no title page. Nothing is known about the provenience of the manuscript. It was donated to the Library of the Hungarian Academy of Sciences together with the 30000-volume library of the late Hungarian Count Gustav

---

153  Sztankovics, "Zakarjás" 117–119, 216–220.
154  The manuscript is kept in the Manuscript Library of the Hungarian Academy of Sciences. Its call number is: K 114, microfilm call number: MF 1173/II. A description of the codex can be found in: Csapodi Csaba, *A "Magyar Codexek," elnevezésű gyűjtemény (K31-K114)*, (Budapest: MTAK, 1973), 109.

Batthyány in 1838. This library was earlier located at the family residence in the town of Rohonc (today: Rechnitz, Austria), hence the name of the codex. The Batthyánys had amassed their book collection from a great array of sources through a succession of centuries, so there is no guarantee that the codex is from either Hungary, or somewhere from Central Europe. Since, however, it came to Budapest from a then-Hungarian town, it deserves a place in the study on Hungarian secret writings.

The codex became the center of academic attention soon after its appearance, but only as long as it was considered to be a potentially valuable ancient Hungarian writing. The initial enthusiasm soon died out, and gave place to disappointment, skepticism and suspicion. By the end of the nineteenth century the academic public had decided to regard it as a forgery, so no serious scholar had studied it for a long time, until the turn of the twentieth and twenty-first century.[155]

Two pages of the Rohonc codex (91-91a)

Having examined the regularities of the character strings in depth, the literature of the codex today agrees that the ciphered text is neither a forgery, nor a hoax, but carries decipherable real content. Having too many

---

155 See also: Benedek Láng, "Why don't we decipher an outdated cipher system? The Codex of Rohonc" *Cryptologia* 34 (2010): 115–144. Gábor Tokai, "Az első lépések a Rohonci-kódex megfejtéséhez", (First steps towards the solution of the Rohonc codex), *Élet és Tudomány* LXV/52–53, LXVI/2 (2010–2011): 1675–1678. and 50–53. Levente Zoltán Király, "Struktúrák a Rohonci-kódex szövegében." (Tructures in the text of the Rohonc codex) *Theologiai Szemle* 54 (2011/2): 82–93.

characters with too few combinations, and lacking spaces between the words, it does not look as if it were trying to convince the reader that it had been written in a natural language. Neither does it seem to have been created to be sold for a fortune to a collector of old books and rarities. In this sense it does not appear to be a hoax either, because with its simple gray bind it looks neither valuable, nor mysterious, not counting the fact that it had been written with unknown characters. Obvious differences can be spotted when comparing the codex to the Voynich Manuscript, with its decorous appearance, and illustrations of mystical galaxies, botanical creatures and nude ladies.

The argument that the codex was written by a lunatic in his enthusiasm cannot be verified. To begin with, it must have been written by several people, which would require the cooperation of a group of nutty maniacs. And even if it was indeed written by one person alone, the returning "grammatical" structures indicate that no spontaneous automatic writing was employed, the author had instead applied certain pre-established rules in the process of writing. For this same reason, the consistent use of the combination of characters convinces me that the old hoax-theory can be completely dismissed. The writer was following a meaningful text, assigning the characters to the various items of this text. Nobody is able to note down such meaningless strings of characters with such rigorously followed rules.

The codex is most certainly a system of code-signs that is the result of a cipher, stenography or structured language.

Can the Rohonc codex possibly be a cipher? The text was obviously not produced by using a simple monoalphabetic cipher. It has way too many characters for that, way too strong repetitions, and a frequency chart that resembles no other natural alphabet. Running a consonant test yields no result either – vowels and consonants cannot be identified, and the entropy of the text is so low that the possibility of the polyalphabetic methods can be ruled out, too. A procedure that employs several alphabets would hide the patterns of the text well. But the codex is full of quickly returning sections with fully or partially identical structures, paragraphs or at least beginnings.

Could the codex have been coded in a homophonic cipher? An important argument for the homophonic system is that one gets the impression that certain signs stand for letters, but not every sign behaves like this: a good number of them seem to denote complete concepts or word parts. A study of the characters also indicates that certain signs could be left out, as if they carried no meanings, just like nullities. If this assumption is right, and the Rohonc codex contains a complex homophonic cipher, then the text should mostly have signs for letters and syllables, and partially for words. The letter-frequency and consonant tests, however, yielded no valuable information in this respect. Certain symbols clearly stand for the names of Christ and Pilate, but whether these could be regarded as nomenclatures is dubious.

The reader of the codex gets the impression that perhaps it is not only the single characters that carry a meaning, but often pairs of symbols, or perhaps triples or quadruples of them. Looking at the composite signs, a rather complex syllable-coding method might emerge. Assuming that sometimes single signs stand for syllables and double signs for single letters also explains the frequent repetitions.

Two further possibilities should be mentioned. The first is that we are dealing with a mere consonant-writing. Since this is basically the same as assuming that the codex was written in shorthand, this will be discussed below. The second is that nomenclatures dominate the text to such an extent that signs for letters are almost completely missing, and the system is virtually made up of word signs, in other words, codes. Such a code system, which requires an enormous amount of work and a good deal good luck to be broken, poses problems similar to that of a structured language, so it should be approached as such.

Could the Rohonc codex be an example of the multiple stenography systems popular in the seventeenth century? The obvious topic of the codex, Christian liturgy does not exclude this option. Shorthand systems were as regularly used for recording prayers and other religious purposes as for making records.

When Reverend James Humphrey left his Massachusetts home in 1776 to fight for independence of his country, he was thoroughly familiar with *Stenography Completed,* the 1727 work of James Weston, so he could use this method to record the religious experiences he had in between the fights. Reverend Alexander Ewing used the method of John Byrom around 1780, and Reverend James Hawkes used that of Henry Barmby for similar purposes.

In these cases making the personal message discreet was just as important as increasing the speed of writing, if not more.[156] It was also not infrequent for a designer of a shorthand system to illustrate the advantages of his work on the Lord's Prayer or other Biblical texts,[157] even complete

---

156  Eric Sams, "Cryptanalysis and Historical Research," 94.

157  William Fordyce Mavor, *Universal Stenography, or a new compleat system of short writing* (S. l.: Harrison, s. d.).

gospels were printed in shorthand.[158] A fragment from the Bible from 1886 uses Pitman's system to code the New Testament.[159] The basic constituents of the symbols are simple, but the characters that they make up are rather complex, and, due to the regularities of the text, they are repeated every so often. Just by looking at the pages of the shorthand gospel without the character table one gets lost pretty easily and cannot decide how to decipher the character strings.

There are several arguments, however, against the theory that the Rohonc Codex would be a shorthand scheme that we have no key to. Shorthand systems are meant to be economical and they are fundamentally letter-based, even if they do contain many abbreviations and word signs. The characters of the Rohonc Codex (those that appear to be basic units), are not in the least stroke-like. On the contrary, most of them take a lot of time and effort to draw. This makes this writing *slow*, whereas the vital feature of shorthand is that it is *fast*. Furthermore, shorthand systems are usually not secretive, this is why they leave plain texts and recognizable numerals in the text, as page numbers, for example (even if many shorthand systems do offer signs to be used for numbers too). They aim at teaching the reader, not excluding him. This, however, cannot be said of the Rohonc Codex, where there are no signs, page numbers, chapter headings, or enumerations that would refer to the cultural background of the codex. Finally, shorthand systems basically go from left to right, which is the way for right-handed people to write quickly without smearing the ink, whereas the text of the codex is written from right to left.

It is not entirely excluded for the Rohonc codex to be an early and not widespread shorthand design that cannot or does not wish to be as practical as more successful systems, and which is more secretive in nature, like Pepys's system of nullities. One can presume that the author was trying to put into practice a language constructed by himself, and this idea leads into the next topic, that of artificial languages.

How could one decide whether the Rohonc codex was written in such an artificial language? The fact that the text is totally incomprehensible does not rule out the possibility of human design. Some of the most well-known and "most philosophical" constructed languages also look bewildering

158 *The New Testament of our Lord and Saviour Jesus Christ in Taylor's system of Short Hand as improved by George Odell* (London: G. Odell, 1843). For this rare text, see Bibliothèque Sainte Geneviève, Paris, Réserve, delta 68 223.

159 *The new testament of our Lord and saviour Jesus Christ, printed in en easy reporting style of phonography by Isaac Pitman* (London: Frederick Pitman, 1886), Bibliothèque Sainte Geneviève, Paris, Réserve, delta 68 226.

without their key, their pictograms do not resemble anything, their structure seems illogical for the superficial observer. Only the most talented and lucky codebreaker would be able to break the languages constructed by Kircher or Wilkins. The idea therefore, that the codex is written in such a constructed language is not to be discarded. His author perhaps did not want to conceal or encrypt anything, it is just our bad luck that the table for the character keys and the description of the system are missing. Not even the absence of spaces should necessarily indicate intentional secrecy. The majority of structured languages does not intentionally hide spaces (why would they?) but neither do they emphasize them more than the Rohonc codex does.

Historians of structured languages distinguish between *a posteriori* language designs (that are based on existing languages) and the more "philosophical" *a priori* ones (those that are not). The codex does not seem to belong to those languages that have been designed in search of the lost ancient languages of Adam. Nor does it belong to the philosophical languages designed by Wilkins that offered to classify the entire world.[160] Most likely it is one of the seventeenth-century attempts to create a common writing that is more practical than perfect.[161] These focused on producing such a character-writing that everybody can read in their own language, therefore the name "universal character" or "escriture universelle" (universal writing). Such a system would need a very high number of characters to cover all the different basic concepts and verbs, as pointed out by Francis Bacon and John Wilkins too.[162]

The most famous of the many common writing projects is the *Common Writing* of Francis Lodwick. Many of these designs, however, were never printed. We know from scattered correspondence that in the years around 1630 three Frenchmen, des Vallées, Jean le Maire and D. P. Champagnolles, an Englishman, Philip Kinder, an Irishman, the Reverend Johnson, and a Swedish writer, Benedict Skytte, all working independently, came up with a version of artificial language where the words are represented by symbols. Sadly, none of these have survived – perhaps they were not all completed, perhaps they are lost or are still lying in oblivion in a manuscript library somewhere.[163] Champagnolles' language design must have been pretty

---

160  Slaughter, *Universal languages and scientific taxonomy*.
161  Knowlson, *Universal Language Schemes*, chapter 2.
162  Ibid. 53–56.
163  Slaughter, *Universal languages and scientific taxonomy*, 109–120. Rhodri Lewis, *Language, Mind and Nature: Artificial Languages in England from Bacon to Locke* (Cambridge: Cambridge University Press, 2007), 24–42.

good since he could translate Homer's Iliad for King Charles I with no problem. Still, it was never published, for his widow had asked for too large a
fee for it. Another language, Reverend Johnson's Wit-spell was withheld for
technological reasons – its characters were simply too elaborate to be typeset. The Rohonc codex' text could be any of these projects, or even the end
product of a seventh!

The chronology may undermine this hypothesis. The known history
of universal languages in Hungary started a long time after the presumed
birth date of the Rohonc codex, and they were considerably more primitive
than the codex, except for one (Georg Kalmár's version), which was very
complex, but not completely finished. Nevertheless, there may have been
similar unpublished designs even in the Central European region. Or perhaps this language may have been created in Western Europe in the early
17th century, either by an author whose other books are known today, or by
someone whose name we have not yet heard of.

Accepting the assumption that the Rohonc codex is an artificial language put into practice, one is right to assume also that its characters or
combination of characters stand for complete words, concepts, frequent
connectives and pronouns. It is quite possible that its symbols denote the
*words* of a universal language instead of the *letters* of a particular natural
language. If this was the case, one would need a dictionary for this language, a list that assigns the combination of characters to our modern-day
concepts. In the language designs that survived intact, this list is made up
of several thousand items – in the thick book of Wilkins the lexicon alone
makes up almost three hundred pages.

In conclusion, one should not expect the codex to behave like a cipher
in which the *letters* are coded and where nomenclatures only make up
the minor part of the text. One should rather treat the text as a code language where the whole *words* and sentences are the single units, and the
letter-by-letter cipher text is the minority. As a result, tools of codebreaking
should be used, and not those of cryptanalysis (frequency analysis, vowel
test, word-pattern analysis and so on). The initial and ending character
strings standing before and after the illustrations are very often repeated
with smaller or bigger variations, so they offer themselves as good starting
points for breaking the code,[164] just like the character strings (also repeated
with small variations) identified as numbers.[165]

---

164 Such as on pages 60a, 64a, 65, 68a, 69, 69a, 71, 72, 89a, 91a, 93a, 96, 98.
165 Gyürk Ottó, "Megfejthető-e a Rohonci-kódex?" (Is the Rohonc codex decipherable?) *Élet és Tudomány* 25 (1970), 1923–1924.

Studying these led both Gábor Tokai and Levente Zoltán Király to find a breaking point, first working independently, later in cooperation. They have identified the numeral system of the language, the names of the evangelists mentioned in the text, and have reconstructed the order of the loose pages. They have started the compilation of the code dictionary mentioned above. This research demonstrates that the text contains strong structures and therefore cannot possibly be the work of a lunatic. It is a structured and planned text that describes a given content: a religious text, a Bible commentary with a collection of prayers.[166]

---

166  Király, "Struktúrák a Rohonci-kódex szövegében."

# 9. Summary

This research on the cipher use of early modern Hungary was based on nearly three hundred code keys that survived mostly in manuscripts, and more than sixteen-hundred ciphered letters, about four hundred in manuscripts, the rest published. Considerable amount of "external" sources and comments connected to various forms of cryptology was also taken into account.

A historian of the period emphasized the particularly great number of surviving ciphers from the Hungarian region.[1] How far this is true as compared to other countries of the region (such as Poland, the German states, France or Spain) is still an open question that systematic research has to confirm. This much-needed large-scale comparative analysis would include a methodical study of the nomenclature collections, a typology of the enciphered letters, and a collection of comments on cipher use and on the practice of secrecy. It could be a study of similar structure with similar research questions as this present work, except on a greater scale, covering all of the European sources. Only after that is completed can one satisfactorily place the Hungarian sources and evaluate their richness.

What are the main conclusions of the present work, and how successfully could this research answer the initial research questions?

Despite the fact that the majority of the surviving sources are from the field of politics (diplomacy, envoy's reports, military correspondence, etc.), cryptography extended beyond central diplomacy to be used by various social layers on a day-to-day basis. It was not necessarily a privilege of men, several sources testify that women connected to politics in this way or another used claves too. Apparently, the only criterion for cipher use was literacy.

Just as the users were not all politicians, the purpose of ciphering was not necessarily political either: private life, love affairs, extremely intimate relationships, shame, excessive drinking, military weakness, fear, family feuds, moral sins, details of missionary work, religious conviction, scientific recipes, magic of the talisman were all topics that cried for enciphering. A close examination of the relation of cipher and plain texts provides a deeper understanding of the secrecy concept of the people in the past. What they deemed worthy of encrypting today sometimes seems to lack any sense. Levels of secrecy and privacy can be identified: hardly anything

---

1   Várkonyi, "A tájékoztatás hatalma."

was ever completely encrypted, most encrypted sources made some sense to the reader without a clavis too, and only a more concrete understanding required more elaborate tools of decrypting. Some sources encode certain information, only to give away the code key in the same source (as in the diaries of Haller, Szaniszló or Cementes, or the talisman scripts of Krakow). As the level of decoding was gradual, so was access to the secret: one community had more direct access to a particular letter, codex, diary or message than the other. Secret as content and secrecy as practice sometimes parted: the handbooks of the magic of talisman encrypted the not-so-mysterious names of spirits, while the Rohonc codex was not meant to be encrypted (or so we assume), yet its content is not accessible to us now.

An important facet of the this research focused on the history of cryptographic technology. As the sources allowed to, there was an attempt to map up, how much the cipher users understood the way it worked, whether they realized how important it was to protect the key, how they exchanged claves and how often they replaced them. It was astonishingly difficult in early modern Hungary to decipher a homophonic code, at least this is what the available sources indicate. One area of the monograph where it could be challenged is this: future research should identify a more organized and more successful codebreaking office related to the Vienna Court.

In the three-hundred-year-long period under study, certain trends might be highlighted. Central diplomacy abandoned the monoalphabetic ciphers and gradually turned to more complex homophonic methods. By the end of the period, not only letters of the alphabet, but also syllables had separate signs or numbers in the ciphers, while nullities and code words were more and more extensively used. Parallel to this development, simpler enciphering techniques appeared on lower levels of society in the practice of various professions. The further we descend from diplomatic routines, the more dominant monoalphabetic ciphers become. This was probably due to the lack of professional code breakers on the given level, to the less vital nature of the secret to be protected, and not least that complex homophonic methods were not known and available to everyone. The libraries of the period did carry the reference books that could even have strengthened the ciphering techniques of people outside the spheres of politics, yet hardly anyone used these resources, it looks. Politics may have been the unique source of advanced ciphering methods – the further we get away from it, the simpler methods we find. Future research may find more evidence of knowledge transferred from the Turkish-Ottoman culture, however, there is no sign at the moment that such investigations would yield any result, particularly because the Turks themselves do not seem to have been aware of their rich Arabic heritage in the field of cryptography.

Various types of everyday users became part of the history of ciphers. The widespread use of ciphers and their growing popularity must have been related to the fact that in the three-partite Hungary, partly occupied by the Turks, partly living under Austrian direction, and partly balancing between the two in Transylvania, a particularly large portion of the population was living in the frontier zone and participated (or was forced to participate) in the network of information flow as possessors and transmitters of secrets. The depth they submerged into cryptography and the aims for which they used ciphers indicate a great variability in their attitudes to secrecy.

While many conclusions of local significance might be drawn (and have been drawn) from this large-scale research – regarding technology usage, knowledge transfer, etc. – where I find it most fruitful are the two following claims: 1) histories of cryptography should combine internalistic and externalistic approaches, and 2) investigations into ciphers should take into account the secrecy studies of the same periods, if we really want to understand how this technology was used in real life.

# 10. Appendix

## 10.1. List of cipher tables from early modern Hungary

### Columns of the table

**Location of manuscript:** The call number (in an archive or manuscript collection) of the original copy of the clavis.

**Date:** The year/period when a key was made and / or used.

**Users:** The writer, owner, user and addressee of the key, if available.

**Language:** The base language that was encrypted with the help of a given cipher table – if it can be determined at all, using the alphabet of the table, the table of nomenclatures or other external information relating to the correspondence.

**Type of cipher:** Monoalphabetic, strong or weak homophonic. Abbreviations of this columns: Mono: monoalphabetic, Homo: Homoalphabetic, Weak homo: only a few letters are assigned to homophones.

**Size:** The size of the code table, the approximate number of signs/numbers listed in the code alphabet or the nomenclature table. This number is always estimated, and together with the column that gives the method of encryption, it roughly indicates the strength of the key.

| Location of manuscript | Date | Users | Language | Type of cipher | Size |
|---|---|---|---|---|---|
| Milano State Archives, Sf 650/3,5, photocopy: http://vestigia.hu/ | 1488 | Cipher table prepared by Francesco Oliva for the Hungarian king (Matthias) | Italian | Homo with graphic signs | 140 |
| 44 cipher tables, 19th century copies by Antal Gévay: OSZK Quart. Lat 2254. | 1529–1570 | Habsburg rulers (Charles V and Ferdinand, I), Austrian and Hungarian magnates and political actors (bishop Miklós Gerendy, Hieronymus Laski, János Szapolyai, Johann Malvezzi, Eduardo Provisionali, Carolus Rym, Angelus Caraffa, Rym von Eesenbeke, Gaspar Seredy, David Ungnad, Johann von Tarnow (Ossiek), Antal Verancsics, Christopher Teuffenpach, Archbishop Johann Weze, Albert von Wys, Giambattista Castaldo, Michael Czernowitsch | German, Latin with some Italian and French | Mono, homo and weak homo | 20–130 |
| MNL-OL, R 316, Miscellanea, 27. fol. 1–2 | 1530 | Ferdinand I and János Szapolyai (note: Antonius Verantius, Joannis Regis secretarius) | Latin | Mono | 23 |
| Military History Archives 1548/3. | 1548–1549 | Ferdinand I and his ambassador in Constantinple, Johann Malvezzi | Latin | Homo | 110 |
| 9 cipher tables in the collection of the Staatzkanzlei: HHStA Staatskanzlei Interiora Kt. 12–14. "Chiffrenschlüssel" | 1540–1570 | Ferdinand I and the Habsburg court with Pál Bornemissza, Giambattista Castaldo, Andreas Dudith, György Frater, István Brodarics, Ferenc Zay | Latin, German, Italian | Homo | 35–200 |
| 9 cipher tables: ÖStA HHStA Türkei I. Karton 28. Konv. 2. 1571. s. d. fol. 171–180. | 1571 c. | Maximilian I and his ambassadors in Constantinople (Carolus Rym?) | Latin | Mono, homo and weak homo | 25–70 |

| Source | Date | | Language | Homo and nomenclator tables | 40–120 |
|---|---|---|---|---|---|
| 5 reconstructed cipher tables: Lech Szczucki, Szepessy Tibor, eds. *Epistulae / Andreas Dudithius*, Vol. 2–4. | 1574–5 | Andreas Dudith and the Vienna Chancellery | Latin and Italian | Homo and nomenclator tables | 40–120 |
| Reconstructed cipher table of Bálint Balassi: Révay, *II. Rákóczi Ferenc*, 42. | 1577–1588 | Bálint Balassi, András Balassa (1577) and Sándor Kapy (1588) | Hungarian | Mono | 23 |
| HHStA, Ung Akt. Misc Fasc 422 Conv 1 fol 75 | 1621 | Ferdinand II and Jacobus Curtis | Latin | Mono | 24 |
| Reconstructed cipher table on the basis of the letters in Budapest, University Library Ms G. 4. Fol. Tom. V.: Donáth Regina, "A diplomáciai titkosírás XVII. Századi használatához," *Magyar Könyvszemle*, 1964, 55–62 | 1628 c. | Ferdinand III and his ambassador in Constantinpole, Johann Ludwig Kuefstein | Latin, German and Italian | Weak homo | 35 |
| Archbishop's Archives, Esztergom, AEV n. 148/3 and n. 159, published: Tusor Péter, "Pázmány biboros olasz rejtjelkulcsa: C.H. Motmann 'Residente d'-Ungheria'", *Hadtörténelmi közlemények* 116 (2003) 535–581 | 1634–1635 | Cornelius Heinrich Motmann and Archbishop Péter Pázmány | Italian | Homo | 150 |

| Location of manuscript | Date | Users | Language | Type of cipher | Size |
|---|---|---|---|---|---|
| 6 reconstructed cipher tables from Transylvanian archives: Ötvös Ágoston, *Rejtelmes levelek első Rákóczy György korából, Vámos, Vadai, „Pázmány Péter és I. Rákóczy György titkosírása,"* | 1634–1648 | Péter Pázmány, György Rákóczi I. and his delegates | Hungarian | Mono and weak homo | 22–100 |
| Published cipher table: MTT III/5. 144–146. | 1637 | György Lippay and György Rákóczi I. | Hungarian | Homo | 90 |
| Reconstructed cipher table: Szilágyi Sándor, ed. I. *Rákóczi György svéd és franczia szövetkezéseinek történetéhez,* 52 | 1643 | György Rákóczi I. | Latin | Homo | 80 |
| Reconstructed cipher table: MTT III. 3. vol. 28–30. | 1644 | János Kemény and György Rákóczi I. | Hungarian | Mono | 24 |
| 5 cipher tables from the archives of the Mednyánszky family: MNL-OL P 497, 3. | 1658 | Jónás Mednyánszky and György Rákóczi II | Latin, Hungarian | Mono, homo, pigpen | 22–200, |

| | | | | |
|---|---|---|---|---|
| 1660–1690 | 3 cipher tables from the archives of the Teleki family: MNL–OL P 1238 Collection of Mihály Teleki, miscellaneous documents, cipher keys, some published: Szilágyi Sándor, ed. - Erdélyi Országgyűlési Emlékek 16. 1675–1679, 678–683 | Mihály Teleki and his correspondents | Hungarian, Latin | Mono and weak homo | 30–360 |
| 1663–71 | 3 cipher tables in HHStA, Ung Akt. Spec Verschwörerakten IV. Fasc. 312. Konv. A. fol. 4., Fasc. 314. Konv. B. 1671. I-III. fol. 76–78; Fasc. 317. Konv. D. 1670–1671 fol. 77. | Ferenc Nádasdy and Ferenc Frangepán | Latin | Mono and homo | 160–400 |
| 1664–1668 | 22 cipher tables related to the Wesselényi conspiracy: HHStA Ungarische Akten Specialia Verschwörerakten VII. Varia (Pressburger Kommission etc.) Fasc. 327. Konv. D. Chiffres 1664–1668 | Hungarian political actors, Miklós Zrínyi, Jónás Mednyánszki, Pál Szepesi, Mihály Bory, Ferenc Nádasdy | Hungarian and Latin | Mono, weak and proper homo | 40–1300 |

| Location of manuscript | Date | Users | Language | Type of cipher | Size |
|---|---|---|---|---|---|
| 2 cipher tables in HHStA Ungarische Akten Specialia Verschwörerakten III. Zrinyische Akten Fasc. 296. Konv. B 1668–1669 fol. 77–80. | 1669 | Andreas Gembicki and Péter Zrínyi | Latin | Mono and nomenklators | 40–70 |
| 4 Reconstructed cipher tables: MTT III. vol. 22. 436–446. | 1677–1678 | Dániel Absolon, Bálint Nemessányi, Mihály Teleki | Hungarian, Latin | Mono and homo | 30–200 |
| 6 cipher tables (some of them in two copies) from the letter collection of palatine Pál Esterházy: MNL–OL, P 125 No. 11977O–75, including instructions on the use of cryptography | 1680 c. | Palatine Pál Esterházy and his correspondents (Mátyás Benyovszky, Mihály Apafi, Imre Thököly) | Hungarian and Latin | Weak homo | 80–350 |
| Reconstructed cipher table of Sándor Pál's diary: Jakab Elek, *Sándor Pál kapithia s az erdélyi nemzeti fejedelemség utolsó évei*, MTT 19 (1874): 162–194 | 1687–1690 | Pál Sándor | Hungarian and Latin | Mono | 30 |

| | | | | | |
|---|---|---|---|---|---|
| 77 cipher tables (some of them duplicates) from the archives of Ferenc Rákóczi II that he took into emigration, originals: MNL–OL G 15 Caps. C. Fasc 43.; 19th century handwritten copies: MTA, Manuscript Collection, 4951/5, Some published: Révay, *II. Rákóczi Ferenc* | 1703–1711 | Ferenc Rákóczi II and his correspondents (Joseph Voynovich, Sándor Nedeczky, Dániel Esterházy, István Ebeczky, László Kökényesdi) generals, delegates, allies, and his wife including also a few tables of the Habsburg Emperor and his generals decrypted by Rákóczi. The collection also includes the famous Clavis musicalis | Latin, French, Hungarian, German | Homo (including a few mono) | 40–750, av: 160 |
| 18 cipher tables (some of them duplicates) from the Archives of Ferenc Rákóczi II that he took into emigration, originals: MNL–OL G 15 Caps. C. Fasc 44, 19th-century handwritten copies: MTA, Manuscript Collection, 4951/5, Some published: Révay, *II. Rákóczi Ferenc* | 1703–1711 | Ferenc Rákóczi II and his correspondents, delegates and allies (including the ambassadors of the French Court, Rivier and Bonnac, and the Polish Elżbieta Helena Sieniawska) | French | Homo | 100–550 av: 350 |
| 7 cipher tables (some of them duplicates), originals: MNL–OL P. 396 -1, (Acta Rakocziana) 185 (no. 10543–6), and 31 (no. 11345), from the archives of the Károlyi family | 1703–1711 | Rákóczi's entourage | Hungarian? | Homo and mono | 60–2700 av: 80 |

| Location of manuscript | Date | Users | Language | Type of cipher | Size |
|---|---|---|---|---|---|
| 34 cipher keys (with many duplicates) from Pál Ráday's political documents: Ráday Archives C64-4d2-10 and 25. 19th century handwritten copies: MTA, Manuscript Collection, 4951/5, Some published: Révay, II. Rákóczi Ferenc | 1703–1711 | Ferenc Rákóczi II, Pál Ráday and their correspondents and delegates Domokos Brenner, Ernst Jablonszky, János Pápai, Sándor Nedeczky, Ferenc Horváth, Máté, Thalaba István Dobozi, Ádám Mányoki, Gáspár, Pápai, József Vojnovich, Charlotte Amalie von Hessen-Wanfried (Rákóczi's wife), János Körtvélyessy | French, Latin, Hungarian and some German | Homo | 60–400 |
| Reconstructed cipher table: AR I. vol. 4. Appendix | 1704 | Ferenc Rákóczi II and Miklós Bercsényi | Hungarian | Mono | 25 |
| Military History Archives E. 1705/18 | 1705 | Sándor Károlyi and Miklós Bercsényi, generals of Ferenc Rákóczi II | Hungarian | Mono | 26 |

## 10.2.    List of ciphertexts from early modern Hungary

### Columns of the table

**Publication:** The bibliographic data of the published text.

**Manuscript:** The call number (in an archive or manuscript library) of the original copy of the ciphertext.

**Date:** The date when a ciphertext was written.

**Users:** The number of the letters to be found in the given publication or under the given call number (unless there is only one), and the writer, signer, and addressee of the message, if available.

**Language:** The language of the plain text.

**Type of cipher:** Monoalphabetic, strong or weak homophonic. Abbreviations of this columns: Mono: monoalphabetic, Homo: Homoalphabetic, Weak homo: only a few letters are assigned to homophones.

**Solved:** y(es) or n(o), depending on whether the plain text is available, or whether key is provided in the source publication and whether the ciphertext can be read using the key available.

| Publication | Manuscript | Date | Users | Language | Type of cipher | Solved? |
|---|---|---|---|---|---|---|
| Gyula Décsényi, "Mátyás király leveleskönyve a gróf Khuen-Héderváry család könyvtárában," Magyar Könyvszemle, 19 (1891): 169–175; György Rácz, ed. A Héderváry-kódex hasonmás kiadása. | | 1470–1472 | Janus Pannonius? | Latin | Mono, pig-pen cipher | y |
| Iván Nagy and Albert B. Nyáry, eds. Magyar diplomacziai emlékek Mátyás király korából 1458–1490. III, 14–15. | Mf. MNL-OL, Mf. 8620. | 1482 | Matthias Corvinus to Ercole d'Este, prince of Ferrara | Latin | Graphic signs | y |
| 8 letters: Iván Nagy and Albert B. Nyáry - Magyar diplomacziai emlékek Mátyás király korából 1458–1490. III., 13–17, 90–91, 166–168, Albert Berzeviczy, ed. Aragóniai Beatrix magyar királyné életére vonatkozó okiratok (MHH 4. Dipl. 39.), 437, 38, 39, 445. | Microfilm copy on the basis of the Modena State Archives: MNL-OL, Mf. 8620. | 1482–1486 | Beatrix of Aragon, Queen of Hungary and Matthias Corvinus, king of Hungary and Eleonor of Aragon, princess of Ferrara, Cardinale Ippolito I. d'Este, Ercole d'Este, prince of Ferrara | Italian | Graphic signs | y and n |
| 50 letters related to Hungarian history in the Modena State Archives | Photocopies: http://vestigia.hu/ | 1482–1519 | Beatrix of Aragon, Queen of Hungary and Eleonor of Aragon, princess of Ferrara, Cardinale Ippolito I. d'Este and others | Latin and Italian | | y and n |
| Miklós Vértesy, "Titkos írás egy Corvinában," Magyar Könyvszemle, 77 (1961): 167–169. | | 1491 | Beatrix of Aragon, Queen of Hungary | Latin | Mono graphic signs | y |

| Reference | Source | Description | Date | Language | Cipher | Quoted |
|---|---|---|---|---|---|---|
| Albert Berzeviczy, ed. Aragóniai Beatrix magyar királyné életére vonatkozó okiratok, (MHH 4. Dipl. 39.), 184. | State Archives of Milan | Tamás Bakócz, bishop of Győr, Maffeo Trivilliense envoy of Milano | 1491 | Latin | | y |
| Péter Kasza: Stephanus Brodericus: Epistulae, 636. | BN T.6. 43 r-v | István Brodarics to Sigismund, king of Poland | 1525 | Latin | Mono, graphic signs | y |
| | 18 reports: HHStA, Ung. Akt. Allg. Akt. Fasc. 9–18. | Ambassadors to János Szapolyai | 1528–1531 | Latin | Mono, graphic signs | y |
| Armand Dezső Herzfelder, "Kolozsvári Czementes János könyve" Magyar Könyvszemle (1896): 276–301, 351–373. | OSZK Oct. Hung. 484. | János Cementes of Kolozsvár, diary | 1530–1586 | Latin and Hungarian | Mono, graphic signs | y |
| József Bartha, "Putnoki levél," Magyar Könyvszemle, 1898: 128–130. | OSZK fol. Hung 887 (?) | Petrus Presbiter to Emerico de Putnok | 1531 | Hungarian | Mono, graphic signs | y |
| MTT IV/9. 291–292; Péter Kasza, Stephanus Brodericus: Epistulae, 2012; 636. | MNL-OL, E 185, fol. 52–53. | István Brodarics to Tamás Nádasdy | 1532 | Latin | Graphic signs | y |
| 2 letters: Századok 1878, 600 and 603. | | Gábor Sanchez, resident of Ferdinand I to his king | 1536 | Latin | | Partially quoted |
| 13 letters: MTT III/1. 731–791, Századok 1878 793. no. 2. | | Ferdinand I and Johann von Wese, archbishop of Lund | 1537–1538 | Latin | Plaintext | y |
| 7 letters, Antal Gévay, Gesandtschaft König Ferdinands I. an Sultan Suleiman I.1540–1541, 105–137. | ÖStA HHStA Türkei I. Karton 5. Konv.2. 1541. fol. 1–47. | Hieronym Laski to Ferdinand I | 1541 | Latin | | y |
| 13 letters: MTT III/1. 260–269, 501–558; III/2. 506–519. | | György Fráter and Johann von Wese, archbishop of Lund, Ferdinand I | 1542–1543 | Latin | | y |

| Publication | Manuscript | Date | Users | Language | Type of cipher | Solved? |
|---|---|---|---|---|---|---|
| Vilmos Fraknói, ed., Monumenta Hungariae Historica 3. Monumenta Comitialia regni Hungariae 2. 1537 – 1545 - XI, 522–525. | | 1543 | Gabor Werner to Ferdinand I | Latin | | y |
| 8 letters Révay, Titkosírások, 66–67. | War History Archives, 1548/3–21 and 1549/3. | 1548 | Ferdinand I and Johann Malvezzi | Latin | Homo | n |
| MTT III/5. 113–114. | | 1548 | Sultan Suleiman to György Fráter | Latin | | y |
| 42 letters: MTT III/15. 478–677. | | 1552–1553 | Ferdinand I and Giambattista Castaldo | Latin | | Regesta |
| 3 letters: MTT IV/6. 224–230. | | 1553–1554 | András Báthory and Tamás Nádasdy | Hungarian | Graphic signs and letters | n |
| László Szalay, ed., Verancsics Antal m. kir. helytartó, esztergomi érsek összes munkái 3. Első portai követség 1553–1554. MHH 2. Script.4, 271–274. | | 1554 | Antal Verancsics to Ferdinand I | Latin | | y |
| 4 letters: MTT IV/7. 130–32, 249–250. | | 1555–1556 | László Kerecsényi and Tamás Nádasdy | Hungarian | Graphic signs | n |
| | 5 letters: ÖStA HHStA Türkei I. Karton 18. Konv 2 and 19. Konv. 1–2, 5. 1564. | 1564 | Albert de Wyss, Emperor Maximilian I, and Ferdinand I. | Latin | | y |

| | | | | | |
|---|---|---|---|---|---|
| 10 letters: ÖStA HHStA Türkei I. Karton 26–30. | 1570–1574 | Emperor Maximilian I and Carolus Rym, David Ungnad | Latin | | y |
| 14 letters: ÖStA HHStA Türkei I. Karton 28. Konv. 1. 1571. X-XII. fol. 44–47, 52–54, 65–66. Konv. 2. 1571. s. d. fol. 108, 110–111, 113, 114–116, Konv.3. 1571.fol. 33–87. | 1571 c. | Ambassadors (including Carolus Rym) to the Habsburg court | Latin | Graphic signs | mostly: n |
| 6 letters: ÖStA HHStA Türkei I. Karton 32, 34, 37, 43, 44, 93, 110. | 1577–1581 | Friedrich Breuner, Sinzendorff, David Ungnad, Emperor Rudolf II | German | | y |
| 5 letters: Béla Stoll, ed. Balassi Bálint, Összes versei, 260–394 | 1577–1588 | Bálint Balassi, András Balassi, Sándor Kapy | Hungarian and Latin | Mono | y |
| 4 letters: ÖStA HHStA Türkei I. Karton 45. Konv. 1. 1581.IX. | 1581 | to Ambassador Breuner | Latin | | y |
| ÖStA HHStA Türkei I. Karton 48. Konv. 3. 1583.04-06. fol. 137–144., 147–151. | 1583 | by Ambassador Breuner | German | | n |

| Publication | Manuscript | Date | Users | Language | Type of cipher | Solved? |
|---|---|---|---|---|---|---|
| 3 letters: MTT II/11. 162–187. | | 1597 | Princess Maria Kristierna and Princess Maria | German | Numbers between 10 és 50 | n |
| 2 letters MTT III/7. 57, 445. | | 1600 | David Ungnad to Rudolf I and Barvitus | Latin | | Regesta |
| | 9 letters: ÖStA HHStA Türkei I. Karton 93. Konv. 1, 2 and 3. | 1611–1616 | Emperor Matthias II, Michael Starzer, and Hanns von Mollart, head of the Hofkriegsrat | German | | y |
| | HHStA, Ung Akt. Misc Fasc 422 Conv 1 fol 72–79. | 1621 | Emperor Ferdinand II and Jacobus Curtis | Latin | Mono | n |
| MTT III/9. 658–659. 218. | | 1626 | Gábor Bethlen to Georg Wilhelm of Brandenburg | Latin | | y |
| Regina Donáth, "A diplomáciai titkosírás XVII. századi használatához," *Magyar Könyvszemle*, 1964, 55–62. | 16 letters: ELTE University Library, G. 4. Fol. Tom. V. | 1628 | Ambassadors in Constantinople (Johann Ludwig Kuefstein) to Ferdinand III | German | Homo | y |
| 3 letters: MTT III/21. 685–697 and III/22, 95–96. | | 1630 | Weighard Schulitz to Johann von Khospott | Latin, German | | y |
| Károly Szabó, ed. *Erdélyi Történelmi Adatok*, 4, 1 – 103 | missing | 1630–1644 | Gábor Haller, diary | Latin and Hungarian | Pigpen and letter transposition | y |

| | | | A secret correspondent to the imperial court | | Graphic signs | solved in a separate letter |
|---|---|---|---|---|---|---|
| 2 letters: Péter Tusor, "Pázmány bíboros olasz rejtjelkulcsa: C.H. Motmann 'Residente d'Ungheria': A római magyar agenzia történetéhez", Hadtörténelmi közlemények 116 (2003) 535–581 | 2 letters: ÖStA HHStA Türkei I. Kt. 112. Konv. 5. fol. 1–28. | 1632 | Cornelius Heinrich Motmann to Archbishop Péter Pazmany | Italian | Homo | y |
| | Archbishop's Archives, Esztergom AEV n. 148/3 and n. 159 | 1634–1635 | | Italian | | |
| 49 letters: Ágoston Ötvös, Rejtelmes levelek első Rdkóczy György korából, Révay, Titkosírások, 87–107; Vámos, Vadai, "Pázmány Péter és I. Rákóczy György titkosírása." | Batthyány Library, Alba Iulia? | 1634–1648 | György Rákóczi I and his ambassadors, and Péter Pázmány | Hungarian | Weak homo and mono | y |
| 3 letters: MTT III/18. 428, 631. | | 1638–1644 | György Rákóczi I and György Rákóczi II | Hungarian | | Regesta |
| 30 letters: Antal Beke and Samu Barabás, eds., I. Rákóczi György és a porta, 127–130, 162–163, 423–439, 480–82, 489–502, 593–595, 635–6, 641–2, 666–686, 694–96, 868–880. | | 1639–1646 | György Rákóczi I and his ambassadors (István Tholdalaghi, István Körössy, István Rácz, István Réthy, György Hajdú and István Szalánczi) | Hungarian | | y |
| 45 letters: Sándor Szilágyi, ed. Levelek és okiratok I. Rákóczy György keleti összeköttetései történetéhez. | | 1639–1646 | György Rákóczi I and his diplomatic relations | Latin and Hungarian | | y |

| Publication | Manuscript | Date | Users | Language | Type of cipher | Solved? |
|---|---|---|---|---|---|---|
| | 26 letters: MNL-OL, E 190, Arch Fam. Rákóczi, 43. 5. | 1642–1659 | György Rákóczi I, György Rákóczi II, Zsigmond Rákóczi, Ákos Barcsay, Zsuzsanna Lórántffy, Jónás Mednyánszky | Hungarian | Mono and homo | Mostly: n |
| 13 letters: Áron Szilády and Sándor Szilágyi, eds. Török-magyarkori állam-okmánytár III–VII. 5 vols. | | 1643–1685 | György Rákóczi I, György Rákóczi II and Zsigmond Rákóczi | Hungarian | | y |
| 4 letters: Sándor Szilágyi, ed. Okmánytár I. Rákóczy György svéd és franczia szövetkezéseinek történetéhez. | | 1643–1646 | György Rákóczi I and his alliances | Latin and German | Mono | y |
| 2 letters: Sándor Szilágyi, ed., I. Rákóczi György svéd és franczia szövetkezéseinek történetéhez 1643 (MHH 4. Dipl. 21.), 50–55. | | 1643–1644 | György Rákóczi I and Linnardt Tornsenson | Latin and German | Homo | y |
| 8 letters: MTT III/3. 28–56 | | 1644 | János Kemény and György Rákóczi I | Hungarian | Mono | y |
| 18 letters: Sándor Szilágyi, ed., A két Rákóczi György fejedelem családi levelezése. (MHH 4. Dipl. 24) | | 1644–1647 | György Rákóczi I, György Rákóczi II and Zsigmond Rákóczi | Hungarian | | y |
| 27 letters: MTT III/10. 224–228, 286–287, 432–433, 445–447, 654–676, III/11. 229–300; III/13. 229–257; 291–292, 617–622. | | 1646–1658 | The correspondence of Prince Zsigmond Rákóczi with Johann Heinrich Bisterfeld, János Daniel, Jónás Mednyánszky, András Klobusicki, György Rákóczi II, György Rákóczi I, István Szentpáli, János Kemény | Latin and Hungarian | | y and n |

| Reference | Date | Description | Language | Notes | |
|---|---|---|---|---|---|
| 46 letters: Sándor Szilágyi, ed. *Erdély és az északkeleti háború I–II* | 1648–1659 | György Rákóczi II and his diplomatic relations | Latin and Hungarian | | y |
| 3 letters: MTT III/14. 106–108, 225–230. | 1651 | Jónás Mednyánszky, Zsigmond Rákóczy, and András Klobusicki | Hungarian | | y |
| Sándor Szilágyi ed., *Erdélyi Országgyűlési Emlékek 13. 1661–1664*, 427–470. The enciphered parts: 444, 451, 469, 471. | 1653 | János Simonius, diary | German | Only the vowels substituted | y |
| Sándor Szilágyi ed., *Erdélyi Országgyűlési Emlékek 11. 1649–1658*, chapter 24: 185–186. | 1654 | Ferenc Thordaj to György Rákóczi II | Hungarian | | y |
| 6 letters: Széchy, *Miklós Zrínyi*, vol. 3. 335–338, vol 4. 252–269. | 1654–1657 | Miklós Zrínyi to prince György Rákóczi II. | Hungarian | Homo | y |
| MTT II/6. 86–89. | 1655 | Jónás Mednyánszky and János Kemény | Hungarian | Numbers | n |
| 57 letters: Sándor Szilágyi, ed., *Okmánytár II. Rákóczi György diplomacziai összeköttetéseihez.* (MHH 1. Dipl. 23.) | 1655–1656 | The ambassadors of György Rákóczi II to the prince | Hungarian | | y |
| 2 letters: Sándor Szilágyi, "II. Rákóczi György fejedelem összeköttetése Nádasdy Ferenczel," *Századok 7* (1874): 441–476: 474–475. | 1659 | Ferenc Nádasdy to György Rákóczi II | Hungarian | | |

| Publication | Manuscript | Date | Users | Language | Type of cipher | Solved? |
|---|---|---|---|---|---|---|
| 299 letters: Teleki 1, 2, 3, 4, 6, 7 and 8. | | 1659–1679 | Mihály Teleki and Mihály Apafi I, Dénes Bánffy, Mihály Bessenyei, Béthune, Kata Bornemissza, István Dalmády, István Ébeni, Péter Faigel, Louis Forval, Toussaint de Forbin-Janson, Simon Kemény, János Nemes, Mihály Pataki, András Radics, Dominique Reverend, Ferenc Rhédey, Pál Szepesi, István Naláczi, Pál Wesselényi, Dániel Absolon, Mária Széchy, Judit Vér, Imre Thököly, Mihály Thúry | Hungarian and Latin | | y, with the exceptions: Teleki 1: 220–21, 3: 582, 8: 9–10, 10–11, 19–20, 20–21, 22– 26, 27, 30–32, 37–39, 40, 42, 43, 45, 51–52, **88, 96, 306** |
| | 3 letters: MNL-OL, P 125 No. 11967–9. | 1660–1710? | Palatine Pál Esterházy | ? | numbers between 10 és 50 | n |
| | 2 letters: HHStA, Ung. Akt. Spec Fasc 310 Conv A fol 17, 32–35. | 1662–1663 | Ferenc Wesselényi, István Vitnyédi, Ferenc Nádasdy | Hungarian | Mono | y and n |

| Source | Year | Correspondents | Language | Cipher type | Solved |
|---|---|---|---|---|---|
| 3 letters: MTT II/4. 64–65 | 1663 | | Hungarian | | y |
| 5 letters: ÖStA HHStA Ungarische Akten Specialia Verschwörerakten VII. Varia Fasc. 327. Konv. D. Chiffres 1664–1668. | 1664–1668 | Anonymous letters, probably related to the Wesselényi movement | ? | Numbers | n |
| Mihály Héder, Benedek Láng, Szabolcs Lévai, "Filológiai okok egy monoalfabetikus titkosírásfejtő szoftver mellett," Magyar Könyvszemle, 129 (2013/4): 511–519. one letter solved  2 letters: MNL-OL. E 199. Fasc. 8. pallium 1. | 1664–1670 | Ferenc Wesselényi | Latin | Mono | y and n |
| 2 letters: Áron Szilárdy and Sándor Szilágyi, ed. - MHH 4. Dipl. VI.: Török–Magyarkori Állam–Okmánytár. vol. IV, 233–234, 294–95. | 1665 | Mihály Czermeni to Mihály Apafi | Hungarian | | y |
| 4 letters: József Jankovics, ed., Bethlen Miklós levelei, vol. 1. 143–147, 185–186, 379.  MNL-OL P. 659. Fasc. 14. 329; Fasc. 31. 753; Fasc. 29. 740; Fasc. 25. 703. | 1666 | Miklós Bethlen, Mihály Apafi, Mihály Teleki, László Gyulafi | Hungarian | Draft of enciphered letters | y |
| HHStA Ungarische Akten Specialia Verschwörerakten III. Zrinyische Akten Fasc. 296. Konv. B 1668–1669 fol. 75–83. | 1669 | Andreas Gembicki to Péter Zrinyi | Latin | Mono | key is attached |

| Publication | Manuscript | Date | Users | Language | Type of cipher | Solved? |
|---|---|---|---|---|---|---|
| 3 letters: MTT III/13. 515–517. | | 1675 | Toussaint de Forbin-Janson and Mihály Teleki | Latin | | y |
| 6 letters: MTT III/13. 513–535. | | 1675–1678 | Mihály Teleki and Toussaint de Forbin-Janson, Reverend, Lanfranc de Forval | Latin | | y |
| 32 letters: MTT III. vol. 22. 436–446, Teleki 8. 179–216, Teleki 7. 371–373, 450–452, 466–469., MTT III/6. 5–59 | | 1677–1678 | Dániel Absolon, Bálint Nemessányi, Mihály Teleki | Hungarian and Latin | Homo | y |
| MTT III/9. 488. | | 1678 | Imre Thököly to Louis XIV | Latin | | y |
| | 6 letters: OSZK Fol. Hung. 1389/ 1: 18–167. | 1678–1693 | Letters related to the Kuruc battles between D. Reverend, Imre Thököly, Ferenc Galambos | French and Hungarian | Homo | y and n |
| Károly Torma, Történelmi Tár, 1889 (12). 230–269, 503–522, 708–727, (13), 1890. 77–101, 307–327, 493–510, 757–770, (14), 1891. 267–295. | | 1682–1711 | Zsigmond Szaniszló, diary | Hungarian with some Latin | Mono | y |
| 10 letters: MTT III/10. and 11. | | 1685 | János Sobieski and Mihály Teleki | Latin | | y |
| 2 letters: MTT III/10. 742. and MTT III/13. 696–697. | | 1685 | Mihály Inczédi to Mihály Teleki | Hungarian | | y |
| Áron Szilárdy and Sándor Szilágyi, eds. - MHH 4. Dipl. VIII. Török–Magyar-kori Állam–Okmánytár VI, 506–508. | | 1685 | Miklós Draskovich and István Kalmánczay | Hungarian | | y |

| Published source | MS / Archive reference | Date | Author / content | Language | Mono/Homo | y/n |
|---|---|---|---|---|---|---|
| Elek Jakab, *Sándor Pál kapithia s az erdélyi nemzeti fejedelemség utolsó évei*, MTT 19 (1874): 162–194 | | 1687–1690 | Sándor Pál, diary | Hungarian and Latin | Mono | y |
| Bay Mihály diáriuma (MHH II. 23/2.) 461–578. | MNL OL. G. 15. Caps A.1. Fasc 24. fol. 75–124r. | 1692 - 1693 | Mihály Bay, diary | Hungarian and Latin | Mono and homo | y |
| *Sándor Gáspár Naplója: Késmárki Thököly Imre és némely főbb híveinek naplói* MHH II. 23/2.) 627–646, 651–708. | MNL-OL. G. 15. Caps A.1. Fasc 24. fol. 1–28. | 1693 | Gáspár Sándor, diary | Hungarian | Homo | y |
| 505 letters: AR I. vol. 1–10. | | 1704–1711 | Miklós Bercsényi and Ferenc Rákóczi II, János Bottyán, Gáspár Pápai, Antal Brenner, Gabriel Golovkin, Constantinus Kantamír, Sándor Nedeczki, Antal Esterházy, Dániel Esterházy, Sándor Károlyi, Ádám Vay, Pál Ráday, Ferenc Horváth | Hungarian (some Latin) | | y |
| | 100 letters: MNL-OL. G 15. Caps. C Fasc 39. | 1704–1706 | Ferenc Rákóczi II (often using pseudonyms: Nathanaël Sylver, Pompeio Cesoni) and his contacts in Poland | French | Homo | y |
| Kálmán Benda, *Ráday Pál iratai*, (1703–1706), 284–96. | Ráday Archives, I. d/2–3 | 1705 | Pál Ráday, diary | Hungarian | Homo | y |
| Kálmán Benda, *Ráday Pál iratai*, (1703–1706), 274–5. | Ráday Archives, I. c. 1107 | 1705 | Ferenc Rákóczi II to Pál Ráday | Hungarian | Homo | y |
| | 7 letters: Military History Archives E. 1705/4–17 | 1705 | Sándor Károlyi, Miklós Bercsényi, Ferenc Rákóczi II, the Court Military Council and Egger v. Lanzenfeld | Hungarian and German | Mono | y and n |

| Publication | Manuscript | Date | Users | Language | Type of cipher | Solved? |
|---|---|---|---|---|---|---|
| 30 letters: Kálmán Benda, *Ráday Pál iratai*, (1703–1706), 74–77, 195–6, 220–24, 238–40, 265–270, 276–7, 297–8, 299–307, 310–315, 324–326, 480–483, 489–495, 508–511, 555–563, 577–8, 582–5, 614–615, 618–9, 622–3, 317–8, 390–1, 284–96. | Ráday Archives, I. d/2–4, 2–10, 2–13, 2–17, 2–18, and 2–24. | 1705–1707 | Pál Ráday and Hermelin Olai, Jablonski Daniel Ernest, János Pápai, László Kökényesdi, József Vojnovich | Latin | Homo | y |
| | 19 letters: Ráday Archives C64-4d2-10. | 1705–1706 | László Vetési Kökényesdi and Pál Ráday, Ferenc Rákóczi II, Tournon | Hungarian (some French) | Homo | y |
| | 2 letters: MNL-OL G 15 Caps. D. Fasc 81. | 1706 | Ferenc Rákóczi II and his envoys (András Bay) | Hungarian | Homo | y and n |
| | 8 letters: MNL-OL G 15 Caps. C. Fasc 36. | 1706 | Ferenc Rákóczi II and his envoys in Constantinople | Hungarian | Homo | y |
| | 23 letters: MNL-OL G 15 Caps. C. Fasc 33. | 1706 | Ferenc Rákóczi II and his envoys in Constantinople (Ferenc Horváth, János Pápai) | Hungarian | Homo | y |
| | 5 letters: MNL-OL P. 396–1, (Acta Ra-kocziana) 2, 20, 23, (no. 379, 7950–52) MNL-OL P. 398, (Rákoczi letters) (no. 35409) | 1706–1710 | Sándor Károlyi, János Pongrácz, Ferenc Szluha, Gábor Nagyszegi, Krisztina Barkóczy | Hungarian | Mono | y |

| | | | | | | |
|---|---|---|---|---|---|---|
| | 10 letters: MNL-OL G 15 Caps. D. Fasc 79. | 1706–1707 | Ferenc Rákóczi II and his ambassadors (Gáspár Pápai) | Hungarian | Homo | y |
| | 3 letters: MNL-OL G 15 Caps. D. Fasc 82. | 1707 | Ferenc Rákóczi II and his diplomatic contacts | French | Homo | y and n |
| | 15 letters: MNL-OL G 15 Caps. D. Fasc 80. | 1707 | Ferenc Rákóczi II and his envoys in Constantinople (János Pápai, Ferenc Horváth, Mihály Hentér) | Hungarian | Homo | y |
| | 3 letters: MNL-OL G 15 Caps. E. Fasc 109. | 1708 | Ferenc Horváth of Ládony, Constantinople, to Ferenc Rákóczi II | Hungarian | Homo | y |
| Kálmán Benda, *Pápai János törökországi naplói* (two letters published) | 9 letters: MNL-OL G 15 Caps. E. Fasc 109. | 1708 | Ferenc Rákóczi II and his ambassadors in Constantinople (János Pápai, Ferenc Horváth) | Hungarian | Homo | y |
| Kálmán Benda, *Pápai János törökországi naplói* (two letters published) | 30 letters: MNL-OL G 15 Caps. H. Fasc 226 | 1710 | Ferenc Rákóczi II and János Pápai | Hungarian | Homo | y |
| | 3 letters: MNL-OL, P 237 (archives of the Festetics family, misc. documents 10. d. 2. items 38–46. | 1710–1711 | Ferenc Rákóczi II, one of them probably to his wife, Charlotte Amalie von Hessen-Wanfried | Latin | Numbers | y |
| | 10 letters: MNL-OL G 15 Caps. J. Fasc 256/e | 1711 | Ferenc Rákóczi II and various correspondents (including Mihály Mikes) | Hungarian | Homo | y |

| Publication | Manuscript | Date | Users | Language | Type of cipher | Solved? |
|---|---|---|---|---|---|---|
| Imre Bánkúti, "Források Kassa 1710–1711. évi védelméhez," Hadtörténeti Közlemények 2003, 910–921 | 3 letters: MNL-OL G 15. Caps. H. Fasc. 237. | 1711 | Dániel Esterházy and Ferenc Rákóczi II | Hungarian | | y |
| Béla Köpeczi, ed. II. Rákóczi Ferenc Válogatott levelei, 68. | MNL-OL G 15. Caps. H. Fasc. 253. | 1711 | Ferenc Rákóczi II and Ádám Vay | Hungarian | Plaintext | y |
| Ödön Sztankovics, trans., "Zakarjás János és Fáy Dávid délamerikai jezsuita misszionáriusok úti levelei (1749–1756)", Földrajzi Közlemények, 1910 (38.), 115–128, 215–236. | ELTE University Library, G. 689 | 1749–1756 | János Zakarjás to father József Bartakovics | Latin and Hungarian | Language change and Hungarian runic | y |

# Acknowledgements

I would like to thank the following scholars, friends and scholar-friends for their help: Balázs Ablonczy, Gábor Almási, Leopold Auer, Craig Bauer, Dóra Bobory, Gergely Buzás, Enikő Békés, Sándor Bene, András Cieger, Rumen István Csörsz, Ágnes Deák, Claire Fanger, Gábor Farkas, István Fazekas, Ottó Gecser, Mihály Héder, Gábor Kármán, Péter Kasza, László Z. Karvalics, Dóra Kerekes, Levente Zoltán Király, Judit Klement, Szabolcs Lévai, Karl de Leeuw, Petr Mata, Veronika Novák, Beata Megyesi, Gábor Klaniczay, István Monok, Géza Pálffy, Csaba Pléh, Jolanta Rzegocka, Dóra Sallay, Christiane Schaefer, Klaus Schmeh, Attila Sunkó, Gábor Tokai, Péter Váradi, Ágnes R. Várkonyi, and the members of the Philosophy and History of Science Department at the Budapest University of Technology and Economics, particularly: Márta Fehér, Tihamér Margitay, János Tanács, Gábor Zemplén and Nóra Molnár, and finally my wife, Márta Tarnai.

For the extraction and briefing of a large part of the printed sources, I employed a research assistant, Dániel Kálmán, for the thorough work of whom, I am grateful. The more extensive, Hungarian version of this book profited a lot from the help of the editors of the Balassi publishing house. Karl de Leeuw, editor of the present series at Atlantis - Amsterdam University Press, was so kind as to read the whole text carefully and to comment and correct it in many ways.

I thank the following libraries and archives for their help: Hungarian National Archives, Ráday Archives, Haus-, Hof-, und Staatsarchiv, National Széchényi Library (Manuscript Department), War History Archives (Budapest), Library of the Hungarian Academy of Sciences (Manuscript Department), ELTE University Library (Manuscript Department), Biblioteca Apostolica Vaticana, Archivum Secretum Vaticanum, Bibliothèque Saint-Geneviève (Paris). A previous, larger version of this book has been published in Hungarian, I thank the Balassi Publishing House for all the work they invested into this previous book.

I am grateful to the Collegium de Lyon, where thanks to an Eurias fellowship, I could concentrate exclusively on my research for a year, and to the Hungarian National grant, OTKA K 101544, which provided me with the necessary infrastructure. Last but not least, this book could be finished thanks to the funding provided by the Hanse-Wissenschaftskolleg, Institute for Advanced Study, Delmenhorst, Germany.

# Earlier publications

Parts of this book have been published in the following articles:

Benedek Láng, "Why don't we decipher an outdated cipher system? The Codex of Rohonc," *Cryptologia*, 34 (2010): 115–144.

Benedek Láng, "People's secrets: Towards a social history of Early Modern cryptography," *The Sixteenth Century Journal*, 45/2 (2014): 291–308.

Benedek Láng, "Ciphers in Magic: Techniques of Revelation and Concealment," *Magic, Ritual, and Witchcraft*, 2015/2, 125–141.

Benedek Láng, "Shame, love and alcohol: Private ciphers in early modern Hungary," *Cryptologia* 39/3 (2015): 276–287.

Benedek Láng, "Real-Life Cryptology: Enciphering Practice in Early Modern Hungary," in Katherine Ellison and Susan Kim, eds. *A Material History of Medieval and Early Modern Ciphers: Cryptography and the History of Literacy*, (Routledge, 2017), 223–240.

# Bibliography

## Manuscript Sources

ELTE – Eötvös Loránd Tudományegyetem, Egyemeti könyvtár (ELTE University Library)
    G. 4.    Fol. Tom. V. Johann Ludwig Kuefstein's letters to Ferdinand III
    G. 689  letters of János Zakarjás

MNL OL – Magyar Nemzeti Levéltár Országos Levéltára, Budapest (Hungarian National Archives, Budapest)
    E 190    Archives of the Hungarian Treasury, Rakóczi family archives
    E 196    Archives of the Hungarian Treasury, Thurzó family archives
    E 199    fasc. 8, Archives of the Hungarian Treasury, Enciphered drafts of Ferenc Wesselényi
    G 15     Archives of the Rákóczi War of Independence, Caps. C. Fasc 33, 36, 43 and 44. Caps. D 80, 81, Caps. E. Fasc 109. Caps. F. Fasc 160; Caps. H. Fasc 226 and 237.
    P 125    Esterházy family archives
    P 398    Károlyi family archives
    P 497    Mednyánszky family archives
    P 1238  Mihály Teleki Collection, Miscellenous documents, Cipher keys

MTA – Magyar Tudományos Akadémia (Hungarian Academy of Sciences), Manuscript Department, 4951/5, manuscript copies of the Rákóczi cipher keys

OSZK – Országos Széchényi Könyvtár (National Széchényi Library)
    Quart. Lat 2254, Cipher key collection of Antal Gévay
    Oct. Hung. 484, Diary of János Cementes of Kolozsvár

ÖStA HHStA – Österreichisches Staatsarchiv, Haus-, Hof- und Staatsarchiv, Vienna
    Staatskanzlei Interiora, Chiffrenschlüssel Kt 13–21
    Ungarische Akten, Allg. Akt. Fasc 9–12, 15, 18
    Ungarische Akten Specialia Verschwörerakten
        III.   Zrínyische Akten Fasc. 296. Konv. B. 1668–1669
        IV.   Nádasdysche Akten Fasc. 312 Konv. A. and Fasc. 314. Konv. B. 1671.

V.    Frangepanische Akten Fasc. 317. Konv. D.
VII.   Varia Fasc. 327. Konv. D. Chiffres 1664–1668
Ungarische Akten Misc Fasc 422 Conv 1
Staatenabteilungen Türkei I. Kt. 5, 18–19, 26–35, 43–45, 48, 93–96, 103–4, 110–112.

Ráday Levéltár (Ráday Archives) C64-4d2-10 and 25, I d/2–3, 4, 10, 13, and 24, Political documents of Pál Ráday

Hadtörténelmi Levéltár (War History Archives, Budapest), 1548 and E. 1705

## Edited Sources

Al-Kadi. "Origins of cryptology: The Arab contributions." *Cryptologia*, 16 (1992): 97–126.
*Archivum Rákóczianum* (Rákóczi Archives). 12 vols. Budapest: MTA Tört Blz, Kiad. 1873–1935.
Azizi, Abdelmalek and Mostafa Azizi. "Instances of Arabic Cryptography in Morocco." *Cryptologia* 35 (2011): 47–57.
Beke, Antal and Barabás Samu, eds. *I. Rákóczi György és a porta* (Rákóczi György I. and the Porta). Budapest: MTA, 1888.
Beke, Antal ed. "Pázmány, Lippay és Eszterházy levelezése I. Rákóczy Györgygyel [1629–1637]. 1–3." ("The correspondence of Pázmány, Lippay and Eszterházy with György Rákóczy I [1629–1637]. 1–3." *Magyar Történelmi Tár* (1881): 641–674, (1882): 134–148, 279–325.
Benda, Gyula. *Ráday Pál iratai* (Writings of Pál Ráday). 2 vols. Budapest: Akadémiai, 1961.
Cospi, Antonio Maria. *L'interpretation des chiffres ou reigle pour bien entendre et expliquer facilement toutes sortes de chiffres simples.* Paris: Courbes, 1641.
Della Porta, Giambattista. *De furtivis literarum notis vulgo de ziferis liber quinque.* Naples: Johannes Baptista, 1602.
–. *De occultis literarum notis, seu artis animi sensa occulte aliis significandi.* Strasbourg: Zetzner, 1606.
Devos, J. P. and H. Seligman, eds. *L'Art de Deschiffrer: Traité de Déchiffrement du XVIIe Siècle de la Secrétairerie d'Etat et de Guerre Espagnole.* Belgium: Université de Louvain, 1967.
Domokos, György, Norbert Mátyus, Armando Nuzzo. *Vestigia – Mohács előtti magyar források olasz könyvtárakban* (Pre-Mohács Hungarian sources in Italian libraries). Piliscsaba: PPKE BTK 2015.
Haller, Gábor, *Naplója. 1630 – 1644.* (Gábor Haller's Diary, *1630 – 1644.*). In Szabó Károly, ed. *Erdélyi Történelmi Adatok,* 4. Kolozsvár: 1862, 1–103.
Herzfelder, Armand Dezső. "Kolozsvári Czementes János könyve" (The book by Johannes Cementes of Kolozsvár). *Magyar Könyvszemle* (1896): 276–301, 351–373.
Kircher, Athanasius. *Polygraphia nova et universalis.* Roma: Typographia Varesij, 1664.
Köpeczi, Béla, ed. *II. Rákóczi Ferenc válogatott levelei* (Selected letters of Ferenc Rákóczi II). Budapest: Bibliotheca Kiadó, 1958.

Magyar *Történelmi Tár* (Hungarian Historical Records). Pest: Magyar Tudományos Akadémia, 1855–1934.

Mrayati, Mohamad, Yahya MeerAlam, and M.Hassan at-Tayyan, eds *The Arabic Origins of Cryptology,* vols. 6 *al-Kindi's Treatise on Cryptanalysis* (2003); *ibn Adlan's Treatise* (2003); *ibn ad-Durayhim's Treatise* (2004); *ibn Dunaynir's Book* (2005); *Three Treatises on Cryptanalysis of Poetry* (2006); *Two Treatises on Cryptanalysis* (2007). Riyadh: KFCRIS, 2003–2006.

Nagy, Iván and B. Nyáry Albert, eds. *Magyar diplomácziai emlékek Mátyás király korából 1458–1490* (Hungarian diplomatic sources from the time of King Matthias, 1458–1490). *III.* Budapest: 1877.

Nagy, Iván. ed. *Késmárki Thököly Imre naplója, 1693–1694* (Thököly Imre's diary). Pest: Eggenberger Ferdinánd, 1863.

Ötvös, Ágoston. *Rejtelmes levelek első Rákóczy György korából* (Secret letters from the time of Rákóczi György I). Kolozsvár, 1848.

Selenus, Gustavus. *Cryptomenytices et cryptographiae libri IX.* Luneburg: Sternen, 1624.

Seligman, H. "Un traité de déchiffrement du XVIIe siècle." *Revue des Bibliothèques et Archives de Belgique* 6 (1908): 1–19.

Simándi, Ladislaus. *Corvi albi eremitici nova Musa inconcinna.* Typ. Clari Montis Czestochoviensis, 1712.

Szaniszló, Zsigmond, *Naplói (1682–1711)* (Diaries, 1682–1711). In Torma Károly ed. *Történelmi Tár,* 1889 (12). 230–269, 503–522, 708–727, (13), 1890. 77–101, 307–327, 493–510, 757–770, (14), 1891. 267–295. 1889–1891.

Szilády, Áron and Sándor Szilágyi, eds. *Török-magyarkori állam-okmánytár III–VII* (State documents from the Turkish-Hungarian era). 5 vols. Pest: Eggenberger, 1870–1872.

Szilágyi, Sándor, ed. *Levelek és okiratok I. Rákóczy György keleti összeköttetései történetéhez* (Letters and documents related to György I Rákóczi' s eastern relations). Budapest: Knoll, 1883.

–. ed. *Okmánytár II. Rákóczy György diplomáciai összeköttetéseihez* (Documents related to György II Rákóczi's diplomatic relations). Budapest: Eggenberger, 1874.

–. ed. *Erdély és az északkeleti háború I–II* (Transylvania and the north-eastern war). Budapest: Magyar Tudományos Akadémia, 1890–91.

–. *Okmánytár I. Rákóczy György svéd és franczia szövetkezéseinek történetéhez* (Documents related to György I Rákóczi's Swedish and French alliances). Budapest: Eggenberger, 1873.

Szczucki, Lech and Szepessy Tibor, eds. *Epistulae / Andreas Dudithius.* Vols. 4. Budapest: Akadémiai Kiadó, 1992.

Sztankovics, Ödön ed. "Zakarjás János és Fáy Dávid délamerikai jezsuita misszionáriusok úti levelei (1749–1756)" (Travel letters of missionaries János Zakarjás and Dávid Fáy). *Földrajzi Közlemények* 38 (1910): 115–128, 215–236.

Teleki, Mihály. *Levelezés (Correspondence)*, vol. 4, 1–8. Budapest: Magyar Történelmi Társulat, 1905–1926.

Thaly, Kálmán ed., "Késmárki Thököly Imre és némely főbb híveinek naplói és emlékezetes írásai 1686 – 1705" (Diaries and memorable writings of Imre Thököly of Kežmarok and some of his main followers 1686 – 1705), *Monumenta Hungariae Historica*, II. 23/2. (1868): 461–578.

Trithemius, Johannes. *Polygraphiae libri sex.* Oppenheim: Haselberg de Aia, 1518.

–. *Steganographia: ars per occultam scripturam.* Frankfurt: Becker, 1606.

Tüskés, Gábor, Ilona Kovács, Béla Köpeczi eds. *Correspondance de François II Rákóczi et de la palatine Elżbieta Sieniawska 1704–1727.* Budapest, Balassi: 2004.

Vigenère, Blaise de. *Traicte des Chiffres.* Paris: Abel l'Angelier, 1586.

## Selected Secondary Literature

Ágoston, Gábor. "Információszerzés és kémkedés az Oszmán Birodalomban a 15–17. században" (Intelligence and espionage in the Ottoman Empire in the 15th – 17th centuries). In Tivadar Petercsák and Mátyás Berecz, eds., *Információáramlás a magyar és török végvári rendszerben* (Information flow in the Hungarian and Ottoman fortess systems). 129–157. Eger: Dobó István Vármúzeum, 1999.

Alvarez, David. "The Papal Cipher Section in the Early Nineteenth Century." *Cryptologia* 17 (1993): 219–224.

Assmann, Aleida and Jan Assmann, eds. *Geheimnis und Öffentlichkeit; Geheimnis und Offenbarung; Geheimnis und Neugierde.* Schleier und Schwelle III, Munich: Fink, 1997–1999.

Bauer, Craig. *Secret History: The Story of Cryptology.* CRC: Chapman Hall, 2013.

__. *Unsolved!: The History and Mystery of the World's Greatest Ciphers from Ancient Egypt to Online Secret Societies.* Princeton: Princeton University Press, 2017.

Bauer, Friedrich L. *Entzifferte Geheimnisse: Methoden und Maximen der Kryptologie.* Berlin: Springer, 2000. English translation: *Decrypted Secrets. Methods and Maxims of Cryptology.* Berlin: Springer, 2002.

Bazeries (Commandant). *Les Chiffres secrets dévoilés, étude historique sur les chiffres appuyée de documents inédits tirés des différents dépôts d'archives.* Paris: E. Fasquelle, 1901.

Beckers, Hartmut. "Eine spätmittelalterliche deutsche Anleitung zur Teufelsbeschwörung mit Runenschrift-verwendung." *Zeitschrift für deutsches Altertum und deutsche Literatur* 113 (1984): 136–145.

Biagioli, Mario. "From ciphers to confidentiality: Secrecy, Openness and Priority in Science." *The British Journal for the History of Science,* 45 (2012): 213–233.

__. *Galileo's Instruments of Credit: Telescopes, Images, Secrecy.* Chicago: University Of Chicago Press, 2006.

__. "Venetian tech-transfer: how Galileo copied the telescope." In Albert van Helden, Sven Dupré, Rob van Gent and Huib Zuidervaart, eds., *The Origins of the Telescope* 203–230. Amsterdam: Amsterdam University Press, 2011.

Boglár, Lajos. "The Ethnographic Legacy of Eighteenth Century Hungarian Travellers in South America." *Acta Ethnographica,* 1955, 313–358.

Biaudet, Henry. "Un chiffre diplomatique du XVIe siècle: Étude sur le cod. Nunz. Polonia 27. A. des archives secretes du Sant-Siège." *Annales Academiae Scientiarum Fennice.* Helsinki: 1910.

Bischoff, Bernhard. *"Übersicht über die nichtdiplomatischen Geheimschriften des Mittelalters" Mitteilungen des Instituts fur Österreichische Geschichtsforschung* 62 (1954): 1–27.

Bobory, Dóra. *The Sword and the Crucible: Count Boldizsár Batthyány and Natural Philosophy in Sixteenth-Century Hungary.* Newcastle upon Tyne: Cambridge Scholars Press, 2009.

Bok, Sissela. *Secrets: On the Ethics of Concealment and Revelation.* New York: Vintage, 1989.

Buonafalce, Augusto. "Cicco Simonetta's Cipher-Breaking Rules." *Cryptologia* 32 (2008): 62–70.

Carter, Charles Howard. *The Secret Diplomacy of the Habsburgs, 1598–1625.* New York: Columbia University Press, 1964.

Cecchetti, Bartolommeo. "Le scritture occulte nella diplomazia veneziana." *Atti del Regio Istituto Veneto* 14 (1868–69): 1186–1211.

Cordoba, Ricardo ed. *Craft Treatises and Handbooks: The Dissemination of Technical Knowledge in the Middle Ages.* Turnhout: Brepols, 2013.

Couto, Dejanirah. "Spying in the Ottoman Empire: Sixteenth-Century Encrypted Correspondence." in Francisco Bethencourt and Florike Egmond, eds. *Cultural Exchange in Early Modern Europe* (Volume III) - Correspondence and Cultural Exchange in Europe, 1400–1700. 274–312. Cambridge: Cambridge University Press, 2007.

Dávid, Géza – Pál Fodor, "Oszmán hírszerzés Magyarországon." (Ottoman intelligence in Hungary). In Tivadar Petercsák and Mátyás Berecz, eds., *Információáramlás a magyar és török végvári rendszerben* (Information flow in the Hungarian and Ottoman fortress systems) 197–207. Eger: Dobó István Vármúzeum, 1999.

Davids, Karel. "Craft Secrecy in Europe in the Early Modern Period: A Comparative View." *Early Science and Medicine*, 10 (No. 3, Openness and Secrecy in Early Modern Science) (2005): 341–348.

de Leeuw, Karl. "The Black Chamber in the Dutch Republic and the Seven Years' War, 1751–1763." *Diplomacy and Statecraft* 10 (1999): 1–30.

–. "The Black Chamber in the Dutch Republic during the war of the Spanish Succession and its aftermath, 1707–1715." *The Historical Journal* 42 (1999): 133–156.

–. "Cryptology in the Dutch Republic: a case-study" in idem and Jan Bergstra, eds. *The History of Information Security: A Comprehensive Handbook*. Amsterdam: Elsevier, 2007: 324–364.

–. and Jan Bergstra, eds. *The History of Information Security: A Comprehensive Handbook*. Amsterdam: Elsevier, 2007.

– and H. van der Meer. "A Turning Grille from the Ancestral Castle of the Dutch Stadholders." *Cryptologia* 19 (1995): 153–165.

Devos, J. P. *Les chiffres de Philippe II (1555–1598) et du Despacho Universal durant le XVIIe siècle*. Brussels: Académie Royale de Belgique, 1950.

Dulong-Sainteny, Claude, "Les signes cryptiques dans la correspondance d'Anne d'Autriche avec Mazarin, contribution à l'emblématique du XVIIe siècle." *Bibliothèque de l'école des chartes* 140 (1982): 61–83.

Eamon, William. *Science and the Secrets of Nature: Books of Secrets in Medieval and Early Modern Culture*. Princeton: Princeton University Press, 1994.

Gillogly, James J. "Breaking an Eighteenth Century Shorthand System." *Cryptologia* 11/2 (1987): 93–98.

Engel, Gisela, Brita Rang, Klaus Reichert and Heide Wunder, eds. *Das Geheimnis am Beginn der europäischen Moderne*. Frankfurt am Main, Klostermann, 2002.

Farkas, Gábor Farkas, András Varga, Tünde Katona, Miklós Latzkovits, István Monok, eds. *Magyarországi magánkönyvtárak II. 1588–1721* (Hungarian private libraries II. 1588–1721). Szeged: Scriptum, 1992.

Farkas, Gábor Farkas, ed. *Magyarországi jezsuita könyvtárak 1711-ig, II, Nagyszombat 1632–1690* (Hungarian Jesuit libraries til 1711, II, Nagyszombat 1632–1690). Szeged, Scriptum, 1997.

Hausner, Gábor, Tibor Klaniczay, Sándor Iván Kovács, István Monok, Géza Orlovszky, eds. *A Bibliotheca Zriniana története* (History of the Bibliotheca Zriniana). Budapest: Argumentum Kiadó, 1992.

Hilaire-Pérez, Liliane and Catherine Verna. "Dissemination of Technical Knowledge in the Middle Ages and the Early Modern Era: New Approaches and Methodological Issues." *Technology and Culture* 47 (2006): 536–565.

Hilaire-Pérez, Liliane and Anne-Francoise Garcon eds. *Les chemins de la nouveauté: Inventer, innover au regard de l'histoire*. Paris, 2004.

Hull, David. "Openness and secrecy in science: their origins and limitationism." *Science, Technology and Human Values* 10 (1985): 4–13.

Jankovics, József, István Monok, eds. *Dudith András könyvtára* (Library of Andreas Dudith). Szeged: Scriptum, 1993.

Epstein, Stephan R.. "Craft Guilds, Apprenticeship, and Technological Change in Preindustrial Europe." *The Journal of Economic History* 58 (1998): 684–713.

Findlen, Paula. *Athanasius Kircher: The Last Man Who Knew Everything*. New York: Routledge, 2004.

Fletcher, John Edward. *Athanasius Kircher und seine Beziehungen zum gelehrten Europa seiner Zeit.* Wiesbaden: Otto Harrassowitz, 1988.

Fodor, Pál. "An anti-Semite Grand Vizier? The crisis in Ottoman-Jewish Relations in 1589–91 and its Consequences." In idem, ed. *In Quest of the Golden Apple: Imperial Ideology, Politics, and Military Administration in the Ottoman Empire.* 191–206. Istanbul 2000.

Ginzburg, Carlo. *Il Nicodemismo: Simulazione e dissimulazione nell'Europa del '500.* Turin: Einaudi, 1970.

Godwin, Joscelyn. *Athanasius Kircher's Theatre of the World: The Life and Work of the Last Man to Search for Universal Knowledge.* Rochester, Vt.: Inner Traditions, 2009.

Kahn, David. *The Codebreakers. The Story of Secret Writing.* London: Weidenfeld and Nicolson, 1967.

–. "The Future of the Past – Questions in Cryptologic History." *Cryptologia* 32 (2008): 56–61.

–. *The Reader of Gentlemen's Mail: Herbert O. Yardley and the Birth of American Codebreaking.* New Haven, CT: Yale, 2004.

Karttunen, Liisi. "Chiffres diplomatiques des nonces de Pologne vers la fin du XVIe siècle: Extraits des archives des princes Chigi à Rome." *Annales Academiae Scientiarum Fennice.* Helsinki: 1911.

Kerekes, Dóra. *Diplomaták és kémek Konstantinápolyban* (Diplomats and spies in Constantinople). Budapest: L'Harmattan, 2010.

–. "Hírszerzés a XVI-XVII században" (Intelligence in the 16th-17th centuries). *Irodalomismeret* 13 (2003): 63–70.

__. "Kémek Konstantinápolyban: A Habsburg információszerzés szervezete és működése a magyarországi visszafoglaló háborúk idején (1683–1699)" (Spies in Constantinople, the organization and functioning of the Habsburg intelligence, 1683–1699). *Századok* 141 (2007): 1217–1258;

–. "Titkosszolgálat volt-e a Habsburgok titkos levelezői intézménye?" (Was the 16-17th Century Habsburg "Secret Correspondence" a Secret Service?). In Csaba Katona, ed. *Kémek, ügynökök, besúgók: Az ókortól Mata Hariig* (Spies, agents, informers: from Antiquity to Mata Hari) 97–137. Szombathely: Magyar Nemzeti Levéltár Vas Megyei Levéltára, 2014.

Kiss Farkas, Gábor. "'Difficiles Nugae' Athanasius Kircher magyarországi kapcsolatai" ('Difficiles Nugae' Kircher's contacts in Hungary). *Irodalomtörténeti Közlemények* 109 (2005): 436–463.

Kovács, Ilona, "Exil et Littérature: La période 1711–1735 dans l'oeuvre de François II Rákóczi." *Cahiers d'études hongroises* 7 (1995): 20–28.

Kőszeghy, Péter. *Balassi Bálint, Magyar Alkibiadész* (Baling Balassi, the Hungarian Alcibiades). Budapest: Balassi Kiadó, 2008.

Knowlson, James. *Universal Language Schemes in England and France, 1600–1800.* Toronto, University of Toronto Press, 1975.

Láng, Benedek. "Ciphers in Magic: Techniques of Revelation and Concealment." *Magic, Ritual, and Witchcraft,* 2015/2, 125–141.

__. "People's Secrets: Towards a Social History of Early Modern Cryptography." *The Sixteenth Century Journal* 45.2 (2014): 291–308.

–. "Shame, Love and Alcohol: Private Ciphers in Early Modern Hungary." *Cryptologia* 39.3 (2015): 276–287.

__. *Unlocked Books, Manuscripts of Learned Magic in the Medieval Libraries of Central Europe.* University Park, PA: Penn State University Press, 2008.

__. "Why don't we decipher an outdated cipher system? The Codex of Rohonc." *Cryptologia,* 34 (2010): 115–144.

Leong, Elaine and Alisha Rankin, eds. *Secrets and Knowledge in Medicine and Science 1500–1800.* Surray: Ashgate, 2011.

Lerville, Edmond. *Les Cahiers secrets de la cryptographie.* Paris: Rocher, 1972.

Lochrie, Karma. *Covert Operations: The Medieval Uses of Secrecy.* Philadelphia: University of Pennsylvania Press, 1999.

Long, Pamela O. *Openness, Secrecy, Authorship: Technical Arts and the Culture of Knowledge from Antiquity to the Renaissance.* Baltimore: Johns Hopkins University Press, 2001.

Király, Levente Zoltán. "Struktúrák a Rohonci-kódex szövegében." (Tructures in the text of the Rohonc codex) *Theologiai Szemle* 54 (2011/2): 82–93.

Macrakis, Kristie. "Confessing secrets: secret communication and the origins of modern science." *Intelligence and National Security* 25 (2010): 183–197.

Markó, Árpád, "A versíró Rákóczi" (The poet Rákóczi). *Magyar Könyvszemle* 26 (1936): 259–264.

McMullin, Ernan. "Openness and secrecy in science: some notes on early history." *Science, Technology and Human Values* 10 (1985): 14–23.

Meister, Aloys. *Die Anfänge der modernen diplomatischen Geheimschrift.* Paderborn: Ferdinand Schöningh, 1902.

__. *Die Geheimschrift im Dienste der päpstlichen Kurie von ihren Anfängen bis zum Ende des 16. Jahrhunderts.* Paderborn: Ferdinand Schöningh, 1906.

Monok, István ed. *A Rákóczi-család könyvtárai, 1588–1660* (Libraries of the Rákóczi family). Szeged: Scriptum, 1996.

__. "Csanaki Máté könyvjegyzéke" (Booklist of Máté Csanaki). *Magyar Könyvszemle* (1983): 256–262.

__. ed. *Erdélyi Könyvesházak II: Kolozsvár, Marosvásárhely, Nagyenyed, Szászváros, Székelyudvarhely* (Transylvanian Libraries II: Kolozsvár, Marosvásárhely, Nagyenyed, Szászváros, Székelyudvarhely). Szeged: Scriptum, 1991.

__, Noémi Németh, András Varga, eds. *Erdélyi Könyvesházak III. 1563 – 1757: A Bethlen–család és környezete, Az Apafi–család és környezete, A Teleki–család és környezete, Vegyes források* (Transylvanian libraries, the Bethlen, Apafi and Teleki libraries). Szeged, Scriptum, 1994.

Newman, William and Anthony Grafton, eds. *Secrets of Nature: Astrology and Alchemy in Early Modern Europe.* Cambridge, MA: The MIT Press, 2001.

Newman, William. "Alchemical symbolism and concealment." In Peter Galison and Emily Thompson, eds. *The Architecture of Science,* 59–77. Cambridge, MA: MIT Press, 2000.

Nummedal, Tara. *Alchemy and Authority in the Holy Roman Empire.* Chicago: The Chicago University Press, 2007.

Özgen, Elif. "The connected world of intrigues: the disgrace of Murad III's favourite David Passi in 1591." *Leidschrift* 27 (2012): 75–100.

Pálffy, Géza. *The Kingdom of Hungary and the Habsburg Monarchy in the Sixteenth Century.* Boulder, Colorado–Wayne, NJ: Center for Hungarian Studies and Publications, Inc., 2009.

Paravacini Bagliani, Agostino, ed. *Il Segreto / The Secret,* Micrologus, vol. 14. Florence: Sismel, 2006.

Pasini, Luigi. "Delle scritture in cifra usate dalla Repubblica Veneta." In *Il Regio Archivio Generale di Venezia.* Venezia: Pietro Naratovich, 1873.

Pauler, Gyula. *Wesselényi Ferencz nádor és társainak összeesküvése: 1664–1671, vol. 2.* (Palatine Wesselényi Ferenc's conspiracy, 1664–1671). Budapest: Akadémia, 1876.

Pellerey, Roberto. *Le lingue perfette nel secolo dell'utopia.* Roma-Bari: Laterza, 1992.

Pesic, Peter. "François Viète, Father of Modern Cryptanalysis – Two New Manuscripts." *Cryptologia* 21.1 (1997): 1–29.

Petercsák, Tivadar and Mátyás Berecz, eds., *Információáramlás a magyar és török végvári rendszerben* (Information flow in the Hungarian and Ottoman fortress systems). Eger: Dobó István Vármúzeum, 1999.

Platania, Gaetano. "La Polonia nelle carte del cardinale Carlo Barberieni Protettore del regno." *Accademie e Biblioteche d'Italia* 56 (n. s. 39) (1988) n. 2. 38–60.

Preto, Paolo. *I servizi segreti di Venezia.* Milan: il Saggiatore, 1994.

Principe, Lawrence M. "Robert Boyle's Alchemical Secrecy: Codes, Ciphers and Concealments." *Ambix* 39 (1992): 63–74.

Révay, Zoltán. *II. Rákóczi Ferenc és korának rejtjelezése (XVIII. század)* (Cryptology of the era of Ferenc II. Rákóczy). Budapest: Magyar Néphadsereg Híradó Főnökség Kiadása, 1974.

—. *Titkosírások. Fejezetek a rejtjelezés történetéből* (Ciphers, Chapters from the History of Cryptology). Budapest: Zrínyi Katonai Kiadó, 1978.

Rockinger, Ludwig von. "Über eine bayerische Sammlung von Schlüsseln zu Geheimschriften des sechzehnten Jahrhunderts." *Archivalische Zeitschrift* 1892: 21–96.

Sacco, L. *Manuel de Cryptographie.* Paris: Payot, 1951.

Schmeh, Klaus. *Codeknacker gegen Codemacher: Die faszinierende Geschichte der Verschlüsselung.* Dortmund: W3L, 2014.

—. *Nicht zu knacken: Von ungelösten Enigma-Codes zu den Briefen des Zodiac-Killers.* Hanser, 2012.

Seligman, H. "Un traité de déchiffrement du XVIIe siècle." *Revue des Bibliothèques et Archives de Belgique* 6 (1908): 1–19.

Simmel, Georg. "The Sociology of Secrecy and of the Secret Societies." *American Journal of Sociology* 11 (1906): 441–498.

Simonetta, Marcello. *The Montefeltro Conspiracy: A Renaissance Mystery Decoded.* London: Doubleday Books, 2008.

Singh, Simon. *The Code Book: The Science of Secrecy from Ancient Egypt to Quantum Cryptography.* New York: Doubleday, 1999.

Slaughter, Mary M. *Universal languages and scientific taxonomy in the 17th century.* Cambridge: Cambridge University Press, 1982.

Snyder, Jon R. *Dissimulation and the Culture of Secrecy in Early Modern Europe.* Berkeley: University of California Press, 2012.

Speziali, Pierre. "Aspects de la cryptographie au XVI siècle." *Bibliothèque d'humanisme et Renaissance* 17 (1955): 188–206.

Szakály, Ferenc. *Mezőváros és reformáció. Tanulmányok a korai magyar polgárosodás kérdéséhez.* (Oppidum and Reformation: studies on the early Hungarian formation of bourgeoisie). Budapest, 1995.

Széchy, Károly. *Gróf Zrínyi Miklós 1620–1654 (Count Miklós Zrínyi 1620–1654)* vols. 5. Budapest: Magyar Történelmi Társulat, 1896–1902.

Stix, Franz. "Die Geheimschriftenschlüssel der Kabinetskanzlei des Kaiser." *Nachrichten von der Gesellschaft der Wissenschaften zu Göttingen, Philologisch-Historische Klasse,* Neue Folge, Fachgruppe II, 1936: 207–226, and 1937: 61–70.

Stolzenberg, Daniel. "The Universal History of the Characters of Letters and Languages: An Unknown Manuscript by Athanasius Kircher." *Memoirs of the American Academy in Rome* 56/57 (2011/2012): 305–321.

Strasser, Gerhard. "Die kryptographische Sammlung Herzog Augusts: Vom Quellenmaterial für seine Cryptomenytices zu einem Schwerpunkt in seiner Bibliothek." *Wolfenbütteler Beiträge* 5 (1982): 83–121.

___. *Lingua Universalis: Kryptologie und Theorie der Universalsprachen im 16. und 17. Jahrhundert.* Wiesbaden: Harrassowitz, 1988.

___. "The Noblest Cryptologist: Duke August the Younger of Brunswick-Luneburg (Gustavus Selenus) and His Cryptological Activities." *Cryptologia* 7 (1983): 193–217.

Tokai, Gábor. "Az első lépések a Rohonci-kódex megfejtéséhez" (First steps towards the solution of the Rohonc codex). *Élet és Tudomány* LXV/52–53, LXVI/2 (2010–2011): 1675–1678. and 50–53.

Tóth, Ferenc. *Correspondance diplomatique relative à la guerre d'indépendance du prince François II Rákóczi (1703–1711).* Paris-Genève: Honoré Champion, 2012.

Tusor, Péter. "Pázmány bíboros olasz rejtjelkulcsa: C. H. Motmann 'Residente d'Ungheria': A római magyar agenzia történetéhez" (Cardinal Pázmány's Italian Codebook: C. H. Motmann 'Residente d'Ungheria,' On the History of the Hungarian Agenzia in Rome). *Hadtörténelmi közlemények* 116 (2003): 535–81.

Vermeir, Koen. "Openness versus secrecy? Historical and historiographical remarks." *The British Journal for the History of Science*, 45 (2012): 165–188.

Vermeir, Koen and Dániel Margócsy, "States of secrecy: an introduction." *The British Journal for the History of Science*, 45 (2012): 153–164.

Vadai, István, "Két XVII. századi titkosírás megfejtése" (The solution of two, 17th century ciphers). In Ötvös Péter, ed. *Pálffy Kata leveleskönyve: iratok Illésházy István bujdosásának történetéhez (1602–1606)*. 183–189. Szeged: 1991.

Vámos, Hanna, István Vadai, "Pázmány Péter és I. Rákóczy György titkosírása" (The cipher of Péter Pázmány and György Rákóczi I). In Alinka Ajkay and Rita Bajáki eds. *Pázmány nyomában* (Following Pázmány), 461–479. Vác: Mondat, 2013.

___. Kuruc titkosírások megfejtése (Solutions of Kuruc ciphers). In István Mercs, ed. *Kuruc(kodó) irodalom* (Kuruc(izing) literature), 209–221. Nyíregyháza: Móricz Zsigmond Kulturális Egyesület, 2013.

Vadai, István. "Két XVII. századi titkosírás megfejtése" (Solution to two seventeenth-century ciphers). In *Pálffy Kata leveleskönyve: Iratok Illésházy István bujdosásának történetéhez (1602–1606)* (Letter-book of Kata Pálfyy: Texts relevant for István Illésházy's exile), ed. Ötvös Péter, 183–89. Szeged: Scriptum Kft, 1991.

___. "Titkosírás" (Cryptography). In *Magyar Művelődéstörténeti Lexikon* (Encyclopaedia of Hungarian cultural history), vol. 12, ed. Péter Kőszeghy Péter and Zsuzsanna Tamás, 60–65. Budapest, Balassi, 2011.

Várkonyi, Ágnes R. *A rejtőzködő murányi Vénusz* (The hiding Venus of Murany). Budapest: Helikon Könyvkiadó, 1987.

___. "Az elveszett idő: Zrínyi Miklós nádori emlékirata?" (The time lost: a memorandum of Palatine Miklós Zrínyi?) *Hadtörténeti Közlemények* 113 (2000): 269–328.

___. "A tájékoztatás hatalma" (The power of information). In Tivadar Petercsák and Mátyás Berecz, eds., *Információáramlás a magyar és török végvári rendszerben* (Information flow in the Hungarian and Ottoman fortess systems), 9–32. Eger: Dobó István Vármúzeum, 1999.

Vértesy, Miklós. "Titkos írás egy Corvinában," (Secret writing in a Corvina). *Magyar Könyvszemle*, 77 (1961): 167–169.

Éva, Vígh. *Barocco etico-retorico nella letteratura italiana*. Szeged: JATE Press, 2001.

Viterbo, Emanuele. "The Ciphered Autobiography of a 19th Century Egyptologist." *Cryptologia*, 22/3 (1998): 231–243.

Viskolcz, Noémi ed., *Johann Heinrich Bisterfeld (1605–1655). Bibliográfia, A Bisterfeld könyvtár* (*Johann Heinrich Bisterfeld (1605–1655). Bibliography, The Bisterfeld library*). Budapest – Szeged: OSZK, Scriptum, 2003.

Wilding, Nick. "'If you have a secret, either keep it, or reveal it': Cryptography and Universal Language." In Daniel Stolzenberg, ed., *The Great Art of Knowing – The Baroque Encyclopedia of Athanasius Kircher*, 93–103. Fiesole: Stanford University Libraries, Edizioni Cadmo, 2001.

___. "Publishing the Polygraphy: Manuscript, Instrument, and Print in the Work of Athanasius Kircher". In Paula Findlen, ed. *Athanasius Kircher: The Last Man Who Knew Everything*. 283–296. New York: Routledge, 2004.

Zagorin, Perez. *Ways of Lying: Dissimulation, Persecution and Conformity in Early Modern Europe*. Cambridge, MA, 1990.

# Index

Words like cryptography, cryptology and cipher do not appear in the index, because they occur on almost every pages.